THE AUTHOR,
ART, AND
THE MARKET

The Social Foundations of
Aesthetic Forms Series

Jonathan Arac, Editor

THE SOCIAL FOUNDATIONS OF AESTHETIC FORMS

A series of
COLUMBIA UNIVERSITY PRESS
Jonathan Arac, Editor

THE AUTHOR, ART, AND THE MARKET

Rereading the History

of Aesthetics

Martha
Woodmansee

Columbia

University

Press

New York

Columbia University Press
New York   Chichester, West Sussex

Copyright © 1994 Columbia University Press

Library of Congress Cataloging-in-Publication Data

Woodmansee, Martha.
   The author, art, and the market : rereading the
history of aesthetics / Martha Woodmansee.
          p.   cm.—(Social foundations of aesthetic
forms series)
   Includes bibliographical references and index.
   ISBN 0–231–08060–3 (alk. paper)
   ISBN 0–231–10601–7 (pbk.)
     1. Aesthetics, Modern—18th century.
   2. Aesthetics, Comparative.   3. Popular culture.
   I. Title.   II. Series.
   BH181.W66   1994
   111'.85—dc20   94–35564
                                             CIP

Casebound editions of Columbia University Press books
are printed on permanent and durable acid-free paper.

Printed in the United States of America

c 10 9 8 7 6 5 4 3 2 1
p 10 9 8 7 6 5 4 3 2 1

CONTENTS

ACKNOWLEDGMENTS

The research for these essays was begun at the National Humanities Center and completed with the generous support of the Andrew W. Mellon Foundation at Harvard University. I was aided in their writing by the tremendous collegiality of the Department of Germanic Languages there and at Columbia University—for which I would like to express particular thanks to Dorrit Cohn and Inge Halpert. Grants-in-aid from the American Council of Learned Societies and the W. P. Jones Fund at Case Western Reserve University helped me to complete the project. In its final stages I benefited from the services of the University's Freiberger Library—especially the help of Michael Partington, Michael Yeager, and Sue Hanson.

For their helpful responses to this work at various stages in its production I wish to thank M. H. Abrams, Charles Altieri, Nancy Armstrong, Howard S. Becker, Raymond Birn, Marshall J. Brown, James Boyle, Joseph A. Buttigieg, Arthur Danto, Robert Darnton, Cathy Davidson, Mary Douglas, John M. Ellis, Suzanne Ferguson, Barbara Foley, Michael Hancher, E. D. Hirsch, Peter Jaszi, Helmut Kreuzer, Berel Lang, Peter Lindenbaum, Lawrence Lipking, Andrea Lunsford, Colin McLarty, Gary Saul Morson, Mark Rose, Edward Said, Leroy Searle, Ingo Seidler, Patricia Meyer Spacks, Susan Stewart, Udo Strutynski, Nancy Strauss, and Jane Tompkins.

For their generosity and rigor in reading the completed manuscript I am especially grateful to Richard T. Gray, Patricia Harkin, Lawrence D. Needham, and James J. Sosnoski, as also to Clifford Siskin, who read it for Columbia University Press. This would be a better book had I been able to respond to their suggestions more fully.

Finally, I owe a special debt to the friends with whom I have been puzzling over High German Theory since graduate school: Ruth Ann Crowley, Christian Oesterreich, Leslie Strickland, Rose and Dan Subotnik, and Fred Thompson. I could never have finished this book without their help and encouragement. In this context I must also thank three more friends: Margreta De Grazia for showing me how to finish, Gerald Graff for acting as if he knew I would, and Werner J. Dannhauser for his unwaveringly loyal opposition.

Some of these essays have previously been published: portions of "The Interests in Disinterestedness" in *Proceedings of the Tenth Congress of the International Comparative Literature Association* and *Modern Language Quarterly*; "Genius and the Copyright" in *Eighteenth-Century Studies;* "Aesthetics and the Policing of Reading" in *Cultural Critique;* and the first section of "The Uses of Kant in England" in *Verlorene Klassik? Ein Symposium,* edited by Wolfgang Wittkowski. I am grateful for permission to reprint.

FOREWORD

Arthur C. Danto

I have begun to think that the whole form and tenor of philosophical thought in the West was determined, once and for all, by the fact that its initiating—and finest—texts were dialogues. This is not because the dialogic format as such recommended itself to philosophical expression, for in fact the form was rarely used thereafter—by Berkeley, Hume, and Santayana, but never so far as I know by Kant, Hegel, Heidegger, or Dewey, whose thought required vehicles of other kinds. It is, rather, whatever the vehicle, what one might call the deep presuppositions of philosophical thought that are entailed by the dialogue, as well as the way in which philosophers were to conceive their practice, their subject, and their history. Consider *The Republic,* in which the definition of justice quickly emerges as a theme, after which, one by one, attempted definitions by the various speakers, each embodying a different social position, are shown in one or another way defective by their incapacity to handle hard cases, or because they violate some shared intuition. Cephalus's proposal that justice is paying one's debts is blocked by the hard case of whether it can conceivably be reckoned just to place a weapon in a madman's hands, even if it is his by rights and you have promised to return it to him. Polymarchus's thought that justice is aiding one's friends and harming one's

enemies is blocked by the reflection that harming is making worse—
and can one seriously consider the proposition that making someone
worse off than they were is what justice consists in? Step by step a
definition emerges that satisfies the speakers that it will withstand
counterexamples and at the same time accommodate our intuitions
about what justice is. But that implies that everyone present, even the
fierce foucauldian *avant la lettre* Thrasymachus, who had insisted that
justice is but what satisfies the interests of power, share the same
concept. Their difficulty has only been in finding a way to express it.
It is as though the concept itself lies outside the progressive efforts to
capture it in terms of explicit necessary and sufficient conditions. Only
that progress has a history, but the history of the successive efforts to
capture it is no part of the concept itself. The concept is timeless and
impersonal, and must be so if the dialogue is to be possible.

This immediately determines the way in which philosophers conceive of their history. Of course there were philosophers before Plato,
and texts before his as well: the pre-Socratic masters did not express
themselves through fragments. But it was wholly natural to see them
as engaged in a kind of dialogue—one could imagine them discours-
ing in the Asphodel Fields the ancients believed in, on the topics of
Being and Becoming, the Many and the One, the deepest and darkest
concepts there are, which the masters sought to snare in powerful
flawed definitions, with only their intuitions to guide them. The shape
of philosophical history is defined by something outside history altogether, so that while history of a certain kind inevitably characterizes
philosophical practice, it does not impinge on philosophical substance,
which is everywhere and always the same, timeless and universal, and
invariant to every rational being. In the great dialogue the *Theaetetus*,
two components in the concept of knowledge are identified, but the
parties to the discussion all agree that the definition is incomplete and
that the discussion must proceed. Knowledge itself of course has a
history, though not so profound a history that we can credit ourselves
with knowing more about the fundamental truths of life than the
Greeks knew, whom we continue to consult, and deem worth consult-
ing, though their world was palpably different from our own. But
philosophers of knowledge continue the dialogue of the *Theaetetus*,
and while they have added a third condition to Socrates' two, they
dispute with consummate sophistication about what is known in the
literature of epistemology as "the fourth condition of knowledge,"
joining, as it were, a dialogue that began with Socrates, Theaetetus,
and the latter's teacher, Theodorus.

Inasmuch as philosophy's self-image is embodied in what is taken for granted in the dialogic form, there is a question, one to which I certainly do not know the answer, of whether the dialogue was the inevitable and natural form for philosophical discourse, or whether there is a powerful determinism in which what began as a literary form came to serve as a matrix of thought, and philosophy became what it is through the fatality of a literary accident. Whichever way we think about the matter, it remains the fact that philosophy cannot easily be thought of or practiced in any way very different from the way in which we encounter it in its first exemplary and perhaps paralyzing texts. Whitehead has written that the whole of Western philosophy is a set of footnotes to Plato, but there may be a deeper sense in which all that philosophy is a tribute to what had to be thought of in place for the philosophical dialogue to be possible.

These reflections are provoked by Martha Woodmansee's stunning book, and in partial explanation of a certain limitation in philosophical thinking—a certain defect, she might say—that tends to blind it to the presuppositions of its own practice, and to its own goals that might be better served by a different kind of practice altogether, which her own book in fact exemplifies. At the very least, if she is right, the tacit distancing of concepts from the endeavor to analyze them from without is wrong, and even philosophically wrong, for it historicizes the latter and dehistoricizes the former when it is possible that concepts too have histories, and that there are in consequence deep discontinuities in philosophical practice—which is not so much a dialogue after all—in which historically situated thinkers pursue an ahistorical prey. But the history of philosophy instead is something more dramatic and abrupt, almost cataclysmic in its pulsing, in which one concept is replaced by another only distantly related to it, even if in fact both have the same name. This is what gives her book an excitement far in excess of that appropriate to the study of the obscure texts she has recovered from whatever Asphodel Field old and forgotten writers retire to, and the restoration of a moment of vanished thought she has nailed down as an exercise in the history of aesthetic reflection. She has not just filled in a missing chapter in a complex historical narrative construed as an explanation of the emergence of a masterpiece of philosophical thought, Kant's *Critique of Aesthetic Judgment*. She will, if right, have replaced what one might call a continuity model of history, which is the model tacit in the structure of history conceived of as dialogic, with a *dis*continuity model in which concepts themselves undergo cataclysmic change, and under which whole new beginnings emerge from the material matrices of thought. It is this promise that makes her book of interest not simply to historians of eighteenth-century thought, for whom it is obligatory, nor even for historians of aesthetics, but for philosophers, whatever their subject, who want to be self-conscious of their practice, and who may find, upon reading this book, that they have to defend themselves from a position very different from the one they thought themselves to occupy. With none of the obscurity or verbal hysteria that have clouded so much of postmodernist writing, Woodmansee has leveled a fundamental challenge to philosophy from an area and discipline that in candor most philosophers have tended to regard as marginal, namely aesthetics.

Consider what Woodmansee terms "disciplinary history," namely the way in which practitioners of an intellectual discipline represent the history of their subject through its representative texts. A famous anthology in aesthetics begins with the canonical writings of Plato and Aristotle, and proceeds to those of Kant and Hegel via Plotinus, Augustine, Shaftsbury, and Hume. It concludes with Schopenhauer, Nietzsche, Heidegger, and Dewey. A lot is left out, it goes without saying, but these omissions can be justified by citing first the indispensibility of these authors, and then the advantage of having substantial and authoritative writings rather than what academic critics call "snippets." The textbook market being what it is, competitive anthologies are bound to appear, each with its special justification. What Woodmansee makes us appreciate is that the form of these conventional textbooks forecloses the fundamental question she means to address, for the energy that drives the anthology, ostensibly historical, in fact is dialogical. It implies a logic of Asphodel Fields, in which as equals and contemporaries, Nietzsche and Aristotle discourse together, and Plato and Kant moot strategies of universalization. Not only the philosophers, but the students themselves are by standard educational practice thrust among the Asphodels, for if they are given examinations, they will be asked to compare Aristotle and Nietzsche on tragedy, or Plato and Hegel on beauty. Or they will write term papers analyzing Dewey's criticisms of platonism, or Nietzsche's animus toward Socrates. Or, if they have a bit of art history, they will be asked how Plato would deal with a work like Van Gogh's painting of his bed. And this is to connect the great aestheticians with one another in a long dialogue, stretching over two millennia in which the same concepts— beauty, pleasure, taste, and art itself—are shared by the participants who differ only in how to lay logical fingers on them. The assumption is that with the right definition, everyone would at last agree and the dialogue come to an end, as the participants in *The Republic* agree, and *The Republic* itself reached its natural terminus.

I cannot forbear situating this philosophy of philosophy against not only the educational practices that presume it, which include the anthology, the compare-and-contrast examination question, and the convergent reading list, with the alternatives that have exacerbated pedagogical and even intellectual consensus in recent years. I refer to those challenges to the canon—THE CANON—that insist that wholly different and incommensurable points of view define the life of the mind, and divide men from women, blacks from whites, gays from straights, Europeans from Third Worlders on the very commonalities that once were taken to underlie academic discourse and made "dialogue" a nice cozy way of talking about academic talking. There is no dialogue, merely confrontation, and the best we can hope for is to acknowledge these differences, and work out schemes in which they can coexist without mutual cooptation. Thus, educational practice would reflect the radical discontinuities that partition us one from another. So the conflict, the deep and one might even say metaphysical conflict, is between whole conceptions of the relationship between concepts and practices that on one side is exemplified by the history of philosophy as philosophers conceive it, and, on the other, as it is conceived of by someone like Foucault or, more benignly, like Richard Rorty—a history of differences misrepresented as a history of samenesses. And I suppose the great philosophical question of the time, barely as yet articulated, is how such a deep division can be overcome. But the very idea of overcoming it may already imply its having been overcome, since there must be some underlying commonality between the parties. And what if there is none? What if the deep truth is absolute discontinuity?

Martha Woodmansee belongs to a generation of what I might call "discontinuists," inspired by Foucault, and sensitive to the radicalisms available today to feminists and others who seek places in the institutions of thought and culture, but question the premises with which thought and culture have been represented traditionally in those institutions. It is against the sharpened sensibility of someone who has internalized the conceptual warfares of recent decades that her powerful and compelling text must be appreciated. She has brought her learning, her analytical powers, and her historical gifts to bear upon a moment in history when literally everything changed, when what was taking place was not a new chapter in an ongoing story but a whole new story misread as a new chapter. And instead of a linear model for reading the history of philosophical aesthetics from Plato to Kant to Hegel to Heidegger to now, that history is dissolved into an archipelago of bodies of thought and theory, only partially related to one another at the surface, but where each arises out of its own set of material conditions that the philosophies reflect each by each. So Kant's text is like some immense tree with a tangled root mass drawing nourishment from changes in the material production of books, the material circumstances of the writers of books, the material situation in which the reading of books is so different from what the latter had been a generation or so earlier that a redefinition of literature emerged as a matter of course, all of this talked about by thinkers far less commanding than Kant, who are rebuilding the philosophy of art to accommodate their particular interests. Aesthetics as a systematic way of thinking about art draws its nourishment from human—all-too-human—requirements very distant indeed from the resounding formulations of universality, unspecific purposiveness, and disinterestedness that so mark the thought of Kant and, through Kant, the later aestheticizings of the art historian Ernst Gombrich and the art critic Clement Greenberg, today felt as impossibly confining by an art world whose material conditions are very different from those of Kant's age. In a way, Woodmansee's analysis is an enlightened and convincing form of Marxist analysis, applied to writers and thinkers long pressed into the shadows in which Kant's luminosity cast them, but who explain the great work that superseded and negated them. She has rescued them, not to give them a second life in a revised canon, nor the immortality of translation and a life in the seminar room, but to better understand whence philosophy derives its energies in one of its great ages, and to better understand how we ought to philosophize against the philosophies of the past.

What is certainly true is that what we think of today as aesthetics is altogether an eighteenth-century achievement. Whatever else they did, the thinkers of the eighteenth century forged a logical connection between aesthetics and art by treating the latter as an object of disinterested contemplation, and a source of a kind of intellectual pleasure. It was an episode in what I have elsewhere spoken of as the philosophical disenfranchisement of art, in the sense that it was an effort, and a massively successful one at that, to extrude art from reality and the stream of life, and in distancing it from the practical, to put it on pedestals where the whole institutional structure of the art world has endeavored to keep it. Woodmansee sees the matter from an opposite direction, not from philosophy down but from practice up, and I cannot help but point out that not even she is able to resist some allegiance to the unificatory virtues of continuity. After all, she has a story to tell, and stories seem to imply continuant subjects. Thus, she suggests that there was a period in which art was conceived of instrumentalistically, and that was replaced by one in which it was conceived of aesthetically. But then it was *art* that was thought of in two different ways, neither of which truly belongs to the essence of art—or at least the concept of Art seems common to the two periods, and hence outside the history. And that connects her two periods, the one she merely alludes to and the other in which she immerses the reader, into a kind of dialogue.

Perhaps narrative all by itself is inconsistent with the kind of story she wants to tell. Or perhaps the very idea of continuity needs rethinking. It may be that the idea of a concept that exists outside the history of its progressive characterization in the course of philosophical inquiry is as much and as little warranted as the idea of the soul is, invoked to give unity to a life it lies outside of. The subject of a lived life, like the subject of a history, may be metaphysically posited, engendered by a kind of grammar, and given some pride of metaphysical place when in truth both soul and concept may simply *be* the histories, and have no reality outside them.

This is hardly the place or the occasion, at the end of what is intended as a tribute by way of foreword to an exemplary and original book, to take such speculations further. Nor in truth would I know how to do philosophy if the presuppositions of the dialogic model collapse, and our concepts in fact so fundamentally historicized as this book implies they are. But philosophy is in a kind of crisis, if you like, in a second dogmatic slumber, and it is not the least virtue of Martha Woodmansee's marvelous work that it might awaken it—awaken us— to a reexamination of the dialogic essence imposed upon our discipline from the start!

The Genius of the Artist with Minerva and Muses by Daniel Chodowiecki
(1726–1801). Frontispiece for Johann Georg Sulzer's *Allgemeine Theorie
der schönen Künste* (1771). Courtesy of the Yale Collection of German
Literature.

THE AUTHOR,
ART, AND
THE MARKET

INTRODUCTION: REREADING THE HISTORY OF AESTHETICS

The fine arts. . . . There they all are together, it goes without saying, whether related or not. . . . What cannot be combined by such philosophy? Painting and dance, rhetoric and architecture, poetry and sculpture, all of them conjured up and projected onto a wall by the magical light of a little philosophical lamp, where they dance forward and back colorfully, and the ecstatic spectators nearly shout themselves breathless for joy.

—*Goethe, "Die schönen Künste in ihrem Ursprung, ihrer wahren Natur und besten Anwendung, betrachtet von J. G. Sulzer"* *(1772)*

The subject of this study is our modern conception of art. Shorthand for the "fine arts" of painting, sculpture, poetry, music, architecture, and sometimes dance, the term *art* designates a sphere of activity that is sui generis—identifiable and distinct from the crafts, the sciences, and all other human activities. Those who make an occupation of reflecting on it, modern philosophers of art or aestheticans, tend to treat this notion as if it were universal and timeless. The individual activities we designate as "arts" are, to be sure, as old as civilization, and recorded speculation about their diverse interrelations dates back to classical antiquity. But, as Paul Oskar Kristeller showed some forty years ago, it was not until the eighteenth century that they came to be thought of as constituting a distinct domain, the "fine arts," or simply "art," which is distinguished from the variety of other human activities.

"The grouping together of the visual arts with poetry and music into the system of the fine arts with which we are familiar did not exist in classical antiquity, in the Middle Ages, or in the Renaissance," Kristeller writes. The ancients undertook comparisons of poetry and painting, and their investigations of imitation "established a kind of link" between painting and sculpture and between poetry and music. The Renaissance witnessed "the emancipation of the three major visual arts from the crafts." It carried forward the comparison of the various arts, focusing especially on painting and poetry, and it "laid the ground for an amateur interest in the different arts that tended to bring them together from the point of view of the reader, spectator, and listener rather than of the artist." In bringing about the emancipation of the natural sciences, the seventeenth century prepared the way for a clearer distinction between the arts and the sciences. "Only the early eighteenth century, especially in England and France," Kristeller concludes, "produced elaborate treatises written by and for amateurs in which the various fine arts were grouped together, compared with each other, and combined in a systematic scheme based on common principles." This development culminated, finally, with the incorporation, in the second half of the century in Germany, of all of this "comparative and theoretical treatment of the fine arts as a separate discipline into the system of philosophy."[1]

The forty years since the appearance of this essay in the *Journal of the History of Ideas* have produced no refutation of Kristeller's thesis. Indeed, the essay has been frequently cited and anthologized. But if his thesis had met with as widespread acceptance as such recognition suggests, why is it that there has been so little effort to develop it? Kristeller could not have pointed the way more clearly: "It is not easy to indicate the causes for the genesis of the system [of the arts]," he observes toward the end of the essay, and then he goes on to suggest several promising lines of research.[2] Is it not puzzling, therefore, that none has been systematically pursued? Let us explore this anomaly briefly by examining several representative moments in the reception of the essay.

Probably nobody did more to disseminate Kristeller's ideas than Morris Weitz by including "The Modern System of the Arts" in the second edition of his anthology, *Problems in Aesthetics*, which appeared in 1970. The fact that a second, much enlarged edition was called for—it is over two hundred pages longer than the first edition that appeared in 1959 and itself came to nearly seven hundred pages—

indicates that the textbook enjoyed wide circulation. *Problems in Aesthetics* collects readings from Plato to Panofsky organized around topics or, as Weitz terms them, "problems"—a variant of which tactic has more recently been employed by Terry Eagleton. The first of these sections of the book, entitled "What is Art?," includes in addition to Kristeller's essay (which, reproduced in full, occupies fifty-five pages) short selections by Plato, Aristotle, Plotinus, Joshua Reynolds, Roger Fry, Dewitt Parker, Jacques Maritain, and Benedetto Croce. If "art" did not emerge until the eighteenth century, we may wonder what Plato, Aristotle, and Plotinus are doing here. When we turn to Weitz's introduction to this section we read:

> The question, "what is art?," is as old as the history of aesthetics. It is, of course, true that before the arts of poetry, music, painting, and sculpture were brought under the category of "Fine Arts," in the eighteenth century, the problem was traditionally specified as "what is the nature of poetry, music, sculpture, or painting?" But essentially the problem has remained the same: to state the defining properties of art. From Plato to the present day, philosophers, critics, and artists have tried to answer this question. It is the very model of a philosophical problem: what do, for example, the works of art, *Oedipus Rex*, the Parthenon, the *Iliad*, Chartres Cathedral, and, to come up to date, Picasso's "Guernica," have in common?[3]

The real cultural difference to which Kristeller had called attention is recognized and then promptly transformed into a terminological difference: "It is, of course, true," Weitz writes, that up until the eighteenth century "the problem was traditionally *specified* as, 'what is the nature of poetry, music, sculpture, or painting?' " But, he continues, *"essentially* the problem has remained the same" (emphasis added). In other words, Plato, Aristotle, and Plotinus may appear to have been writing about one or another of the arts, or about beauty, but they were really attempting to define art in the modern sense in which *Oedipus*, the Parthenon, the *Iliad*, Chartres Cathedral, and the "Guernica" are all art. The universality of this cultural formation, which it had been the chief contribution of Kristeller's investigation to put in question, is therewith reaffirmed.[4]

Weitz's tactic here typifies the way in which philosophers of art have come to terms with Kristeller's essay. Even in their role as historians they are given to citing or alluding to it approvingly and then proceeding to operate as if "art" were timeless and universal. That is to say, their histories are marked by systematic "denial" of the historicity of their subject matter. This manifests itself both in their *selection* of texts and in their *method of reading*.

In their role as historians, philosophers of art are inclined to recognize as relevant to the history of aesthetics only texts that appear to be addressing "problems" currently deemed philosophical and to be addressing them in a philosophical way, that is, in a way that the discipline of philosophy has sanctioned. In a recent essay entitled "The Historicity of Aesthetics," for example, Arnold Berleant writes that "theory necessarily comes after the fact." It "reflects" artistic practice. Its object is to "account for" or "explain" artistic practice.[5] Armed with this disciplinary notion of theory, is it surprising that philosophers of art have been blind to so many of the texts that could shed significant light on the evolution of "art"? Reviews of books, exhibits, and performances, authors' prefaces, textbooks, handbooks, manuals for the consumer, and the like reveal more clearly than ostensibly *pure* philosophical treatises the concrete problems "art" was invented to solve. However, such texts are so patently written not to *explain* but to *intervene* and to *influence* practice that they fall outside the purview of the historians of aesthetics. Insufficiently philosophical to merit their attention, such texts have been relegated to the "history of taste."

A case in point is the review of Gottfried August Bürger's collected poems in which Schiller adumbrated the ideas on the nature and function of art that he would later spell out in greater detail in his letters *On the Aesthetic Education of Man.* Composed in 1790 before he had even read Kant's *Critique of Judgment,* the theory of art he propounds in this review is expressly designed to do battle with the sensationalist verse that was sweeping Germany in the wake of Bürger's chilling ballad, "Lenore," about a young girl carried to her grave by the skeleton of her beloved. Accordingly, as I show in chapter 3, the review reveals a great deal about the cultural politics that gave rise to the modern theory of art.

The impression it leaves that "art" was invented to stem the commercialization of literature—which, not incidentally, was preventing Schiller's own writing from selling—is confirmed by the ponderous manual entitled *The Art of Reading Books* that Johann Adam Bergk brought to market eight years later in 1799. Bergk's object, the topic of chapter 4, is to divert his middle-class readers from the growing literature of "lite" entertainment to which he felt they were turning with dangerous avidity, by instructing them in a highly "refined," cerebral mode of reading. What gives his project such interest is that to characterize this mode of reading Bergk borrows his key concepts from Kant's *Critique of Judgment.* His hope—which undergirds literature curricula to this day—is that readers who have been taught to read as he specifies will come to select suitable reading matter of their own accord. Too sophisticated to be entertained by the lighter fare, they will demand for their leisure the "classics" on which he draws throughout his book for illustration—authors like Lessing, Wieland, Goethe, and Schiller, who can sustain and reward the mode of reading he has taught them.

Writings like Schiller's and Bergk's are crucial to understanding why the ideas to which Kant gave *pure* philosophical form evolved and flourished. However, because they wear their prescriptive intent so boldly, because they aim to *intervene* and to *alter* rather than to *explain* practice, such writings do not appear to be "properly" philosophical. They therefore tend to be overlooked by the philosopher-historians— excluded from the canon of texts relevant to the history of aesthetics. We may pause here to wonder, parenthetically, whether this kind of oversight is not motivated by the "denial" to which I alluded at the outset. For it would seem that by threatening to turn aesthetics into an artifact of the specific historical situation in which Kant lived and worked, these writings by Schiller and Bergk threaten to dissolve this branch of philosophy.

The same aversion to rhetoric that blinds the philosopher-historians to the relevance of such texts pervades their readings of the texts to which they do turn their attention, depleting these texts of their ability to help us understand the underlying motives for the momentous conceptual change that gave us "art." To mention but one revealing example explored in more detail in chapter 4, their treatment of Addison's *Pleasures of the Imagination* is marked by the same double gesture of recognition and denial that I have noted. On the one hand, they pronounce it a founding document. To quote Peter Kivy, writing in 1977, "Most philosophers who worry about such things seem to agree that the discipline of aesthetics, as practiced by professional philosophers today, came into being in Britain early in the eighteenth century and that Addison's *Spectator* papers *On the Pleasures of the Imagination* is the inaugural work, if any single work is."[6] As evidence Kivy cites Jerome Stolnitz's designation of Addison's work as "the starting-point of modern aesthetics" in an essay "On the Origins of 'Aesthetic Disinterestedness' " that appeared in the early 1960s.[7] Locutions like "the inaugural work" and "the starting-point of modern aesthetics" bespeak recognition of the implications of Kristeller's essay—recognition, that is, of the historicity of "art." And indeed Stolnitz cites Kristeller in his essay.[8] But having thus recognized the historical specificity of "art," these philosopher-historians promptly deny the implications of their finding by reading Addison's text as if it were a philosophical treatise—a text designed to define, or more precisely, to *explain* a preexisting practice.

Read with greater sensitivity to the essay's communicative context, it becomes apparent that Addison is attempting not so much to explain a preexisting practice as to *produce* a new practice. *The Pleasures of the Imagination,* as I note in chapter 4, is a pedagogical project, a contribution not in the first instance to aesthetics but to the growing literature on conduct—in the tradition of Gracián, Peachum, Chesterfield, etc.—and, more specifically, to the literature on leisure-time conduct. It takes readers on a guided tour of one after another of the fine arts in order to recommend, as preferable to less "innocent" sources of recreation, the amateur activities that would come to be known as "connoisseurship." Read in this way, Addison's essay contributes a good deal to our understanding of the evolution of "art." It suggests that it was in the first instance as a solution to the "problem" of leisure—in a word, as a "refined" spectator sport—that the arts came together under a single concept. But philosopher-historians like Kivy and Stolnitz read right past Addison's pedagogical rhetoric, noticing only those linguistic features of his essay in terms of which he may be viewed as attempting to give clear formulation to the timeless and universal facts of aesthetic experience. This has the dual consequence of turning Addison into a bungler and preventing his essay from enriching our understanding of the evolution of "art." For read in this way, it appears in the philosophers' histories as a "lively," but superficial—which is to say, ultimately inept—attempt at an aesthetic treatise that is redeemed only by its extraordinary suggestiveness. To quote Monroe Beardsley, it "invited, and to some extent exemplified, a new approach to the *problems* of art and beauty" that subsequent philosophers like Kant would eventually grapple with more successfully (emphasis added).[9] So much for Addison's founding role in the history of aesthetics.

In their selection of texts, then, and in the strategies with which they read them, those who make an occupation of aesthetics tend to deny the history of their subject matter.[10] Surprisingly, this is no less true of Terry Eagleton's recent commentary on the history of aesthetics, *The Ideology of the Aesthetic*. Although Eagleton is anxious to disclaim providing any kind of history,[11] his commentary is closely affiliated with the work of the philosopher-historians. He takes the same "high priori" road as they, selecting for comment the ideas of a few giants arranged chronologically. As a Marxist literary critic, he reads with more sensitivity than they to nonphilosophical, especially political, registers, but he does not present the ideas he extrapolates as emanating from historical persons with motives for theorizing in specific ways. Indeed, he disparages the linking of the ideas contained in texts with the personal motives that inspired those texts (p. 4) in favor of "trac[ing] aesthetic motifs" (p. 3) through time. In short, he is engaged in "thematics"—a thematics that, to cite the book's cover, ranges "throughout modern Western thought" in frank denial of the origins he himself assigns aesthetics in eighteenth-century Germany (p. 13). His book reinscribes the tradition of great minds speaking with one another over and above the historical process that informs Weitz's anthology and the work of the philosopher-historians generally.[12]

This trend will not be reversed in a single volume, of course. A new history that is more sensitive to the historicity of its subject is a task for many scholars, and I view the present volume as but one chapter in this larger project. It explores a single, decisive moment in the evolution of "art"—the moment in late eighteenth-century Germany when "art" achieved something quite close to its modern form. At the center of the volume is the "masterpiece" in which disciplinary histories of aesthetics tell us that nearly a century of effort to theorize "art" came to fruition in 1790. I mean the *Critique of Judgment*, of course, but I hasten to warn the reader that I have little to say about it directly. It is rather as a specter that Kant appears in the present volume, tempting the reader to view its relatively independent chapters as an extended commentary on his masterpiece—commentary designed not to dispute its centrality in the development we are exploring, but to complicate disciplinary accounts of it as a victory of pure philosophical reflection by resituating it in the larger debate over culture in which it originally functioned.

I have thus attempted to foreground texts that disciplinary histories have overlooked. (Translations, except as noted, are my own.)

These include, in addition to the texts mentioned above by Schiller and Bergk, what would appear to be the earliest theorization of "art" in its modern sense, a short essay from 1785 in which Karl Philipp Moritz singles out and exalts as "beautiful works of art" objects produced in studied indifference to the desires of consumers, whether for pleasure or utility.

Having examined some of the professional and economic interests of "difficult" writers like Moritz in mystifying inherited conceptions of artistic production in chapter 1, I take up in chapter 2 an extended debate over the nature of a "book" that legal scholars also joined with the result that many of these ideas about artistic production got incorporated into, and empowered by, laws of intellectual property known as "copyright," or "authors' rights."

The role played by gender in the formation of "art" is the subject of chapter 5, where I briefly examine the "containment" of Germany's first acclaimed woman novelist, Sophie von La Roche—the process by which she was transformed from a promising "artist" into an amateur, a source of inspiration first to female readers and then only to the male writer who helped her into print, Christoph Martin Wieland. La Roche's enshrinement in literary history as "Wieland's muse" enacts the displacement figured in the engraving on the frontispiece of this book, *The Genius of the Artist with Minerva and Muses,* which Johann Georg Sulzer commissioned for the frontispiece of his comprehensive dictionary of the fine arts, *Allgemeine Theorie der schönen Künste* (1771)—for this is the only appearance women make in this pioneering and widely influential work.

This body of theory entered Anglo-American discourse through Coleridge. Finally, therefore, in chapter 6 I turn to Coleridge's effort to impose on England principles of art appreciation gleaned from the *Critique of Judgment.* Reading his *Principles of Genial Criticism* in the context of the powerful forces of opposition he encountered puts the uses of "art" in a perspective from which the main outlines and some of the deep personal and professional stakes in our own contemporary culture wars also become visible. By regrounding aesthetic ideas in this way in their motives in history we may begin to understand how a cultural formation that evolved as recently as "art" could have entrenched itself so thoroughly that we imagine it always to have existed.

The Hack by Friedrich Jacob Tromlitz after Karl Moritz Berggold. From *Triumpf des deutschen Witzes in einer Sammlung der stechendsten Sinngedichte und witzigsten Einfälle deutscher Köpfe,* edited by Christian Friedrich Traugott Voigt (Leipzig: Baumgärtnerische Buchhandlung, 1800), facing p. 58. Courtesy of the Yale Collection of German Literature.

Berggold del.   Tromlitz sc.

Der Fabrikautor.

1. THE INTERESTS IN DISINTERESTEDNESS

Is it merely an accident of construction, a chance of composition that the whole Kantian theory of mimesis is set forth between these two remarks on salary[:] . . . the definition of free (or liberal: freie) *art by opposition to mercenary art . . . [and the statement] that in the Fine-Arts the mind must occupy itself, excite and satisfy itself without having any end in view and independently of any salary[?]*

—*Jacques Derrida, "Economimesis"*

In 1785, five years before the publication of Kant's *Critique of Judgment,* there appeared in the *Berlinische Monatsschrift* a short essay with the long-winded title *Versuch einer Vereinigung aller schönen Künste und Wissenschaften unter dem Begriff des in sich selbst Vollendeten* [*Toward a Unification of All the Fine Arts and Letters under the Concept of Self-Sufficiency*]. In this essay a little-known figure in the history of aesthetics, Karl Philipp Moritz (1756–1793), gave the first unequivocal and systematic expression to what I have called our modern conception of the arts. Works of art, he argued in this and in his subsequent writings, are "self-sufficient totalities" produced simply to be contemplated "for their own sake"—that is, "disinterestedly," purely for the enjoyment of their internal attributes and relationships, independently of any external relationships or effects they might have.[1]

These propositions about the nature and function of art—together with the array of further propositions they entail or suggest about the appropriate methods of classifying, interpreting, describing, and evaluating works of art—have dominated discussion of the arts in the twentieth century.[2] And yet, familiar as the propositions set forth by Moritz are to us today, it is hard to imagine a more radical departure from the two millennia of theorizing about the arts that preceded his essay. For the arts up until this time had been perceived as intervening directly in human life—as imparting and empowering beliefs, as communicating truths (and of course also falsehoods) in a pleasing form—and their value and excellence as works of art had been measured, *instrumentally,* in terms of their success (or failure) in serving these broad human purposes. Moritz, by contrast, presents us with the image of all these purposes being "rolled back" into the work of art itself, there to reside as the purely "internal purposiveness" [*innere Zweckmäßigkeit*] of the parts with respect to the whole:

> In contemplating a beautiful object . . . I roll the purpose back into the object itself: I regard it as something that finds *completion* not in me but *in itself* [*in sich selbst Vollendetes*] and thus constitutes a whole in itself and gives me pleasure *for its own sake* [*um sein selbst willen*]. . . . Thus the beautiful object yields a higher and more disinterested [*uneigennützigeres*] pleasure than the merely useful object.[3]

Art, according to this new way of thinking, is a discrete realm of ultimate purpose. Its value is *intrinsic.*

Through the mediation of Kant, in whose *Critique of Judgment* they came to fruition,[4] these radically new ideas about the nature of art and about the attitude appropriate to it took hold and, with astonishing rapidity, became the reigning theory of the arts. How is this dramatic shift in the theory of art to be explained? I propose to look first at the theoretical context in which Moritz worked—that is, the occurrence in France of the earliest explicit attempt to provide a general theory of the fine arts, and the reception of this theory by Moritz's precursors in Germany. Second, I shall turn to Moritz's contribution to this project. Close reading of his essay of 1785 will suggest that profound changes in the social and economic situation of the arts during his lifetime prompted his departure from inherited tradition and gave rise to the modern theory of art and the aesthetic experience. Finally, I shall examine the nature of these changes in somewhat greater detail.

I

It was suggested above that "art" in its modern sense, as comprehending all and only the "fine" arts, is the product of a rather recent remapping of human activities. An important milestone in this development was the Abbé Charles Batteux's treatise, *Les beaux arts réduits à un même principe* [*The Fine Arts Reduced to a Common Principle*]. Batteux distinguished the *mechanical arts*, which have as their objective the satisfaction of man's needs, from the arts "whose end is pleasure." In the latter class, which he designated the *fine arts*, Batteux placed music, poetry, painting, sculpture, and the art of gesture, or dance. Architecture and eloquence did not seem to him to fall neatly into either category, so he established yet a third class in which the objectives of both utility and pleasure are combined.

> The arts of the first kind employ nature as they find it, solely for use and service. Those of the third kind bestow a certain polish upon it in order to suit it for use and for pleasure. The fine arts do not use nature at all, but instead only imitate it, each according to its own manner.[5]

With the publication of Batteux's treatise in 1746 the formation of the modern system of the fine arts was nearly complete.

Batteux brings the arts together under the concept of imitation— a concept that he claims to have discovered in Aristotle, but which, as I note below, he conceives in a distinctly non-Aristotelian fashion. In "reducing" the arts to this "common principle" Batteux hopes to clarify for "amateurs" what he imagines to have become too rich a fund of artistic rules and precepts. "We read, we study, we thirst after knowledge," he writes, but our efforts are eluded "because of the infinite number of parts." Let us therefore think of "all these rules as so many branches of the same trunk": if we "trace them to their source," we shall find "one principle so simple as to be readily comprehended and yet so comprehensive as to absorb all of the little rules of detail" (pp. xvi–xvii). Such is the principle of imitation.

The project of Batteux's treatise is to demonstrate "from the known qualities of the human mind" that the imitation of nature is the arts' "common object" and that they differ from each other only "in the means they employ in the execution"—"colors, sounds, and gestures" in the case of painting, music, and dance, and "speech" in the case of poetry (p. 4). In the principle of imitation

> we have, on the one hand, the link, or kind of brotherly tie, by which all the arts . . . are united, tending to one common end and regulated by common principles; and on the other hand, the particular differences by which they are separated and distinguished from each other. (p. 5)

For Batteux, as for most neoclassical critics, the imitation of nature necessarily involves idealization. To please a polite audience the artist must improve upon nature, he must create an imitation that

> copies it, not slavishly, but rather, selecting objects and features, presents them in all the perfection they are capable of: in a word, an imitation in which one sees nature not as it is in itself but as it could be, and as it can be conceived by the mind. (p. 29)

Thus we are told that Molière, when he wanted to depict a misanthrope, "did not look around Paris for an original" to copy; instead, by drawing on "all of the marks of a gloomy temper that he was able to observe among men" along with those his genius could supply, he "represented [*figura*] a unique character" (p. 31). Derived by abstraction from a class of particulars, this composite ideal is called "beautiful nature" [*la belle nature*] (p. 32). Art, for Batteux, is the "imitation of nature, agreeable to taste; that is, [the] imitation of beautiful nature."[6] This unifying principle established, he proceeds in the body of his treatise to extract from it the rules for the individual arts and their respective genres.

Expounded by D'Alembert in his famous "Discours préliminaire" for the *Encyclopédie* (1751), Batteux's ideas exerted enormous influence both in France and abroad. In Germany they fell on especially fertile soil. By the time the first of an impressive series of translations and adaptations of his treatise appeared there in 1751,[7] native speculation had issued in a new branch of philosophy that shared—indeed, was defined by—the very interests that had inspired Batteux. This was the nascent "science of sensuous knowledge" [*anschauende Erkenntnis*] that Alexander Baumgarten, its founder, denominated "aesthetics."[8] One of its chief goals was a general theory of the arts. Despite the corroboration Batteux's treatise obviously lent to their project, however, the German aestheticians did not receive him with unequivocal enthusiasm. A heated debate ensued, engendering refutations and defenses of his unifying principle until well into the 1770s.[9] But the vehemence of his opponents is deceptive. Indeed, a study of their writings would make an interesting chapter in the history of critical—or metacritical—misprision. For while they present their own opposing views on the arts as absolutely new, they in fact barely go beyond translating Batteux into their own idiom. It was, in short, in willful misreadings of Batteux that the forefathers of idealist aesthetics carved out their intellectual space.

One of the most gifted among them, and "the most vital single influence" on the intellectual development of the young Moritz,[10] was Moses Mendelssohn. Mendelssohn attempted to sketch the broad outlines of a general theory of the arts in an essay entitled *Betrachtungen über die Quellen und die Verbindungen der schönen Künste und Wissenschaften [Reflections on the Sources and Relations of the Fine Arts and Letters]* which appeared in 1757 in the *Bibliothek der schönen Wissenschaften und der freyen Künste.* This essay synthesized the two decades of vigorous philosophical speculation on the arts set in motion by Baumgarten. And thanks to Mendelssohn's mastery of the vernacular—Baumgarten had written in crabbed Latin—his essay established the direction in which the theory of art would evolve in subsequent decades.

What Batteux had been content merely to allude to in passing—and then only in the most general terms as the "pleasure" of an audience—is at the center of Mendelssohn's concern. "What phenomena are accompanied by greater movement of the driving wheels of the human soul than the fine arts?" he asks at the beginning of his *Betrachtungen.*[11]

> Poetry, eloquence, beauty in shapes and in sounds penetrate through the various senses to our souls and rule over all our dispositions. They can make us happy or depressed at will. They can stir our passions and then soothe them, and we willingly submit to the power of the artist who causes us to hope, to fear, to be angry, to be soothed, to laugh, and to shed tears. (p. 168)

For Mendelssohn the unity of the arts is grounded in the powerful effects they exert upon an audience—in the capacity they exhibit to *move* us. He deems it the central task of a general theory of the arts to explain this fact of experience. Assuming the explanation to lie in some essential similarity among art objects (an assumption he shares with Batteux), Mendelssohn asks: "But what do the diverse objects of poetry, of painting, of eloquence and of dance, of music, of sculpture and architecture, what do all these objects of human contrivance have in common such that they can concur in [this] single purpose?" (p. 168).

Mendelssohn believes that one answer to this question may be dismissed without further ado: Batteux's proposition that "the common property is the imitation of nature" (p. 169). Now, this is hardly a fair summary of the French writer's position, suppressing as it does his critical qualifier—Batteux, as we have seen, had been careful to explain that the arts imitate *beautiful* nature, not nature pure and simple—but it clears the way for Mendelssohn's alternative view. For, reduced to this "most sterile proposition," the French treatise is opened to his objection: "What if *Batteux* were asked why nature pleases us? And why does imitation please? Wouldn't he be as perplexed as that Indian sage at the well-known question: *And what does the giant tortoise stand on?*" (p. 169) Having thus "disposed" of the French critic, Mendelssohn proceeds to develop the ideas that Batteux's qualifier, "beautiful," had been designed to convey. He thereby brings into the center of discussion a concept of great significance to the theoretical shift we are tracing.

Imitations of nature please us, Mendelssohn asserts, insofar as they possess a still more fundamental ingredient of pleasure: perfection [*Vollkommenheit*]. For nothing so pleases the human soul as perfection. This has been conclusively demonstrated by (Wolffian) psychology, Mendelssohn writes (p. 169). And it may be taken as further established—this time by the investigations of Baumgarten—that art is sensuous (or concrete) knowledge. Thus, it may be concluded that "to please our souls" the arts must render perfection sensuous. And as this is their ultimate purpose, "we can presume the following principle to be certain: the essence of the fine arts and letters consists in the sensuous expression of perfection [*sinnlicher Ausdruck der Vollkommenheit*]" (p. 170). This we call "beauty," and it is what is really meant, he contends, by phrases like "the imitation of beautiful nature."

But could this be what Batteux meant by the phrase? For the standard to which he had held the arts is conspicuously absent from Mendelssohn's definition. Batteux had called for the perfection of *nature*, for an imitation of and truth to nature as it ideally is. But Mendelssohn's principle of perfection places no such constraints on the arts. It calls only for the creation of a beautiful object. "Any perfection capable of being rendered concrete or sensuous," he writes, "may produce an object of beauty":

> This includes all perfections of outer form, that is, of lines and shapes; the harmony of diverse tones and colors; the relation among the parts of a whole; all the faculties of our souls; all the dexterities of our bodies; and even the perfections of our external circumstances, such as honor, comfort, and riches . . . if they can be rendered perfectly concrete. (p. 170)

In short, although it may, a work of art *need not* reflect nature. Its beauty and excellence are a function not of its correspondence to some hitherto-existing reality, but rather of the purely internal relationships (of harmony, symmetry, and the like) established among its component parts.

This new conception of the work of art as a freestanding, harmonious, concrete whole is, to be sure, still entangled in Mendelssohn's *Betrachtungen* with elements of the imitation theory. When he descends from the heights of abstraction to suggest how the artist actually implements the principle of perfection, he cites the procedure of the novelist Samuel Richardson. Since a model for such an ideal character as Sir Charles Grandison probably did not exist in nature, Richardson

> undertook to form him as man ought to have been according to the *provenient grace* of God. He chose an ideal beauty as his model and sought in nature the traits that, taken together, constitute such a perfect character. He beautified nature. (p. 174)

Here and elsewhere when he comes to talk about individual elements of a work, Mendelssohn reverts to a (Platonized) imitation theory. The drift of his argument, however, is toward art understood simply as the creation of a beautiful object. He summarizes this view:

> *The artist must raise himself above commonplace nature, and as the re-creation of beauty is his sole aim, he is always free to concentrate it in his works so that it will the more strongly move [rühre] us.* (p. 173)

For nearly three decades this new direction in speculation about the nature of art would remain anchored in the instrumentalist framework so emphatically reaffirmed in Mendelssohn's requirement that the work of art move us. It is first dislodged by his pupil, Karl Philipp Moritz, whose own attempt at a general theory of the arts is directed expressly against such instrumentalism.

II

A number of features of Moritz's *Versuch einer Vereinigung* serve to situate the essay in the development I am tracing: the title itself, the fact that Moritz dedicated the essay to Mendelssohn, and the express assertion in the opening sentence that, in recent theory, the "principle of pleasure" has replaced the "principle of imitation" as the ultimate end or purpose of the fine arts (p. 3).[12] With this succinct summary of the tradition he will sublate, Moritz asserts that the *craftsman* alone is constrained by considerations of instrumentality. Objects of *mechanical art*—Moritz uses a clock and a knife as examples—

> have their purposes outside themselves in the person who derives comfort from their use; they are thus not complete in themselves; in and of themselves and without the potential or actual achievement of their external purposes they have no essential value. (p. 4)

The *artist*, by contrast, is under no such constraints, for a work of *fine art* "does not have its purpose outside itself, and does not exist for the sake of the perfection of anything else, but rather for the sake of its own internal perfection" (p. 4). It follows that the effects of a work of art on an audience are irrelevant to its value. Now a function of purely internal relationships, the value of art is intrinsic. In short, although he adopts Mendelssohn's principle of perfection, Moritz abandons its rationale—the aim of affecting an audience.[13] In this way he completes the gradual remapping of human activities of which "art" in its modern sense is the product—that is, art understood as an activity that is sui generis, totally distinct from all other human activities. The artist's sole end or purpose in Moritz's model of art consists in the creation of a perfectly "coherent harmonious whole" [*übereinstimmendes harmonisches Ganze*] (p. 8).

Although Moritz offers little in the way of argument for this portentous departure, the spirit of a powerful precedent pervades his exposition. This precedent is not to be found in the earlier criticism of the arts, but in the religion of Moritz's youth, which posited absolute *self-sufficiency*, or freedom from dependence upon anything external to Himself, as a necessary condition of the pure perfection of the Deity. When Moritz observes that the beautiful object "does not exist for the sake of the perfection of anything else, but rather for the sake of its own internal perfection," he is simply transferring an essential property of the Deity to the work of art. Indeed, it is by recourse to this theological analogue that he defines all of the different components in his model of art: not only the nature of the work of art and of its connection to the world outside it, but also the nature of the processes by which it is produced by an artist and received by an audience.

Earlier I noted that Moritz describes the mode of reception appropriate to a work of art as unselfish or "disinterested pleasure" [*uneigennütziges Vergnügen*] in the object "for its own sake" [*um sein selbst willen*].[14] This is precisely the attitude deemed appropriate to the Deity in the quietest brand of German Pietism in which the young Moritz was indoctrinated by his father.[15] In his autobiographical novel *Anton Reiser*, the first volume of which appeared the same year as the *Versuch*, Moritz describes the quietist teachings in this way:

> [They] are concerned for the most part with that ... total abandonment of the self and entry upon a blissful state of nothingness, with that complete extermination of all so-called *self-ness* [*Eigenheit*] or *self-love* [*Eigenliebe*], and a totally disinterested [*uninteressierte*] love of God, in which not the merest spark of self-love may mingle, if it is to be pure; and out of this there arises in the end a perfect, blissful *tranquillity* which is the highest goal of all these strivings.[16]

This summary of the highest stage and ultimate goal of human piety and felicity is transported almost verbatim into Moritz's theory of art, where it serves precisely to characterize what we now term the "aesthetic attitude." The contemplation of a beautiful work of art, Moritz observes in the *Versuch*, is accompanied by a "sweet astonishment" [*süße(s) Staunen*], a "pleasant forgetfulness of ourselves" [*angenehme(s) Vergessen unsrer selbst*]:

> As the beautiful object completely captivates our attention, it diverts our attention momentarily from ourselves with the result that we seem to lose ourselves in the beautiful object; and precisely this loss, this forgetfulness of ourselves, is the highest degree of pure and disinterested [*uneigennützigen*] pleasure which beauty grants us. (p. 5)

The mode of reception described here follows just as necessarily for Moritz from the nature of the work of art as does religious piety from the nature of the Deity. God is an end in Himself, perfectly self-sufficient. To love Him selfishly—as a source of private gains—would be to make of Him a mere instrument or means of pleasure. We are thus enjoined to love God disinterestedly, for His own sake. An analogous relationship is established between the work of art and the "aesthetic" attitude. "Beauty in a work of art is not pure and unalloyed for me," Moritz writes, "until I completely eliminate the special relation to myself and contemplate it as something which has been brought forth entirely for its own sake, so that it is something complete in itself" (p. 5). In its origins the theory of art's autonomy is clearly a displaced theology.

How is so exponential an expansion, such an elevation of the function of the arts to be accounted for? Traditionally this has been attributed to secularization: with the erosion of orthodox belief beginning in the Renaissance, art has inherited the task of interpreting human experience. Such explanations find support in high romantic celebrations of art such as Schiller's *Aesthetic Letters* and Wordsworth's *Prelude;* but like the masterpieces from which they draw their support, they are silent about the more fundamental material impulses responsible for this valorizing of art.[17] One of the chief interests of Moritz's essay is that it alerts us to these impulses.

Having discussed the nature of the beautiful work of art and the mode of reception appropriate to it, Moritz turns in the final section of his essay to the artist. At issue is what the artist's attitude ought to be toward *his* audience and toward *his* work. (It is important to retain the masculine pronoun for, as I suggest in chapter 5, only men can become "artists" in the modern sense Moritz seeks to define.) With the same show of logical rigor displayed in his earlier discussion, Moritz enjoins the artist to subordinate all pragmatic considerations to the perfection of his work. "The true artist," he writes,

> will strive to bring the highest internal purposiveness or perfection [*innere Zweckmäßigkeit oder Vollkommenheit*] into his work; and if it then meets with approval [from its audience], he will be happy; but he has already achieved his real purpose by completing the work. (p. 8)

Moritz would have us believe that this concept of the artist's enterprise is simply a logical extension of his definition of art. However,

the vehemence and detail with which he enforces his injunction suggest that more than logical coherence is at stake. The artist is warned:

> But if the thought of approval is your main consideration, and if
> your work is of value to you only insofar as it brings you fame,
> then . . . you are working in a self-interested manner: the focal
> point of the work will fall outside the work; you are not creating
> it for its own sake and hence will not bring forth anything whole
> and self-sufficient. You will be seeking a false glitter, which may
> dazzle the rabble momentarily, but will vanish like fog before the
> gaze of the wise. (pp. 7–8)

The venerable end of giving pleasure to an audience has taken on
unsavory associations indeed: to seek to *please* is here to *curry favor*
with an audience, and this in turn seems to mean indulging its appetite
for spectacle. Such disparaging remarks recur, creating an image of a
contemporary audience anything but receptive to the arts—at least to
the arts that concern Moritz. It is an audience sharply and most
unevenly divided between the many and the few, between the "thou-
sands who have no eye for the beautiful" and the "men of taste" who
make it their chief occupation in life to love and serve art, Moritz
writes, much as the philanthropist loves and serves humankind—
ardently, but without any hope of private gain. By contrast, the many—
"the rabble," as he terms them—seek only "diversion" [*Ergötzung*]
and "pleasant sensations" [*angenehme Empfindungen*], with the consequence that the beautiful work of art is "passed by with indifference"
and the "theaters play to empty houses"—a source of great anguish to
the "noble" few [*die Edlen*].[18]

Such is the world depicted in Moritz's essay. It is a world with so
little use for the beautiful work of art that it cannot but cast doubt on
the disinterestedness of his theoretical project. To see that this is so,
one need only compare the way in which the two competing theories
of art—Mendelssohn's instrumentalist theory and the new theory put
forward by Moritz—would make sense of such widespread indifference to art. In terms of the earlier theory, art that fails to affect and so
to achieve the approval of an audience is without merit. On the new
theory of art's autonomy, however, such unfortunate facts of reception
have no such unfortunate consequences. They are indicative not of an
imperfect work, but of the imperfect sensibility, or piety, of the audience; because for Moritz, as we have seen, the beautiful work of art
does not exist in order to provide pleasure or amuse; it exists, like

God, for its own sake—that is, for the sake of its own internal perfection. By suggesting to Moritz how the question of a work's value—indeed, of its very status as a work of art—might be shifted from considerations of reception to the purely internal consideration of the harmonious interaction of its parts, the quietist creed of his youth inspired a new theory of art in which, as it were, a virtue is made of necessity, and the relative ineffectuality of beautiful art, instead of rendering its value problematic, can be construed as evidence of its very excellence.

The picture of "art" that emerges from Moritz's *Versuch*, then, is of a category designed to "resolve" a concrete dilemma of the contemporary art world. Examination of the situation of the arts in eighteenth-century Germany will help to shed light on the nature of this dilemma.

III

The eighteenth century witnessed momentous changes in the production, distribution, and consumption of art. I shall focus here on the transformation of the book market, not only because it was by this that the philosophers and critics who fashioned the modern theory of art were most affected, but because literature was the first among the arts to undergo the changes I intend to trace.

The rise of the middle classes in eighteenth-century Europe increased dramatically the demand for reading material. A variety of new institutions emerged to meet this growing demand: new literary forms like the novel, reviews and periodicals, circulating and lending libraries to facilitate distribution, and the professional writer. The possibility of actually making a living by the pen is a product of this development—of the emergence, that is, of a sufficiently large and literate middle class to support writers through the purchase of their works. This is especially true of Germany where, in contrast to England and France, the patronage of authors had never been widespread.[19] With few exceptions—such as the court at Weimar—the petty princes and provincial aristocracy in absolutist Germany took little interest in the arts, and practically none in vernacular literature. As J. G. F. Schulz complained in 1784, they were

> more concerned with their soldiers or deer, hogs and horses.
> And if they do read anything in print, it has to be French or

Italian. So they don't know our scholars and don't want to know them. Even less do they seek out and reward literary merit.[20]

However, German absolutism greatly retarded the formation of a middle class—and hence the very preconditions of an energetic world of arts and letters. The creation of these conditions was in large measure the work of a few hundred civic-minded literati—philosophers and poets from Leibniz to Lessing—who divided their time between "their work" and a variety of projects aimed at extending literacy in the broadest sense: the establishment of theaters, the founding of reading societies and periodicals, and so on. Mendelssohn's *Betrachtungen* are the product of one such enterprise. The comparative grace and lucidity with which the essay synthesizes two decades of obscure school-philosophical speculation on the arts reflect the objectives of the periodical for which it was commissioned— Friedrich Nicolai's *Bibliothek der schönen Wissenschaften und der freyen Künste* [*Library of Humanities and Fine Arts*], in the founding and operation of which Mendelssohn and, to a lesser degree, Lessing collaborated.[21] First published in 1757 and modeled on Addison's *Spectator*, the *Bibliothek* was designed to "foster liberal learning and good taste among the Germans" by making the subject matter of aesthetics accessible for the first time to educated laymen as well as to scholars.[22]

The pedagogical motive sounded here is reflected in the literary output of the German ideologues of enlightenment, or *Aufklärer*. However, it also plays a larger role in their theorizing about the arts than is generally recognized. The creation of a literate middle class is a prime rationale in the first comprehensive German poetic, Johann Christoph Gottsched's *Versuch einer critischen Dichtkunst* (1730). This aim causes him and his successors in the generation of Lessing and Mendelssohn to place an extremely heavy emphasis on the pragmatic—that is, upon the effects of the arts, and especially of literature, on an audience. Questions about the nature of artistic imitation are invariably subordinated to the purpose of such imitation—to instruct an audience, or increasingly, to *move* an audience, as the theorists speculate that the distinctive power of literature, as a "sensuous mode of discourse," lies in its ability to instruct the heart as opposed to the head. Mendelssohn's departure from Batteux is an instance of this tendency. And it is in his exploration of the principles and techniques of *subliminal* instruction—later to be held suspect as manipulation—

that Lessing's deviation from neoclassical imitation theory may be seen to lie.[23]

The efforts of the *Aufklärer* to extend literacy and to create a climate in which a literature in the vernacular might begin to develop were remarkably successful. By the 1760s we begin to read of the spread of the reading habit—of the new "reading craze" [*Lesewut*] or "reading mania" [*Lesesucht*]. In the following decades a veritable "reading plague" [*Leseseuche*] is reported to be sweeping the German lands. It is said to have extended even into the lower classes and to have infected women especially. "In no other country has the reading hobby [*Leseliebhaberei*] made such progress as in Germany," the *Weltbürger* proclaims in 1791.

> Formerly nobody engaged in reading except actual scholars or people studying to become scholars. The remainder of the nation was content with the Bible and a few devotional works. But now all this has changed. The sciences have not only ceased to be the property of a certain class; at least a superficial knowledge of them has become a necessity among all the educated classes. One now finds the works of good and bad writers in the dressing rooms of princes and under the workbench; and the nation's gentility, so as not to appear coarse, decorate their rooms with books instead of tapestries. In the last century a soldier with a book in his hand would have been occasion for the most biting sarcasm; in ours an officer who isn't well-read would be contemptible. Our mothers dressed the children in the morning and went about their business; our daughters, however, spend the morning reading poems and magazines, and in the evening wander through the solitary valley with a novel in the hand. Indeed, the peasants are already reading the *Noth- und Hülfs-Büchlein* to each other in the village inn.[24]

In reality the new hobby cannot have been anywhere near as widespread as the *Weltbürger* implies, for it is estimated that as late as 1800 only some 25 percent of the population at most was literate; but the ebullient tone is entirely justified, because this figure is nearly double what it had been only a generation before.[25]

By the 1780s the demand for reading material had sufficiently increased to entice, if not to support, an astonishing number of would-be writers. Reporting a decade later on the "rapid progress" literature was making in Germany, the London bookseller James Lackington notes with undisguised awe that there are "seven thousand living authors in that country," a veritable "army of writers," and "every body reads."[26] This questionable advantage of Germany over England is echoed in G. C. Lichtenberg's observation that if England's forte is "race horses" [*Rennpferde*], Germany's is "race pens" [*Rennfedern*].[27] Such observations are borne out by contemporary catalogues of German literary output.[28] Because of the relative lack of vocational opportunity for the sons of the middle classes in absolutist Germany, the number of would-be writers so proliferated that there developed a kind of literary proletariat—about whose obtrusive presence complaints were filed at the Leipzig book fairs: "One is overcome by nausea and disgust at these otherwise renowned scholars," one visitor complains in 1795. "They have manuscripts for every occasion and by the dozen."[29] The writers who flourished in this climate were those who were able and willing to cater to popular taste.

Although won over relatively slowly from a predominantly devotional literature, the middle-class reading public in Germany had developed, by the last quarter of the century, a voracious appetite for the entire spectrum of light entertainment—from sentimental love stories and novels of education, to tales of ghost-seers and exorcists, and an aggressively escapist literature of adventure and intrigue. An advertisement in the Leipzig newspaper *Reichsbote* gives an idea of this trend. "In all reputable lending libraries you will find the following highly entertaining works," it begins, and then lists

> *Celestine's Garters* (3d ed.); *Corona. The Necromancer; The Ghost of My Girl, Her Appearance and My Wedding Feast; The Chamber of Horror, a Ghost Story* (*Library of Ghost Stories*, vol. i); *Kunigunde, or The Robbers' Cave in the Forest of Firs; Lisara, the Amazon from Abyssinia, a Romantic Portrait; Legends from the World of Ghosts and Magic* (new ed.); *The Suicide, a Tale of Terror and Wonder; Escapades in Sorcery, a Comic Tale; The Old Man of the Woods, or The Underground Dwelling; The Strange Adventures of an Englishman in America; Diverting Anecdotes and Side-Splitting Cross-Cuts* by G. C. Cramer.[30]

Literary entertainment was becoming an industry.

The significance of this trend, especially for "serious" or difficult writers, is the subject of the "Vorspiel auf dem Theater" ["Prologue in the Theater"] (1798) in *Faust*. A spirited altercation between a dramatic poet and a theater producer intent on a box-office success provides the occasion for Goethe to spell out what Moritz had earlier hinted at—namely, why the instrumentalist aesthetic worked out by the generation of Mendelssohn, in which a work's excellence is measured by its capacity to affect an audience, was felt to be incompatible with artistic integrity. The message of the "Vorspiel" is that this aesthetic has been coopted into the service of purely escapist ends by a growing entertainment industry. For shorn of its original moral-didactic intent, it is this aesthetic of *effects* that is propounded by the theater producer. Pondering the (now familiar) question of how to captivate an audience that, while "not accustomed to the best," has "read an awful lot," he exclaims:

> PRODUCER: Above all, let there be sufficient plot!
> They like to look, so let them see a lot.
> You give the audience a solid eyeful,
> So they can gasp and marvel all the time,
> You'll grip them by sheer quantity of trifle,
> Your popularity will climb.
> Mass calls for mass in order to be won.
> Each ends up choosing something for his own;
> Who brings a lot, brings bits for everyone,
> And they will all be happy going home.
> You stage a piece—serve it in pieces, do!
> Why, it's a snap to make this kind of stew;
> It's served as fast as cooked up in your head.
> What use is it to bring a whole instead,
> The public shreds it anyway for you.
>
> POET: You do not sense how cheap this is, how tawdry,
> How shamefully the true artist is thus maligned!
> The charlatan's ragout of tricks and bawdry,
> I see, is now an axiom in your mind.
>
> PRODUCER: Such reprobation leaves me cool:
> To affect an audience you must choose the tool
> That is adapted to your timber.
> The wood you are to split is soft, remember,
> Just look for whom you will have striven!
> This one may be by boredom driven,
> That one is comatose from overfeeding,
> And, what is most reluctantly forgiven,
> A lot arrive here fresh from journal-reading.[31]

But the urgings of this savvy market analyst are to no avail, for it takes "strong[er] drink" to please the new reading public than Goethe's poet is willing to supply. What the poet had expected to stage was a "perfect whole" [*ein Ganzes*]. Turning Moritz's precept into practice, he protests that the job of pandering to the public taste is beneath his dignity as a "true artist" [*echten Künstler*] and tells the producer to find some other "lackey" [*Knecht*].

The vast majority of writers, many of them succumbing to the commercial pressures depicted here, churned out imitations and variations on proven popular themes with unprecedented rapidity.[32] Those who did not—the "true artists" of Goethe and of Moritz—sold poorly. Just how poorly is suggested by the following anecdote in a letter from Heinrich von Kleist to his fiancée. He is describing a visit in 1800 to a lending library in Würzburg.

> Listen to what I found there and I shall need to say no more about the tone of Würzburg.
> "I should like to have a few good books."
> The collection is at your disposal, sir.
> "Perhaps something by Wieland."
> I hardly think so.
> "Or by Schiller, Goethe."
> You would not be likely to find them here.
> "Why is that? Are all these books out? Do people read so much here?"
> Not exactly.
> "What sort of people do the most reading here then?"
> Lawyers, merchants, and married women.
> "And the unmarried women?"
> They are not permitted to apply for books.
> "And students?"
> We have orders not to give them any.
> "But if so little is read, could you tell me then where in heaven's name the works of Wieland, Goethe, and Schiller have got to?"
> Begging your pardon, sir, but these books are not read here at all.
> "I see. You have not got them in the library?"
> We are not allowed to.
> "Then what sort of books have you got here along all these walls?"

Romances of chivalry, those and nothing else. To the right those with ghosts, to the left without ghosts, according to taste. "Aha, I see!"[33]

In short, the public's insatiable appetite for literature did not extend to the German poets. By and large too demanding for the general reader, their works found an audience only among the elite—government officials in the large towns, university-trained professional men, doctors, lawyers, preachers, teachers, and, of course, fellow poets. There developed in late eighteenth-century Germany the high- and lowbrow cultures that we take for granted today.[34]

The beginning of this bifurcation of culture had been discerned by the keen eye of Friedrich Nicolai as early as 1773. "Our writers have reference almost exclusively to themselves alone, or to the scholarly estate [*den gelehrten Stand*]," he writes.

> This little estate, about 20,000 strong, has such contempt for the remaining 20 million speakers of German that it doesn't take the trouble to write for them. . . . The 20 million repay the contempt of the 20 thousand with obliviousness—they hardly know that the scholars exist.

And then Nicolai goes on to predict with uncanny accuracy just where this development was headed:

> Since no scholar wants to write for the uneducated and yet the uneducated world has as much need to read as the educated, the job of writing for them must ultimately fall to the authors of Insel Felsenburgs, devotionals, and moral weeklies, whose abilities coincide more closely with their chosen readership than do those of the great scholars, and who are therefore read a great deal more widely than the great geniuses, though they do not edify their readers one iota, indeed, contribute not insignificantly to the failure of the light of the true scholars to reach the uneducated.[35]

With the expansion of the book market to satisfy demands that the *Aufklärer* themselves had devoted so much of their time and energies to stimulate, these writers began to see the goal of their efforts recede, betrayed by the profit motive of a free market and by the laws of supply and demand. Nicolai's prediction of the 1770s is confirmed by later observers—among them Johann Adam Bergk, whose *Die Kunst, Bücher zu lesen* [*The Art of Reading Books*] I examine below. Writing in

1799, Bergk criticizes the easy optimism displayed by Kant in his influential essay of 1784, "What Is Enlightenment?":

> Reading is supposed to be an educational tool of independence, and most people use it like sleeping pills; it is supposed to make us free and mature, and how many does it serve merely as a way of passing time and as a way of remaining in a condition of eternal immaturity [*Unmündigkeit*]![36]

Observations such as these increase in frequency and pathos beginning in the 1780s, as does the tendency, evident in Nicolai's condemnation of elitist writers, to project and so rationalize their discontents with the literary market economy. However, not all of the *Aufklärer* share Nicolai's populism; and instead of blaming themselves, they lash out at the hacks and at unscrupulous publishers and book dealers for thinking of nothing but their own selfish "interests." "The need to read, which is becoming more and more generally felt, even in those classes of society where the state is wont to contribute so little in the field of education," Schiller complains,

> instead of being used by good writers for more noble purposes, is being misused by mediocre pen-pushers and avaricious publishers to peddle their poor merchandise without regard for the cost in public taste and morality.... Mindless, tasteless, and pernicious novels, dramatized stories, so-called journals for the ladies, and the like are the treasures of our public libraries, and they are completely destroying the few healthy principles that our playwrights had left intact.[37]

Increasingly, however, the *Aufklärer* vent their frustrations on the reading public itself. Unable to reach the new broad-gauge audience on whose approval they depended for a livelihood, the *Aufklärer* decry the public for wanting only to be "diverted" [*ergötzt*], "moved" [*gerührt*], "stimulated" [*gereizt*]. Displaying a lack of fellow-feeling without parallel in the English letters of this period,[38] they condemn the unwitting public for its "addiction" to the "pleasant sensations" [*angenehme Empfindungen*] manufactured by the growing literature industry; and like the "true artist" of Goethe's "Vorspiel" they turn their backs on it. "Since one cannot hope to build and to plant," Schiller remarks, in one of the most extreme expressions of this impulse, "it is at least something to inundate and destroy. The only possible relationship to the public is war."[39]

It is Moritz, however, who converts the *Aufklärer*'s discontents into a viable weapon of cultural politics. Like the majority of writers at this time, Moritz had a deep personal stake in the commercialization of literature. It was as a professional writer that he sought to escape his humble beginnings. In addition to the novels *Anton Reiser* and *Andreas Hartknopf* for which he is best known today, Moritz wrote travelogues[40] and books and essays on topics ranging from history, philosophy, language, and aesthetics to psychology and mythology; he also edited a number of periodicals, including one for experimental psychology.[41] His short career was enormously productive—it had to be in an age in which royalties were calculated by the page. And in this respect at least it was a success: his writings earned him a reputation in polite circles and even a measure of the recognition he craved from the best minds of the period—ranging from Goethe and Schiller to some of the younger generation of romantics, such as Tieck, Wackenroder, and the brothers Humboldt (who attended Moritz's lectures at the Royal Academy of the Arts to which he was appointed in 1789), Schelling, Jean Paul, and the brothers Schlegel.[42] However, his efforts to win the esteem of the elite were continually being frustrated by financial worries. The pressing need for money caused Moritz to take on three or four different projects at a time, with the consequence, as his brother writes to Jean Paul,

> that he never completely finished a work until handing it over to the publisher. It was usually only on the basis of a rough plan sketched out in his mind that he determined the number of pages and negotiated the modest honorarium, whereby he naturally had to say that it was already finished, that it only needed fleshing out. And in a certain sense this was correct—that is, if by finished one means the existence of the work in his imagination and by fleshing it out, committing it to paper. And then he would not even begin to write until the compositor was already waiting for the manuscript, and even then did not write more than he needed at any given time.[43]

The end results of the different projects, completed in such extreme haste because of the urgently needed honoraria, frequently exhibit striking similarities to one another. Moritz was a shameless recycler of his ideas. "No one understood the art of invisible self-plagiarism better than Reiser [Moritz]," his friend Klischnig observes in his *Erinnerungen* [*Recollections*]. "With only a few small changes he inserted whole pages of his earlier works on language in the later ones, without this—as far as I know—coming to the attention of a reviewer."[44] But evidently it did not go entirely unnoticed by his publishers.

Moritz's fast and loose ways with publishers precipitated a kind of boycott of his writings at the book fair of 1788, contributing to the failure of his volume *Über die bildende Nachahmung des Schönen [On the Formative Imitation of the Beautiful]*.[45] This is a longer and more complex treatment of the ideas first presented in the *Versuch*. Moritz wrote it while in Italy in 1786–88—instead of the travelogue for which his publisher, Joachim Heinrich Campe, had advanced him the funds to make the trip—and he considered it his best work to date. "Everything I shall ever write on any subject is contained in the treatise on the formative imitation of the beautiful," he wrote Campe, "and after this treatise it will never be possible for me to write anything superficial again, not even if I try to make myself do so."[46] But the public did not share Moritz's enthusiasm for the work. Because of the "strangeness of your fanciful philosophy, few people can follow you and even fewer want to follow you," Campe would later write him, "so I am going to have to pulp most of the edition."[47] The public would have preferred a travelogue.

The anecdote is illuminating because it underscores the difficulties faced by German writers of the later eighteenth century when they tried to impose on the public what they felt to be their best writing. What distinguished Moritz's tribulations from those of other demanding writers, however, is that the "fanciful philosophy" to which the public turned so deaf an ear came armed against just such an eventuality. For the chief goal of this philosophy was to sever the value of a work from its capacity to appeal to a public that wanted above all to be diverted. In the *Versuch* Moritz had written:

> If pleasure were not *such a subordinate purpose,* or better yet, only a natural consequence of works of fine art, why wouldn't the true artist try to distribute it as widely as possible instead of sacrificing the pleasant sensations [*angenehmen Empfindungen*] of the many thousands who have no eye for the beautiful for the sake of the perfection of his work?—Should the artist say "but if my work is liked or affords pleasure, I have achieved my purpose," then my answer is: To the contrary! It is because you have achieved your purpose that your work is liked; or, the fact that your work is liked *may perhaps be a sign* that you have

achieved your purpose in the work. But if the actual purpose of your work was the pleasure you wished to effect rather than the perfection of the work itself, then the approval of your work by this or that person will for that very reason be suspect to me. (p. 7)

By shifting the measure of a work's value from its pleasurable effects on an audience to such purely intrinsic considerations as "the perfection of the work itself," Moritz arms his own and all difficult writing against the eventuality of a hostile or indifferent reception.

An answer has thus suggested itself to the question with which I began this discussion: how to account for the momentous shift from the instrumentalist theory of art to the modern theory of art as an autonomous object that is to be contemplated disinterestedly. Close reading of essays like Moritz's *Versuch* suggests that this shift is rooted in the far-reaching changes in the production, distribution, and consumption of reading material that marked the later eighteenth century. As literature became subject to the laws of a market economy, the instrumentalist theory, especially in the affective formulation given it by the generation of Mendelssohn, was found to justify the wrong works. That is, it was found to justify the products of the purveyors of strong effects, with whom more demanding writers could not effectively compete. The theology of art fashioned by Moritz offered such writers not only a convenient but a very powerful set of concepts with which to address the predicament in which they found themselves— concepts by which (difficult, or "fine") art's de facto loss of direct instrumentality could be recuperated as a (supreme) virtue. As Moritz himself says about this entirely new strategy in defense of art:

We do not need the beautiful object in order to be entertained [*ergötzt*] as much as the beautiful object needs us to be recognized. We can easily exist without contemplating beautiful works of art, but they cannot exist as such without our contemplation. The more we can do without them, therefore, the more we contemplate them for their own sake so as to impart to them through our very contemplation, as it were, their true, complete existence. (p. 4)

In the claim that the "true" work of art is the locus of intrinsic value— a perfectly self-sufficient totality that exists to be contemplated disinterestedly, for its own sake—Moritz makes a triumph of defeat and "rescues" art from determination by the market. Only a premature death in 1793 prevented him from savoring his triumph, for the theory he formulated rapidly became the dominant theory of philosophers of art, and by the nineteenth century they had succeeded in instilling in the German public a conception of a high culture, or *Kultur*, to which almost all, whatever they actually read in their spare time, paid verbal homage.

The Works of Darkness. Satire of the Book Pirates by Commission of the Book Dealer Himburg in Berlin (1781) by Daniel Chodowiecki (1726–1801). Courtesy of C. G. Boerner, Düsseldorf.

2. GENIUS AND THE COPYRIGHT

Book, *is either numerous sheets of white paper that have been stitched together in such a way that they can be filled with writing; or, a highly useful and convenient instrument constructed of printed sheets variously bound in cardboard, paper, vellum, leather, etc. for presenting the truth to another in such a way that it can be conveniently read and recognized. Many people work on this ware before it is complete and becomes an actual book in this sense. The scholar and the writer, the papermaker, the type founder, the typesetter and the printer, the proofreader, the publisher, the book binder, sometimes even the gilder and the brassworker, etc. Thus many mouths are fed by this branch of manufacture.*

—Allgemeines Oeconomisches Lexicon (*1753*)

In contemporary usage an "author" is an individual who is solely responsible—and thus exclusively deserving of credit—for the production of a unique, original work. Although this notion has been put in question by structuralists and poststructuralists who regard it as no more than a socially convenient fiction for linguistic codes and conventions that make a text possible, its genesis has received relatively little attention. This neglect is the more surprising in the light of Michel Foucault's observation that "it would be worth examining how the author became individualized in a culture like ours, what status he has been given, at what moment studies of authenticity and attribution began, in what kind of system of valorization the author was involved, at what point we began to recount the lives of authors rather than of heroes, and how this funda-

mental category of 'the-man-and-his-work criticism' began,"[1] Foucault's questions go to the heart of the problem to which I now wish
to turn.

The "author" in the modern sense is a relatively recent invention,
a product of the development we have been exploring—the emergence
in the eighteenth century of writers who sought to earn their livelihood
from the sale of their writings to the new and rapidly expanding
reading public. In Germany especially these new, professional writers
found themselves without the kinds of safeguards of their labors that
today are codified in copyright laws. In response to this problem, and
in an effort to establish the economic viability of living by the pen,
these writers set about redefining the nature of writing. Their reflections on this subject played a critical role in shaping the modern
concept of authorship its modern form.

In the Renaissance and in the heritage of the Renaissance in the
first half of the eighteenth century the "author" was an unstable
marriage of two distinct concepts. He[2] was first and foremost a
craftsman; that is, he was master of a body of rules, or techniques,
preserved and handed down in rhetoric and poetics, for manipulating
traditional materials in order to achieve the effects prescribed by the
cultivated audience of the court to which he owed both his livelihood
and social status. However, there were those rare moments in literature to which this concept did not seem to do justice. When a writer
managed to rise above the requirements of the occasion to achieve
something higher, much more than craftsmanship seemed to be involved. To explain such moments a new concept was introduced: the
writer was said to be inspired—by some muse, or even by God. These
two conceptions of the writer—as craftsman and as inspired—would
seem to be incompatible with each other; yet they coexisted, often
between the covers of a single treatise, until well into the eighteenth
century.

It is noteworthy that in neither of these conceptions is the writer
regarded as distinctly and personally responsible for his creation.
Whether as a craftsman or as inspired, the writer of the Renaissance
and neoclassical period is always a vehicle or instrument: regarded as
a craftsman, he is a skilled manipulator of predefined strategies for
achieving goals dictated by his audience; understood as inspired, he is
equally the subject of independent forces, for the inspired moments
of his work—that which is novel and most excellent in it—are not any
more the writer's sole doing than are its more routine aspects, but are

instead attributable to a higher, external agency—if not to a muse, then to divine dictation.[3]

Eighteenth-century theorists departed from this compound model of writing in two significant ways. They minimized the element of craftsmanship (in some instances they simply discarded it) in favor of the element of inspiration, and they internalized the source of that inspiration. That is, the inspiration for a work came to be regarded as emanating not from outside or above, but from within the writer himself. "Inspiration" came to be explicated in terms of *original genius,* with the consequence that the inspired work was made peculiarly and distinctively the product—and the property—of the writer.[4]

This sketch of the development of the concept of a writer since the Renaissance (which, to be sure, I have oversimplified) may be illustrated by two statements, one made by Alexander Pope (1688–1744) at the very beginning of this development and another by William Wordsworth (1770–1850) speaking from the other side of it. As the first major English poet to achieve wealth and status without the aid of patronage but entirely from the sale of his writings to the reading public, Pope still professes the Renaissance view of the writer as primarily a craftsman whose task is to utilize the tools of his craft for their culturally determined ends. In a familiar passage from his *Essay on Criticism* (1711) Pope states that the function of the poet is not to invent novelties but to express afresh truths hallowed by tradition:

> True wit is nature to advantage dressed;
> What oft' was thought, but ne'er so well expressed;
> Something, whose truth convinced at sight we find,
> That gives us back the image of our mind. (ll. 297–300)[5]

However, Pope also incorporates in the *Essay* the other seemingly anomalous view of the writer as subject to a "happiness as well as care," as capable, that is, of achieving something that has never been achieved before. This the poet can accomplish only by violating the rules of his craft:

> Some beauties yet no precept can declare,
> For there's a happiness as well as care.
> Music resembles poetry; in each
> Are nameless graces which no methods teach,

And which a master hand alone can reach.
If, where the rules not far enough extend,
(Since rules were made but to promote their end)
Some lucky license answer to the full
Th'intent proposed, that license is a rule.
Thus Pegasus, a nearer way to take,
May boldly deviate from the common track.
Great wits sometimes may gloriously offend,
And rise to faults true critics dare not mend;
From vulgar bounds with brave disorder part,
And snatch a grace beyond the reach of art.

(ll. 141–55)[6]

Such moments of inspiration, in which the poet snatches a grace beyond the reach of the rules and poetic strategies that he commands as the master of a craft, are still the exception for Pope. However, from the margins of theory, where they reside in the *Essay* at the beginning of the century, these moments of inspiration move, in the course of time, to the center of reflection on the nature of writing. And as they are increasingly credited to the writer's own genius, they transform the writer into a unique individual uniquely responsible for a unique product. That is, from a (mere) vehicle of preordained truths—truths as ordained either by universal human agreement or by some higher agency—the *writer* bcomes an *author* (Lat. *auctor*, originator, founder, creator).

It is as such a writer that Wordsworth perceives himself. Complaining of the "unremitting hostility" with which the *Lyrical Ballads* were received by the critics, Wordsworth observes that "if there be one conclusion" that is "forcibly pressed upon us" by their disappointing reception, it is "that every Author, as far as he is great and at the same time *original,* has had the task of *creating* the taste by which he is to be enjoyed."[7] Inasmuch as his immediate audience is inevitably attuned to the products of the past, the great writer who produces something original is doomed to be misunderstood. Thus it is, according to Wordsworth, that "if every great Poet, . . . in the highest exercise of his genius, before he can be thoroughly enjoyed, has to call forth and to communicate *power,*" that is, empower his readers to understand his new work, "this service, in a still greater degree, falls upon an original Writer, at his first appearance in the world."

Of genius the only proof is, the act of doing well what is worthy to be done, and what was never done before: Of genius, in the fine arts, the only infallible sign is the widening the sphere of human sensibility, for the delight, honor, and benefit of human nature. Genius is the introduction of a new element into the intellectual universe: or, if that be not allowed, it is the application of powers to objects on which they had not before been exercised, or the employment of them in such a manner as to produce effects hitherto unknown.[8]

For Wordsworth, writing in 1815, the genius is someone who does something utterly new, unprecedented, or in the radical formulation that he prefers, produces something that never existed before.

The conception of writing to which Wordsworth gives expression had been adumbrated a half-century earlier in an essay by Edward Young, *Conjectures on Original Composition.* Young preached originality in place of the reigning emphasis on the mastery of rules extrapolated from classical literature, and he located the source of this essential quality in the poet's own genius. Initially his essay attracted relatively little attention in England; but in Germany, where it appeared in two separate translations within two years of its publication in 1759, it had a profound impact.[9] German theorists from Herder and Goethe to Kant and Fichte elaborated the ideas sketched out by Young, shifting them from the periphery to the very center of the theory of the arts.

One of the reasons for this development, I would suggest, is that Young's ideas answered the pressing need of writers in Germany to establish ownership of the products of their labor so as to justify legal recognition of that ownership in the form of a copyright law.[10] The relevance of his ideas to this enterprise had already been suggested by Young himself when he enjoined the writer to

Let not great examples, or authorities, browbeat thy reason into too great a diffidence of thyself: thyself so reverence, as to prefer the native growth of thy own mind to the richest import from abroad; such borrowed riches make us poor. The man who thus reverences himself, will soon find the world's reverence to follow his own. His works will stand distinguished; his the sole property of them; which property alone can confer the noble title of an author; that is, of one who (to speak accurately) thinks and composes; while other invaders of the press, how voluminous and learned soever, (with due respect be it spoken) only read and write.[11]

Here, amid the organic analogues for genial creativity that have made this essay a monument in the history of criticism, Young raises issues of property: he makes a writer's ownership of his work the necessary, and even sufficient condition for earning the honorific title of "author," and he makes such ownership contingent upon a work's originality.

I

The professional writer emerged considerably later in Germany than in England and France. Pope had long since written his way to fame and fortune in England by the time that writers were even beginning to attempt to live from the sale of their writings alone in Germany.[12] The generation of Lessing (1729–1781) was the first to try to do this, but it had little success. After ten years of struggle Lessing wrote his brother in 1768:

> Take my brotherly advice and give up your plan to live by the pen. . . . See that you become a secretary or get on the faculty somewhere. It's the only way to avoid starving sooner or later. For me it's too late to take another path. In so advising, I'm not suggesting that you give up completely everything to which inclination and genius drive you.[13]

From the point of view of the development of a profession of letters, what Lessing recommends is a step backward to writing as a part-time occupation, an activity pursued by the writer as an official of the court to the degree allowed by the social and ideological as well as contractual obligations of his office.[14] In 1770 Lessing himself would be forced to take such a step and to accept a position as court librarian in Wolfenbüttel. The other two giants of the period, Friedrich Gottlob Klopstock (1724–1803) and Christoph Martin Wieland (1733–1813), met with similar fates.

Despite the rapid expansion of the market for books that began in the 1770s, the prospects of the next generation of writers did not improve substantially, as the biographies of writers like Bürger, Moritz, and Schiller attest. Having made a reputation for himself with his play, *The Robbers,* which he published at his own expense in 1781, the twenty-two-year-old Schiller resolved to break his connections with the Duke of Württemberg and try his luck as a professional writer. He would later describe the decision as precipitate, but at the time Schiller appears to have had little idea of the manifold vicissitudes of casting one's lot with the new reading public. "The public is now everything to me," he writes,

> my school, my sovereign, my trusted friend. I now belong to it alone. I shall place myself before this and no other tribunal. It alone do I fear and respect. Something grand comes over me at the prospect of wearing no other fetters than the decision of the world—of appealing to no other throne than the human spirit.[15]

These high expectations are expressed in the "Announcement" of *Die rheinische Thalie*, a periodical conceived by Schiller in 1784 when he failed to make it as resident dramatist to the Mannheim National Theater. The periodical was just the first of a series of such editorial projects that the poet took on in an effort to earn his living as a writer. Despite his productivity, however, Schiller just barely succeeded in making ends meet; and when his health broke down from overwork in 1791, he followed in Lessing's footsteps and accepted a pension from his Danish admirer, Prince Friedrich Christian von Schleswig-Holstein-Sonderburg-Augustenburg. It is in the form of letters addressed to this benefactor that he conceived *On the Aesthetic Education of Man* in 1793–94. Schiller embraced the patronage of the prince with as much enthusiasm as he had displayed in commending himself to the public less than a decade before. In a letter to a fellow poet who had been instrumental in securing the pension, he welcomed it as the "freedom of thought" for which he had so long yearned; and reflecting back on his struggles, he concluded that it was "impossible in the German world of letters to satisfy the strict demands of art and simultaneously procure the minimum of support for one's industry."[16]

What made it so difficult to live by the pen in eighteenth-century Germany? In chapter 1 I suggested that the "serious" writers like Schiller and Moritz who gave us our modern concept of art found it difficult to compete with the lighter literature that began flooding the market in the last quarter of the century, and we will pursue this problem in greater depth in chapter 3. Here I want to explore an even more fundamental obstacle to succeeding as a writer—one that affected all writers, if not all equally.

As my sketch of writers' struggles suggests, eighteenth-century Germany found itself in a transitional phase between the limited patronage of an aristocratic age and the democratic patronage of the marketplace. With the growth of a middle class, demand for reading material increased steadily, enticing writers to try to earn a livelihood from the sale of their writings to a buying public. But most were doomed to be disappointed, for the requisite legal, economic, and political arrangements and institutions were not yet in place to support the large number of writers who came forward.[17] What they encountered were the remnants of an earlier social order. They expected, as professional writers, to trade in ideas in a country that did not yet have a fully developed concept of intellectual property.[18]

The notion that property can be ideal as well as real, that under certain circumstances a person's ideas are no less his property than his hogs and horses, is a modern one. In the country in which Martin Luther had preached that knowledge is God-given and has therefore to be given freely, however, this notion was especially slow to take hold.[19] At the outset of the eighteenth century it was not generally thought that the author of a poem or any other piece of writing possessed rights with regard to these products of his intellectual labor. Writing was considered a mere vehicle of received ideas that were already in the public domain, and, as such a vehicle, it too, by extension or by analogy, was considered part of the public domain. In short, the relationship between the writer and his work reflected the Renaissance view described earlier. This view found expression in the institutions of the *honorarium*, the form in which writers were remunerated, and the *privilege*, the only legal arrangement that served to regulate the book trade until the last decade of the century when, one by one, the German states began to enact copyright laws.

By the middle of the seventeenth century it had become customary for publishers to offer honoraria to the writers whose works they agreed to print. It would be a mistake, however, to conclude that modest sums of money paid out in this way represented direct compensation for those works. To the contrary, as the definition given by Zedler's *Universal-Lexikon* in 1735 shows, the honorarium was simply a token of esteem:

> *Honorarium*, means acknowledgment or reward, recognition, favor, stipend; it is not in proportion to or equivalent to the services performed; differs from pay or wages, which are specifically determined by contracting parties and which express a relationship of equivalence between work and payment.[20]

The honorarium a writer might expect to receive for his work bore no relationship to the exchange value of that work but was rather an acknowledgment of the writer's achievements—the sum of which began, with time, to vary in proportion to the magnitude of those achievements. As such the honorarium resembled the gifts made to poets by aristocratic patrons. Indeed, as Goethe observes in the twelfth book of *Dichtung und Wahrheit* [*Poetry and Truth*], the relationship between writers and publishers in the first half of the eighteenth century still bore a striking resemblance to that which had existed between the poet and his patron. At that time, Goethe writes, the book trade

> was chiefly concerned with important scientific works, stock works which commanded modest honoraria. The production of poetical works, however, was regarded as something sacred, and it was considered close to simony to accept or bargain for an honorarium. Authors and publishers enjoyed a most amazing reciprocity. They appeared, as it were, as patron and client. The authors, who in addition to their talent were usually considered by the public to be highly moral people and were honored accordingly, possessed intellectual status and felt themselves rewarded by the joy of their work. The book dealers contented themselves with the second rank and enjoyed a considerable advantage: affluence placed the rich book dealer above the poor poet, so everything remained in the most beautiful equilibrium. Reciprocal magnanimity and gratitude were not uncommon: Breitkopf and Gottsched remained intimate friends throughout their lives. Stinginess and meanness, particularly on the part of the literary pirates, were not yet in full swing.[21]

The "beautiful equilibrium" described by Goethe collapsed, however, as the market for literature expanded sufficiently to induce writers to try to make an occupation of it. They began to compare "their own very modest, if not downright meager condition with the wealth of the affluent book dealers," Goethe continues,

> they considered how great was the fame of a Gellert or a Rabener, and with what domestic straits a universally loved German writer must content himself if he does not lighten his burden through some other employment. Even the average and the lesser luminaries felt an intense desire to better their circumstances, to make themselves independent of the publishers.[22]

Eventually writers would demand fluctuating honoraria based on sales (i.e., royalties); in the eighteenth century, however, a flat sum remained customary—upon receipt of which the writer forfeited his rights to any profits his work might bring. That is, his work became the property of the publisher to realize as much profit from as he could. It is the injustices to which this arrangement could lead that Goethe alludes to above, injustices that made it difficult to keep up the pretense that writers were content not to be paid for their work.

Christian Fürchtegott Gellert (1715–1769) was one of the most widely read writers of the period. Yet he had received only 20 Thaler 16 Groschen for his popular *Fabeln*; and while he lived out his final years in only modest comfort, thanks primarily to his patrons and the good will of the Dresden court, his publisher Wendler became a wealthy man. In 1786 the remaindered copies alone of Gellert's works fetched Wendler 10,000 thalers.[23] Some measure of this imbalance must be attributed to Gellert's unwillingness to accept money for his writing. Like other writers of his generation, he viewed writing in the terms Goethe describes above. "At first, on account of the public, I didn't want to take anything from the publisher for the *Geistliche Oden und Lieder,*" Gellert wrote his sister toward the end of his life; "however, as my pension has now stopped, and as my kin are dearer to me than the public, I asked 125 thalers and received 150."[24] Gellert was reluctant, even ashamed to take money for his poetry because he did not conceive of writing as an occupation. Writers of the next generation no longer shared Gellert's attitudes, as we have seen. Indeed, Lessing takes direct issue with them in "Leben und leben lassen" ["Live and Let Live"], a proposal for reorganizing the book trade that he drafted in 1772:

> What? The writer is to be blamed for trying to make the off-spring of his imagination as profitable as he can? Just because he works with his noblest faculties he isn't supposed to enjoy the satisfaction that the roughest handyman is able to procure—that of owing his livelihood to his own industry? . . .
>
> But wisdom, they say, for sale for cash! Shameful! Freely hast thou received, freely thou must give! Thus thought the noble Luther in translating the Bible.
>
> Luther, I answer, is an exception in many things. Further-more, it is for the most part not true that the writer received for nothing what he does not want to give away for nothing. Often an entire fortune may have been spent preparing to teach and please the world.[25]

Lessing, who views writing as an occupation, asserts his professional identity in economic terms, raising the issue of fair compensation for his work. Although his position was echoed by other writers intent upon living by the pen, the older conception of writing as a "priceless" part-time activity lived on in the institution of the honorarium.

If I have given the impression so far of casting publishers in the role of villains in the economic exploitation of the writer, let me hasten to correct this impression. Although they were faring much better than writers, publishers by this time were experiencing their own tribulations in the form of unauthorized reprints. The practice of reprinting books without the permission of their original publishers— a practice that would eventually be impugned as "piracy"—had existed since the late fifteenth century. In the eighteenth century, however, as reading became more common and the book trade became a profitable business, it grew to epidemic proportions, for the development of legal institutions had not kept pace with the dramatic growth of the book trade. The only legal institution available to publishers in eighteenth-century Germany was the privilege. An invention of the feudal princes to protect branches of trade they deemed essential to their court economies, privileges had first been extended to printers in the sixteenth century to enable them to realize a profit on their investment in the production of a book before that book could be reprinted. Thus, the book privilege had as its intent not the recognition of the rights of authors, but the protection of printers. In this it resembled the English copyright act that was passed by Parliament in 1709 on the petition of the booksellers.[26] However, unlike the Statute of Anne, as it is known, the privilege was not really a law at all but, as the word itself suggests, a special concession or dispensation conditionally granted to printers or publishers who enjoyed the favor of the court. Thus, in the entry for *Privilegium* in Zedler's *Universal-Lexikon* of 1741 we read:

> Among the consequences of the law is the obligation under which a person is placed to do or to refrain from doing something according to the law. Now just as a law can be waived in its entirety or in part, so too can a lawmaker exempt or grant a person a privilege. This is a special freedom which a lawmaker permits the subject and exempts him from obligation to the law.

The privilege, in short, was not a positive law, but rather, as Fichte would later put it sardonically, an "exception to a natural law" according to which "everybody has the right to reprint every book."[27] In this sense the privilege, like the honorarium, harks back to an earlier conception of writing as a vehicle of something which by its very nature is public—that is, knowledge—and is therefore free to be reproduced at will.

The limited protection afforded a publisher by the privilege was unlike that afforded under the English copyright in another important respect. The privilege extended only to the borders of the territory or municipality that granted it. This system, whereby each separate state and large town could grant a book protection against reprinting, had worked well enough as long as the demand for books was limited. But as demand increased and book trading became lucrative it proved totally inadequate. For eighteenth-century Germany consisted of some three hundred independent states. To safeguard their respective-investments against piracy, writers and their publishers would have had to obtain a privilege in every one of them. To make matters worse, mercantilist economic policies caused some states not only to tolerate piracy but actively to encourage it as a legitimate source of re-venue.[28]

Book piracy affected serious writers and conscientious publishers most of all, exposing problems that have become highly familiar to us in today's conditions of mass-market publishing. The publishers had adopted the practice of using profits from popular books to finance publication of works that, because of the serious or specialized nature of their subject matter, were not likely to succeed in the marketplace. With the growth of piracy, however, this became increasingly more difficult to do. Pirates were naturally attracted to the most popular books. These they would quickly reprint at a lower price than the legitimate publisher had charged. The pirates could easily afford to do this, according to the bookseller Perthes, because they had no previous losses to cover and no authors to pay. The consequence for the legitimate publisher, Perthes goes on to explain, was that he was left with half an edition of the popular item on his shelves.[29] With their profits cut in this way, publishers became hesitant to accept anything that they did not feel confident of turning over quickly. As the bookseller Ganz put it, "Whatever is easiest to write, whatever will enjoy the quickest sales, whatever involves the smallest loss—these are the things that authors must write and dealers must publish as long as the plague of piracy persists."[30] Piracy not only threatened the publishers of the period, then, it also added to the insecurity of serious writers by increasing the difficulties they already had getting their works into print.

Legitimate publishers' resentment of the book pirates and authors' resentment of both triggered an intense debate in which all manner of questions concerning the "Book" were disputed. And here we find another instance of the kind of interplay between discourses to which historians of aesthetics and criticism need to become more sensitive, for it is precisely in this interplay between legal, economic, and social questions on the one hand and philosophical and aesthetic ones on the other that critical concepts and principles as fundamental as that of authorship achieved their modern form.

II

It would be hard to find a more patent example of such interplay than the debate over the book that spanned the two decades between 1773 and 1794. In addition to publishers and legal experts such as Philipp Erasmus Reich, Joachim Heinrich Campe, Johann Stephan Pütter, and Johann Jakob Cella, many of the best-known poets and philosophers of the period contributed: Rudolf Zacharias Becker, Gottfried August Bürger, J.G. Müller von Itzehoe, Adolf Freiherr von Knigge, Kant, Johann Georg Feder, Martin Ehlers, and Fichte, to name just a few.[31] The debate generated so much commentary that it produced an instantaneous *Forschungsbericht,* or survey: Ernst Martin Gräff's *Versuch einer einleuchtenden Darstellung des Eigenthums und der Eigenthumsrechte des Schriftstellers und Verlegers und ihrer gegenseitigen Rechte und Verbindlichkeiten. Mit vier Beylagen. Nebst einem kritischen Verzeichnisse aller deutschen besonderen Schriften und in periodischen und andern Werken stehenden Aufsätze über das Bücherwesen überhaupt und den Büchernachdruck insbesondere* [*Toward a Clarification of the Property and Property Rights of Writers and Publishers and Their Mutual Rights and Obligations. With Four Appendices. Including a Critical Inventory of All Separate Publications and Essays in Periodical and Other Works in German Which Concern Matters of the Book As Such and Especially Reprinting*].[32] The treatise makes good on its promise by reviewing no less than twenty-five of the separate publications and thirty-five of the essays written over the twenty-year period leading up to its appearance in 1794.

The debate was precipitated by the announcement in 1772 of the *Deutsche Gelehrtenrepublik* [*German Republic of Letters*]. In this announcement the poet Friedrich Gottlob Klopstock unveiled a scheme to enable writers to circumvent publishers altogether and bring their works directly to the public by subscription. His aim, he wrote, was

> to ascertain whether it might be possible by arranging such subscriptions for scholars to become the owners of their writings. For at present they are so only in appearance; book dealers are the real proprietors, because scholars must turn their writings over to them if they want to have these writings printed. This occasion will show whether or not one might hope that the public, and the scholars among themselves, . . . will be instrumental in helping scholars achieve actual ownership of their property.[33]

This experiment in collective patronage did not have the direct impact on the structure of the book trade that Klopstock had hoped it might. Subscription was simply too demanding of the time and resources of writers for many other writers to follow his example. And readers had already become accustomed to purchasing their reading matter from the booksellers. This arrangement had the advantage of enabling them to browse before buying and to await the reaction of other readers and the reviews. Furthermore, publishers' names had become an index of quality, a means of orientation for the reader in the sea of published matter.[34] In short, cooperation with the growing distribution apparatus had by this time become virtually unavoidable. It was only on the morale of writers, therefore, that Klopstock's experiment had a direct impact. But here his service was considerable, for Klopstock was the most revered poet of the period. Just by speaking out as he did he helped to create among writers the authority requisite to advancing their interests with the publishers. Thus, the *Gelehrtenrepublik* must be regarded as an important milestone in the development of the concept of authorship—as Goethe seems to suggest in the tenth book of *Dichtung und Wahrheit* when he remarks that in the person of Klopstock the time had arrived "for poetic genius to become self-conscious, create for itself its own conditions, and understand how to lay the foundation of an independent dignity."[35]

If Klopstock's affirmation of the rights of authors seems self-evident to us today, that is because it eventually prevailed. It was anything but self-evident to the author of the entry "Book" in the *Allgemeines Oeconomisches Lexicon* of 1753, which stands as the motto of this chapter. There, where the book is still perceived as a "convenient instrument for conveying the truth," none of the many craftsmen who collaborated in its production is privileged. Listed in the order of their appearance in the production, "the scholar and the writer, the papermaker, the type founder, the typesetter and the printer, the proofreader, the publisher, the book binder" are all presented as deserving equal credit for the finished product and as having an equal claim to the profits it brings: "Thus many mouths are fed by this branch of manufacture." This definition of the book, which now reads like the taxonomy of animals in the Chinese encyclopedia "cited" by Borges, suggests how differently the debate launched by Klopstock might have turned out (indeed, how *reasonable* some other resolution of it would have been).[36] It makes tangible just how much had to change before consensus could build around his bold assertion of the priority of the writer as peculiarly responsible—and therefore uniquely deserving of credit—for the finished product, "Book," which he helped to make. The nature of writing would have to be completely re-thought. And that, as I suggested at the outset of the discussion, is exactly what eighteenth-century theorists did.

The debate in which a good deal of this reflection was carried on focused on the question of whether or not the unauthorized reproduc-tion of books [*Büchernachdruck*] should be prohibited by law. As in-comprehensible as it may seem to us today, the weight of opinion was for a long time with the book pirates. For the reading public as a whole considered itself well served by a practice that not only made inexpensive reprints available but could also be plausibly credited with holding down the price of books in general through the competition it created. And given the taste of a majority of the public for light reading matter, it could hardly be expected to have been swayed by Perthes' objection that piracy was so cutting into the profits of legiti-mate publishers that they could no longer afford to take risks on "serious" literature.

A variety of defenses was offered for book piracy, but the most pertinent to the genesis of the modern concept of authorship are those that sought to rationalize the practice philosophically. Here, as illus-tration, are two such defenses. The first is by a zealous mercantilist who seeks to advance his interests by emphasizing a book's physical foundation:

> The book is not an ideal object. . . . It is a fabrication made of paper upon which thought symbols are printed. It does not contain thoughts; these must arise in the mind of the compre-hending reader. It is a commodity produced for hard cash. Every

government has the duty to restrict, where possible, the outflow of its wealth, hence to encourage domestic reproduction of foreign art objects and not to hinder the industry of its own citizens to the enrichment of foreign manufacturers.[37]

This writer's conclusion would be hard to deny were we to accept his premises. If a book could be reduced to its physical foundation, as he suggests, then of course it would be impossible for its author to lay claim to peculiar ownership of it, for it is precisely the book qua physical object that he turns over to the publisher when he delivers his manuscript and that, in another format, is eventually purchased by his readers.

To ground the author's claim to ownership of his work, then, it would first be necessary to show that this work transcends its physical foundation. It would be necessary to show that it is an emanation of his intellect—an intentional, as opposed to a merely physical object. Once this has been acknowledged, however, it will still remain to be shown how such an object can constitute property—as the following statement by Christian Sigmund Krause demonstrates:

"But the ideas, the content! that which actually constitutes a book! which only the author can sell or communicate!"—Once expressed, it is impossible for it to remain the author's property. ... It is precisely for the purpose of using the ideas that most people buy books—pepper dealers, fishwives, and the like, and literary pirates excepted. ... Over and over again it comes back to the same question: I can read the contents of a book, learn, abridge, expand, teach, and translate it, write about it, laugh over it, find fault with it, deride it, use it poorly or well—in short, do with it whatever I will. But the one thing I should be prohibited from doing is copying or reprinting it? ... A published book is a secret divulged. With what justification does a person expect to have more property in the ideas he expresses in writing than in those he expresses orally? With what justification does a preacher forbid the printing of his homilies, since he cannot prevent any of his listeners from transcribing his sermons? Would it not be just as ludicrous for a professor to demand that his students refrain from using some new proposition he has taught them as for him to demand the same of book dealers ... with regard to a new book? No, no, it is too obvious that the concept of intellectual property is useless. My property must be exclusively mine; I must be able to dispose of it and retrieve it unconditionally. Let someone explain to me how that is possible in the present case. Just let someone try taking back the ideas he has originated once they have been communicated so that they are, as before, nowhere to be found. All the money in the world could not make that possible.[38]

Krause acknowledges that a book is a vehicle of ideas; however, this does not advance the interests of the author an iota; for, as Krause points out, it is precisely for the sake of appropriating these ideas that readers purchase a book in the first place.

Krause's challenge to explain to him how ideas, once communicated, could remain the property of their originator is taken up by Fichte in the essay *Beweis der Unrechtmässigkeit des Büchernachdrucks. Ein Räsonnement und eine Parabel* [*Proof of the Illegality of Reprinting: A Rationale and a Parable*] (1793). Fichte meets the challenge by arguing that a book, in addition to being an emanation of the writer's intellect, is also a verbal embodiment or imprint of that intellect at work. He proceeds by distinguishing between the physical [*körperlich*] and ideal [*geistig*] aspects of a book—that is, between the printed paper and content. Repeating the operation, he then divides the ideal aspects of the book into

> the *material* [*materiell*] aspect, the content of the book, the ideas it presents; and . . . the *form* of these ideas, the way in which, the combination in which, the phrasing and wording in which they are presented.[39]

Then, on the presupposition that we are "the rightful owners of a thing, the appropriation of which by another is physically impossible,"[40] Fichte goes on to distinguish three distinct shares of property in the book. When the book is sold, ownership of the *physical* object passes to the buyer to do with as he pleases. The *material* aspect, the content of the book, the thoughts it presents also pass to the buyer. To the extent that he is able, through intellectual effort, to appropriate them, these ideas cease to be the exclusive property of the author, becoming instead the common property of both author and reader. The *form* in which these ideas are presented, however, remains the property of the author eternally, for

> each individual has his own thought processes, his own way of forming concepts and connecting them. . . . All that we think we must think according to the analogy of our other habits of thought; and solely through reworking new thoughts after the analogy of

our habitual thought processes do we make them our own. Without this they remain something foreign in our minds which connects with nothing and affects nothing. . . . Now, since pure ideas without sensible images cannot be thought, even less are they capable of presentation to others. Hence, each writer must give his thoughts a certain form, and he can give them no other form than his own because he has no other. But neither can he be willing to hand over this *form* in making his thoughts public, for no one can *appropriate* his thoughts without thereby *altering their form*. This latter thus remains forever his exclusive property.[41]

In his central concept of the "form" taken by a thought—that which it is impossible for another person to appropriate—Fichte solves the philosophical puzzles to which the defenders of piracy had recurred, and establishes the grounds upon which the writer could lay claim to ownership of his work—could lay claim, that is, to *authorship*. The copyright laws [*Urheberrecht*] enacted in the succeeding decades turn upon Fichte's key concept, recognizing the legitimacy of this claim by vesting exclusive rights to a work in the author insofar as he is an *Urheber* [originator, creator]—that is, insofar as his work is unique or original [*eigentümlich*], an intellectual creation that owes its individuality solely and exclusively to him.[42] The publisher, formerly proprietor of the work, henceforth functioned as his agent.

The first important legislation designed to regulate publishing rights and contracts was enacted in 1794 in Prussia. Having defined the right to publish as "the authority to reproduce a text in print and to take it to the fairs, to booksellers, and otherwise exclusively to dispose of it," Prussian state law asserts at §998: "As a rule, the bookseller acquires the right to publish only through a written contract with the author."[43] Although the right to publish a text appears to be derived from the proprietary right of its author,[44] nowhere do the Prussian statutes contain an explicit and unambiguous statement to this effect, and they make the bookseller rather than the author the subject of legal protection.

Not until 1810 was the priority of the author's claims explicitly recognized in legislation. This occurred in Baden when the Napoleonic Code was adopted as state law. Laws covering literary property were added to the *Code civile* because, as Johann Nikolaus Friedrich Brauer (1754–1813), the jurist chiefly responsible for adapting the

Code, notes in his commentary, while French legislation deserves the credit for being first to introduce the idea of literary property, it did not "pursue the idea to its conclusion." The French legislation of 1793 "more closely resembles an insurance policy against reprinting than a civil law covering literary property."[45] Accordingly, the chapter "On Literary Property" that the Baden jurists inserted in the section of the *Code civile* devoted to property begins:

> §577. da. Every written transaction is originally the property of the person who composed it, as long as he did not write it on the commission of another and for the advantage of another, in which case it would be the property of the person who commissioned it.[46]

Three years later in 1813 the state of Bavaria would define the object of the author's proprietary rights in the very terms that had been made available by Fichte. According to Article 397 of its Penal Code, which was authored by Ludwig Feuerbach,

> Anyone who publicizes a work of science or art without the permission of its creator, his heirs, or others who have obtained the rights of the creator, by reproducing it in print or in some other way without having reworked it into an original form [*eigentümlicher Form*] will be punished.[47]

Although similar legislation was enacted in one after another of the German states, the situation of serious writers and their legitimate publishers did not immediately improve because the new laws did not reach any farther than the privileges they superseded. Special interstate treaties, or accords, continued to be required until the Prussian state law of 1837 "for the protection of property in works of science and art against reprinting and reproduction" was adopted by the Federation of German States in 1845.[48]

It remains to retrace the path by which Fichte arrived at this concept of the "form" taken by a thought and the radically new conception of writing it implies. In advocating originality, Edward Young had made what proved to be enormously fecund suggestions about the process by which this quality is brought about. An original work, he had conjectured,

> may be said to be of a vegetable nature; it rises spontaneously from the vital root of genius; it grows, it is not made. Imitations

are often a sort of manufacture wrought up by those mechanics, art and labor, out of pre-existent materials not their own.[49]

Young derogates the craftsman's manipulation of inherited techniques and materials as capable of producing nothing but imitations, "duplicates of what we had, possibly much better, before."[50] Original works are the product of a more organic process: they are *vital, grow spontaneously* from a *root,* and by implication, unfold their original form from within.[51] German theorists of the *Genie* period spelled out the implications of these ideas.[52] That is, they expanded Young's metaphor for the process of genial creativity in such a way as to effect the new conception of composition that enabled Fichte, in the final stage of the piracy debate, to "prove" the author's peculiar ownership of his work.

The direction in which their work took them is illustrated by Herder's ruminations on the processes of nature in *Vom Erkennen und Empfinden der menschlichen Seele* [*On Knowing and Feeling*] (1778). What most inspires Herder is the "marvelous diligence" with which living organisms take in and process alien matter, transforming it in such a way as to make it part of themselves:

> Behold yon plant, that lovely structure of organic fibers! . . . With what marvelous diligence it refines alien liquors into parts of its own finer self, grows, loves, gives and receives pollen on the wing of Zypher, stimulates living imprints of itself, leaves, seed, blossoms, fruit; then it ages, gradually loses its impulse to receive and its energy to give anew, dies. . . . The herb draws in water and earth and refines them into its own element; the animal makes the lower herbs into nobler animal sap; man transforms herbs and animals into organic elements of his life, brings them into the processing of higher, finer stimuli.[53]

The ease with which these ideas about the nature of nature could be adapted to rethinking the nature of composition is suggested by the young Goethe's description of writing as "the reproduction of the world around me by means of the internal world which takes hold of, combines, creates anew, kneads everything and puts it down again in its own form, manner."[54] Goethe departs sharply from the older, Renaissance and neoclassical conception of the writer as essentially a vehicle of ideas to describe him not only as transforming those ideas, but as transforming them in such a way as to make them an expression of his own—unique—mind. Herder sums up this new line of thought when he observes that "one ought to be able to regard every book as the imprint [*Abdruck*] of a living human soul":

> Every poem, even a long poem—a life's (and soul's) work—is a tremendous betrayer of its creator, often where the latter was least conscious of betraying himself. Not only does one see in it the man's poetic talents, as the crowd would put it; one also sees which senses and inclinations governed him, how he received images, how he ordered and disposed them and the chaos of his impressions; one sees the favorite places in his heart as well as sometimes his life's destinies: his manly or childish understanding, the stays of his thought and his memory.[55]

This radically new conception of the book as an imprint or record of the intellection of a unique individual—hence a "tremendous betrayer" of that individual—entails new reading strategies. In neoclassical doctrine the pleasure of reading had derived from the reader's recognition of himself in a poet's representations (a pleasure guaranteed by the supposed essential similarity of all men). Thus Pope's charge to the poet to present "something, whose truth convinced at sight we find, / That gives us back the image of our mind." With Herder the pleasure of reading lies instead in the exploration of an Other, in penetrating to the deepest reaches of the foreign, because absolutely unique consciousness of which the work is a verbalized embodiment. Herder describes this new and, to his way of thinking, "active" [*lebendig*] mode of reading as "divination into the soul of the creator [*Urheber*]."[56] Not every writer merits reading in this way, he avers, but with writers who are "worth the trouble"—our "favorite writers"—it is "the only kind of reading and the most profound means of education."

Herder's redefinition of the goals of reading brings us back to the questions with which this discussion began. For his recommendation that we treat a book as a revelation of the personality of its author sets the stage for the entire spectrum of the "man-and-his-work criticism" to which Foucault alluded, as well as for the theoretical tradition that undergirds it: hermeneutic theory from Schleiermacher and Dilthey to a contemporary theoretician like E. D. Hirsch. Despite their many differences, all of these critics share the belief that criticism has essentially to do with the recovery of a writer's meaning, and all take for granted the concept of the author that evolved in the eighteenth century. What we tend to overlook is the degree to which that concept was shaped by the specific circumstances of writers during that period.

Lenore, from *Eight Plates for
Bürger's Poems. First Edition*
(1778) by Daniel Chodowiecki
(1726–1801). Courtesy of
C. G. Boerner, Düsseldorf.

D. Chodowiecki del. et. sc.

3. AESTHETIC AUTONOMY AS A WEAPON IN CULTURAL POLITICS: REREADING SCHILLER'S *AESTHETIC LETTERS*

• It would be hard to find a more extravagant claim for the power of art than Friedrich Schiller's statement near the beginning of the letters *On the Aesthetic Education of Man* that "it is only through beauty that man makes his way to freedom."[1] Schiller makes this statement in defense of the aesthetic inquiry he intends to pursue in the letters. As these began appearing in his journal, *Horen*, in the mid-1790s, Schiller's readers were preoccupied with the revolutionary political struggle convulsing France. With this "most perfect of all the works to be achieved by the art of man—the construction of true political freedom"—hanging in the balance, Schiller writes, "Is it not, to say the least, untimely" to propose to divert readers' attention to the fine arts (p. 7–9)? It would be, he agrees, did not the tendency of events indicate such a measure—had not the struggle for liberty turned into a Reign of Terror.

To Schiller the violent turn of events in France signifies that men are not ready for the freedom they are demanding. "Man has roused himself from his long indolence and self-deception and, by an impressive majority, is demanding restitution of his inalienable rights," Schiller writes in Letter Five. But man "is not just demanding this." In France now, as in America, he is "rising up to seize by force what, in his opinion, has been wrongfully denied him." The absolutist state is

> tottering, its rotting foundations giving way, and there seems to be a *physical* possibility of setting law upon the throne, of honouring man at last as an end in himself, and making true freedom the basis of political associations. Vain hope! The *moral* possibility is lacking, and a moment so prodigal of opportunity finds a generation unprepared to receive it. (p. 25)

Far from establishing a rational state in the place of the Old Regime, the citizens of the new French republic are extending the rule of force. They have proved unable to govern themselves. The lesson to be drawn from the bloody course the revolution was taking is that men are as yet unequipped for self-rule.

In this grave deficiency lies the rationale for the *Aesthetic Letters*. He is justified in diverting attention to the fine arts, Schiller writes, because only aesthetic education can equip men for self-government. Or, as he puts it in the passage from which I quoted at the outset: "If man is ever to solve that problem of politics in practice he will have to approach it through the problem of the aesthetic, because it is only through beauty that man makes his way to freedom" (p. 9). In short, Schiller defines his project in the *Letters* in expressly political terms. He construes "freedom" in keeping with the emancipatory political goals of the Enlightenment, and he makes freedom thus construed the ultimate object of occupation with the arts. Aesthetic education is to result in a rational state—a state governed by principles of liberty, equality, and fraternity.

Why, then, does he depart from this project midstream? For Schiller's readers, even his most sympathetic readers—his editors and translators—have long been troubled by the presence in the *Letters* of another project, one that runs parallel to, eventually displacing the political project just sketched.[2] The goal of this second project is not so much to emancipate mankind as to render emancipation unnecessary. That is to say, by the end of the *Letters* what had been designated the indispensable instrument of emancipation seems to have become identical with it: the experience of beauty in art has become a terminal value. For at the end of the *Letters* aesthetic experience is portrayed as itself the locus of freedom. "Freedom" has lost the distinctly political inflection given it at the beginning of the *Letters* and come to denote the kind of freedom to dream that is the consolation of the subjects of even the most repressive regimes.

The present chapter seeks to shed light on this slippage by examining the cultural-political context in which the *Aesthetic Letters* took shape. I shall focus on a controversy over the nature and function of poetry that Schiller initiated in a review of the collected poems of one of the most popular writers of the period, Gottfried August Bürger. *Über Bürgers Gedichte* [*On Bürgers Poems*], a virtual blueprint of the theory of art elaborated in the *Letters*, reveals quite different considerations at the root of Schiller's extravagant claim for the power of art from those he mentions at the beginning of the *Letters*—not an impassioned interest in human emancipation by peaceful means, but the very material existential considerations of a professional writer in Germany at the end of the eighteenth century. This "occasional" writing makes sense of the puzzling trajectory of the *Letters*, I propose, by suggesting that the emancipatory project announced with such fanfare at their beginning is but a pre-text for the narrowly aesthetic project that gradually displaces it, culminating in the cult of art celebrated at the *Letters*' conclusion.

I

> The aim of the poet is either to benefit, or to amuse, or to
> make his words at once please and give lessons of life. . . .
> He has gained every vote who has mingled profit with
> pleasure by delighting the reader at once and instructing
> him. This is the book that makes the fortune of the
> [*booksellers*] Sosii, that crosses the seas, and gives a long
> life of fame to its author.
>
> —Horace, "The Art of Poetry"

In Gottfried August Bürger (1747–1794) the instrumentalist principles that guided literary practice down through the eighteenth century found one of their most effective partisans. Bürger believed with Horace that a poem ought "at once [to] please and give lessons of life." Whether or not the poem succeeds he considered a matter for its recipients to decide, and he thought that in thus deciding they determined the poem's value.

Bürger is chiefly remembered by English-speaking readers for *Lenore,* a chilling ballad about a girl carried to an early grave by the ghost of her beloved, which took England by storm in the 1790s. The "immediate inspiration of Wordsworth's interest in the ballad"[3] —a connection we will examine in chapter 6—*Lenore* helped to catalyze the revolution in English poetry that got under way with the publication in 1798 of the *Lyrical Ballads.* The notice that accompanied the *Lenore* translation by William Taylor of Norwich in the *Monthly Magazine* for March 1796, where Wordsworth and Coleridge first became acquainted with Bürger, suggests the nature of the German poet's appeal.

> Bürger is every where distinguished for manly sentiment and force of style. His extraordinary powers of language are founded on a rejection of the conventional phraseology of regular poetry, in favour of popular forms of expression, caught by the listening artist from the voice of agitated nature. Imitative harmony he pursues almost to excess: the onomatopoeia is his prevailing figure; the interjection, his favorite part of speech: arrangement, rhythm, sound, rime, are always with him, an echo to the sense. The hurrying vigour of his impetuous diction is unrivalled; yet, it is so natural, even in its sublimity, that his poetry is singularly fitted to become national popular song.[4]

Bürger, who died some two years before the appearance of Taylor's notice, would surely have felt vindicated by its judgment on his poetry as "fitted to become national popular song," for this had been his aim from the beginning. As a young poet in the 1770s, Bürger joined the other Storm and Stress *genies* in calling for the reform of German literature. His ideas about the direction reform ought to take in poetry are set forth in *Herzens-Ausguss über Volks-Poesie* [*Confessions on Popular Poetry*], which he published in 1776 in the *Deutsches Museum.* A short essay that takes its inspiration from Herder's reflections on "Ossian und die Lieder alter Völker" in *Von deutscher Art und Kunst*— the collection of 1773 that did more than any other single publication to kindle the literary revival—Bürger's *Confessions* are the nearest thing to a formal program for poetry that the poet would develop.[5]

Addressing contemporary poets in the direct and personal style of his verse, Bürger begins his *Confessions* by demanding to be told why German poetry should be so exclusive, why Apollo and his muses should reside on top of Olympus where their song delights only the gods and "the few who have strength and wind enough" to ascend the mountain's steep cliffs.

> Should they not descend and walk the earth, as Apollo did in days of old among the shepherds of Arcadia? Should they not leave their radiant garments on high, those garments that have so often blinded mortal eyes, and don human nature? And frequent the homes of mortals, both palaces and huts, and write poetry that is equally understandable and entertaining for all humankind?[6]

Bürger considers broad accessibility essential to poetry, and he faults German poets for doing so little to achieve it. They complain of being appreciated by only a few, yet they write in an idiom so "learned" and "foreign" that they are inaccessible to the majority of their countrymen. Alluding to the heavy French and Greco-Roman influences upon the verse of the period, Bürger complains that German poets would rather paint heavenly than human scenes and would rather paint like the people of other times and places than their own. That is why their songs are not heard "on the lips of the people." They have nothing of relevance to say to the people.

Calling the learnedness that so elevates them above their readership "sheer pedantry" [*Quisquilien-Gelahrtheit*], Bürger enjoins German poets to stop expecting "the many who live on earth" to climb up to them; the poets should instead descend from their lofty heights. Rather than take their cues, secondhand, from the literature of other nations, they should draw their inspiration from the world in which they live. Echoing Luther's insight into what is required of a translator to produce a Bible that captures the imagination of the German people, Bürger commands poets to "get to know the people intimately, explore their imagination and their feeling so you can fill the former with appropriate images and gauge the latter correctly" (p. 317). This, Bürger writes, is the recipe for success among all classes of people:

> I promise that the song of whoever accomplishes this will enchant the sophisticated sage as much as the rough forest dweller, the lady at her dressing table as well as the daughter of nature behind her flax and in the bleach-yard. This is the true non plus ultra of poetry. (p. 318)

Broad appeal is not only essential, it is for Bürger the ultimate test of a poem's excellence. All poetry, he states in the preface to his collected *Poems* in 1778, "can and should be popular. For that is the seal of its perfection [*Vollkommenheit*]" (p. 328).

The centrality of popularity in Bürger's theory of poetry reflects the intense concern of German *Aufklärer* with the formation of a common culture, but his program for extending the boundaries of culture departs sharply from theirs. They aimed to draw ever larger numbers into the orbit they themselves had delineated. Theirs was a pedagogical program designed to impose culture from above. Bürger's contains no such condescension. As Klaus Berghahn has shown, it aimed not to raise the masses into a predefined culture but to enfranchise them.[7] For Bürger identifies with the uneducated—the "peasants, shepherds, hunters, miners, journeymen, boilermen, hatchel carriers, sailors, teamsters, trollops, Tyrolians, and Tyroliennes" (p. 322) whom he hopes to reach in his verse. His aim is to become their spokesman, not their teacher, and in this way to stimulate culture from below.

It is in this spirit that Bürger urges the would-be poet to "get to know the people": "eavesdrop on the ballads and popular songs under the linden in the village, in the bleach-yard, and in the spinning room" (p. 319). From the songs on the lips of common people the would-be poet may hope to glean the language and subject matter from which to fashion verse that all of his countrymen can recognize as an expression of themselves. As evidence for the soundness of his program, Bürger adduces the great national epics. This is how they evolved, he argues; it was "the muse of romance and ballad" who sang

> Orlando Furioso, the Faerie Queene, Fingal and Temora, and— believe it or not—the Iliad and the Odyssey. . . . Truly! These poems were nothing but ballads, romances, and folk songs to the people to whom they were originally sung. And that is exactly why they achieved national acclaim. (p. 320)

Bürger is confident of similarly spectacular results from the reform of German poetry he advocates. "Give us a great national poem of this kind," he urges German poets, "and we shall make it our pocket book" (p. 321).

What enables these masterpieces to speak to so many people, according to Bürger, is that they speak not only to the understanding like "the so-called higher poetry," but also, and more important, to the imagination and the senses (p. 319). This became Bürger's aim, and though he never attempted anything on the scale of the works he names, many of his poems equal these in their mastery of the techniques of engaging *all* of the reader's faculties. Bürger excelled especially in the formally simple, "spontaneous" lyric and in the more complex form of the ballad. In both forms he ranged thematically from the most intimate matters of the heart to problems as public and political as the persistence of feudalism. His goal throughout was to bring his material alive for his readers—to enable them to imagine it as vividly as if they were actually experiencing it.[8]

To see how Bürger sought to achieve such immediacy, let us look at his masterpiece *Lenore* alongside Taylor's occasionally somewhat free English rendering.[9] In a steady stream of translations, imitations, and adaptations the poem gradually overran all Europe, helping more than any other German work of the period—including, J. G. Robertson believes, Goethe's *Werther*, which appeared a few months later—to call the Romantic movement to life.[10] The contemporaneity of the poem contributes to its immediacy. It unfolds against the backdrop of the Seven Years War (1756–63), which many of its original readers would have experienced either directly or indirectly. Peace has been declared when the poem opens. The returning soldiers pass through Lenore's village, but her beloved Wilhelm is not among them. Concluding that he has fallen, Lenore despairs:

> O Mutter, Mutter! hin ist hin!
> Nun fahre Welt und alles hin!
> Bei Gott ist kein Erbarmen.
> O weh, o weh mir Armen!—
>
> [O mother, mother! William's gone!
> What's all besyde to me?
> There is no mercye, sure, above!
> All, all were spar'd but hee!]

Shocked at her daughter's impiety, Lenore's mother bids her pray. What happens is God's will. Lenore must forget Wilhelm and think of her immortal soul:

> Ach, Kind, vergiß dein irdisch Leid,
> Und denk an Gott und Seligkeit!

So wird doch deiner Seelen
Der Bräutigam nicht fehlen.—

[My girl, forget thine earthly woe,
And think on God and bliss;
For so, at least, shall not thy soule
Its heavenly bridegroom miss.]

But Lenore will not be consoled. Wringing her hands and beating her breast, she exclaims:

Lisch aus, mein Licht, auf ewig aus!
Stirb hin, stirb hin in Nacht und Graus!
Ohn' ihn mag ich auf Erden,
Mag dort nicht selig werden.—

[Go out, go out, my lamp of life;
In endless darkness die:
Without him I must loathe the earth,
Without him scorne the skye.]

Night then falls and Lenore, having reached the depth of despair, retires.

Und außen, horch! ging's trap trap trap,
Als wie von Rosseshufen;
Und klirrend stieg ein Reiter ab,
An des Geländers Stufen;

[When harke! abroade she hearde the trampe
Of nimble-hoofed steed;
She hearde a knighte with clank alighte,
And climb the staire in speede.]

A voice asks Lenore to open the door. It is Wilhelm, who entreats her to elope with him:

Auf meinen Rappen hinter mich!
Muß heut noch hundert Meilen
Mit dir in's Brautbett' eilen.—

[Aryse, and mount behinde;
To-night we'le ride a thousand miles,
The bridal bed to finde.]

At first reluctant because of the lateness of the hour, Lenore at last
mounts the steed, and the lovers ride off at a gallop:

> Und hurre, hurre, hop hop hop!
> Ging's fort in sausendem Galopp,
> Daß Roß und Reiter schnoben,
> Und Kies und Funken stoben.

> [And hurry-skurry forth they go,
> Unheeding wet or dry;
> And horse and rider snort and blow,
> And sparkling pebbles fly.]

Several times repeated, these lines operate as a refrain, contributing
to the tempo of the wild ride, which accelerates with every stanza. As
mountains, trees, hedges, towns, and villages hurtle past the couple,
Wilhelm repeats the eerie question:

> Hurrah! Die Toten reiten schnell!
> Graut Liebchen auch vor Toten?—

> [Hurrah! the dead can ride apace;
> Dost feare to ride with mee?]

Wilhelm's query is but one of the many signs that this is no ordinary
elopement. Having passed a funeral procession, the ghostly couple
reaches a cemetery, and there Wilhelm is horribly transformed:

> Ha sieh! Ha sieh! im Augenblick,
> Huhu! ein gräßlich Wunder!
> Des Reiters Koller, Stück für Stück,
> Fiel ab, wie mürber Zunder.
> Zum Schädel, ohne Zopf und Schopf,
> Zum nackten Schädel ward sein Kopf;
> Sein Körper zum Gerippe,
> Mit Stundenglas und Hippe.

> [And when hee from his steede alytte,
> His armour, black as cinder,
> Did moulder, moulder all awaye,
> As were it made of tinder.

> His head became a naked scull;
> Nor haire nor eyne had hee:

His body grew a skeleton,
Whilome so blythe of blee.

And att his drye and boney heele
No spur was left to be;
And inn his witherde hande you might
The scythe and houre-glasse see.]

Thus is Lenore punished for doubting God's wisdom in taking Wilhelm from her. Her heart stops at this horrible sight, and as she expires, spirits perform a *Totentanz,* singing:

Geduld! Geduld! Wenn's Herz auch bricht!
Mit Gott im Himmel hadre nicht!
Des Leibes bist du ledig;
Gott sei der Seele gnädig!

[Be patient; tho' thyne herte should breke,
Arrayne not Heven's decree;
Thou nowe art of thie bodie refte,
Thie soule forgiven bee!]

These final lines drive home the moral of the tale, making it a parable of transgression justly punished. It is difficult to imagine a more exacting implementation than *Lenore* of Horace's instrumentalist injunction to the poet to "delight the reader at once and instruct him." In the original the poem extends to thirty-two stanzas of eight lines each, but it is still capable of chilling the spine even in as drastic an abridgment as this. Bürger's mastery of pace, his galloping rhythms, his vivid visual imagery and onomatopoeic sound effects cooperate to produce a tension difficult to surpass before the invention of moving pictures.

Bürger seems to have taken great pleasure in his mastery of the technology of powerful sensory effects. In a letter to his friend Boie written while he was working on *Lenore* he boasts, for example, that his landlady, to whom he read the poem aloud, "starts up at night in bed [from it]. I'm not even allowed to remind her of [*Lenore*]. Indeed, I myself can't work on it in the evening, for it even makes me shudder a little. When you read it for the first time to our friends in Göttingen, borrow a skull from some medical student, place it next to a dim lamp, and then read. Their hair will stand on end as in Macbeth."[11] Bürger had translated *Macbeth* into German, but he must be referring to lines he will appropriate from *Hamlet* to announce *Lenore*'s completion. "I have a tale to unfold," he writes Boie several months later,

whose lightest word
Will harrow up your souls, freeze your young blood,
Make your two eyes, like stars, start from their spheres
Your knotty and combined locks to part,
And each particular hair to stand on end,
Like quills upon the fretful porcupine.
(Act I, V, 15–20)[12]

Nor is Bürger overreaching. Readers of the *Göttinger Musen-Almanach für 1774*, where *Lenore* was first published, agreed on its power. Indeed, some were sufficiently shaken to express resentment at such an assault on their nerves. "When I read it, it took hold of me so," Herder complained,

> that that afternoon I saw naked skulls on all the church pews. The deuce of a man, to terrify people that way! Why and for what purpose? I wish some one else would sing in the same way about the devil fetching the poet.[13]

Subsequent ballads like *Des Pfarrers Tochter von Taubenhain* (also translated by Taylor for the *Monthly Magazine*, where it appeared as *The Lass of Fair Wone*) and *Der wilde Jäger* (translated by Walter Scott and entitled *The Chase*) employ the techniques perfected in *Lenore* to more social-critical ends. Formally even more flamboyant than *Lenore*, *Der wilde Jäger* tells the story of a count so consumed by a passion for hunting that he allows nothing to stand in his way. He ravages a farmer's fields and a shepherd's flocks, and in defiance of God even violates a hermit's cottage before he is finally stopped and a voice speaking from the heavens condemns him to expiate his sins as a hunter by living until Judgment Day as a hunted creature. In *Der Bauer. An seinen Durchlauchtigen Tyrannen* [*The Peasant. To His Illustrious Tyrant*] no such supernatural intervention is required to bring about justice because the victims of aristocratic arrogance, who are able only to plead for mercy in *Der wilde Jäger*, are prepared to take action in their own defense. The peasant of the poem's title disputes his sovereign's authority even as he indicts his abuses of that authority.

> Wer bist du, Fürst, daß ohne Scheu
> Zerrollen mich dein Wagenrad,
> Zerschlagen darf dein Roß?
>
> Wer bist du, Fürst, daß in mein Fleisch
> Dein Freund, dein Jagdhund, ungebläut
> Darf Klau' und Rachen hau'n?

Wer bist du, daß, durch Saat und Forst,
Das Hurra deiner Jagd mich treib,
Entatmet, wie das Wild?—

Die Saat, so deine Jagd zertritt,
Was Roß, und Hund, und Du verschlingst,
Das Brot, du Fürst, ist mein.

Du Fürst hast nicht, bei Egg' und Pflug,
Hast nicht den Erntetag durchschwitzt.
Mein, mein ist Fleiß und Brot!—

Ha! du wärst Obrigkeit von Gott?
Gott spendet Segen aus; du raubst!
Du nicht von Gott, Tyrann!

[Who are you, Prince, that without hesitation
Your coach wheel runs over me,
Your steed tramples me down?

Who are you, Prince, that in my flesh
Your friend, your hunting dog, unpunished
Sinks its claws and teeth?

Who are you, that through standing corn and forest
The "Hurrah" of your hunt drives me,
Breathless, like wild game?

The corn, such as your hunt treads down,
What steed and dog and you devour,
That bread, you Prince, is mine.

You, Prince, have not, with harrow or plow,
Have not sweat through the harvest day.
Mine, mine the industry and bread!

Ha! You would claim authority from God?
God dispenses blessings; you plunder!
You're not from God, Tyrant!] [14]

Confident of his strength as producer of the grain on which his sovereign depends for his very subsistence, the peasant can only laugh at the other's presumption that he rules by divine right.

The power of this poem, its capacity to engage readers' sympathy for the peasant and his cause, derives no less from the character traits with which Bürger has endowed this figure than from the vividness of his representation of aristocratic brutality. A forerunner of Kleist's rebel, Michael Kohlhaas, the peasant is uncomplicated, hard working, and sincere, as well as very angry. These "primitive" virtues, which are conveyed by the rough style as well as the content of his utterances—by the blank verse, the omission of an occasional article and auxillary, etc.—serve to legitimize the peasant's anger, winning readers to the apocalyptic resolution that the final explosive tercet heralds. We have been prepared for it by Bürger's handling of the pronouns especially: by repeatedly addressing the prince in the form of *you* reserved for inferiors while emphatically asserting his own proprietary rights to the fruits of his labor ("That bread, you Prince, is mine . . . / Mine, mine the industry and bread!"), the peasant conveys his resolve to rise up and overthrow his "illustrious tyrant."

At the opposite end of the spectrum thematically but marked by equal intensity are Bürger's love lyrics. In a variety of forms and styles from the tightly wrought *Das Mädel, das ich meine* [*The Lass I Woo*] to the volcanic *Elegie, als Molly sich losreißen wollte* [*Elegy When Molly Wanted to Tear Herself Away*] he gives expression to his evolving feelings for Augusta ("Molly") Leonhart, with whom he fell passionately in love shortly before marrying her sister Dorette in 1774. Composed toward the beginning of their relationship (before the couple was united, first in a ménage-à-trois with Dorette, then after the latter's death in 1784, in marriage to one another, which ended with Molly's death in childbirth in 1786), *Ständchen* [*Serenade*] employs sensuous sound effects imitative of the strumming of a lute to envelop the reader in the poet's intense longing to be united with his beloved.

> Trallyrum larum höre mich!
> Trallyrum larum leier!
> Trallyrum larum das bin ich,
> Schön Liebchen, dein Getreuer!
> Schleuß auf den hellen Sonnenschein,
> In deinen zwei Guckäugelein!
>
> [Trallyrum larum hear me!
> Trallyrum larum softly!
> Trallyrum larum that's what I am,
> Sweet darling, your faithful one!
> Open up the bright sunshine
> In your two little peeping eyes.]

Having thus awakened his beloved, the poet relates in the four stanzas that follow how he has come to her in the night while all else sleeps—

the husband with his wife, the various birds with their respective mates. "When, oh when will it also be allowed me / To unite with you?" he inquires. Then, having assured his beloved how "fervently" he "yearns to love" her, to "refresh himself" in her arms, he lulls her back to sleep in the final stanza. It echoes the first, aurally caressing the reader even as the poet would his beloved:

> Nun lyrum larum gute Nacht!
> Gott mag dein Herz bewahren!—
> Was Gott bewahrt ist wohl bewacht.—
> Daß wir kein Leid erfahren.
> Ade! schleuß wieder zu den Schein,
> In deinen zwei Guckäugelein!

> [Now lyrum larum and good night.
> May God watch o'er your heart.
> What God o'ersees is well o'erseen.
> Let us come to no harm.
> Ade, now close again the shine
> In your two little peeping eyes.]

Ständchen was set to music many times, as were Bürger's other love poems and ballads, by composers from Haydn to Beethoven. Thus arranged to be sung at social gatherings around the piano, they could more readily serve the function in people's lives that Bürger demands in the *Confessions* when he calls for poetry that frequents palaces and huts as freely as in ancient times—there to cheer and console, to entertain and to stir to action: "Living breath . . . to bless and benefit humankind in this vale of tears!" (p. 320).

In his challenge to Bürger in *Über Bürgers Gedichte,* Schiller will pronounce these uses the domain of "occasional verse," and exhorting the poet to "disentangle himself from the present and, bold and free, soar up into the world of the ideal" (p. 258), he will oppose to Bürger's conception of poetry as a kind of "pocket-book" companion to life in *this* world the proposition that it is the poet's job to present the reader an *other,* better world.[15] Bürger, however, had anticipated this departure from his program. In the preface to the 1789 edition of his *Poems* [*Gedichte*], which occasioned Schiller's assault on the Horatian principles that govern Bürger's practice, he had warned:

> Anyone who denies [the primacy of popularity] in theory or in practice puts the whole business of poetry on a false track and

works against its true purpose. He draws this universal, human art out of the sphere of influence that it belongs to, pulls it away from the marketplace of life and exiles it to a narrow cell like that in which the surveyor measures and calculates or in which the metaphysician expounds on something obscure or unintelligible before his few students. (pp. 352–53)

Bürger accurately predicts the consequences of the "metaphysics" that Schiller will elaborate for poetry: its banishment from "the marketplace of life" to the academy, where it is sustained by scholars and the small circles of disciples they are able to win for it through their lectures.

Favorable reaction to his poetry in the magazines encouraged Bürger to bring out a separate volume. Published in 1778 with engravings by the famous and much sought-after Daniel Chodowiecki (1726–1801), this first edition of Bürger's *Poems* [*Gedichte*] was in every respect a success. Bürger had negotiated a handsome contract with the Göttingen printer, Johann Christian Dieterich, guaranteeing him 800 Reichstaler, and within only six months he managed to accumulate some 1,200 subscribers. Before the book went to press the number had grown to around 2,000 and included eighteen heads of state—among them the queen of England—and an impressive number of well-known statesmen and literati.[16] Similarly, the reviews, although not all favorable, could wax as enthusiastic as this encomium by Wieland in the *Teutscher Mercur:*

Who will not soon know *Bürger's Poems* by heart? In what home, in what corner of Germany will they not be sung? I at least know of nothing of this sort more perfect in any language; nothing that is so fitting, so enjoyable, so amiable and pleasant to both connoisseurs and amateurs, youths and men, the people and the clergy, to each according to his sensitivity. . . . True *popular poetry* [*Volkspoesie*] . . . so lovely, so polished, so perfect! And with all that, as light as a breath of air. And with all this ease and grace, it is so lively and pithy, so full of strength and vigor! Body and spirit, image and thing, thought and expression, inner music and the outer melody of the versification, everything always complete and whole! And in which poet does the *utile dulci* flow together more purely, more sweetly, more vigorously than in this one?[17]

Not only were critics as discriminating as Wieland much impressed with Bürger's first volume; it appears also to have been as big a hit with the general audience as Wieland predicted. Three pirate editions of the volume had appeared by 1779;[18] and it inspired such a rash of imitations that Bürger would feel it necessary to address himself to the problem in the preface of his next edition.

By the time this new, enlarged edition of *Poems* appeared in 1789, Bürger was one of Germany's most popular poets—in a word, something of the *Volksdichter* he had called for in his *Confessions*. It must therefore have come as a shock to him, and to the literary world as a whole, to read in the review of the volume carried in January 1791 by the *Allgemeine Literatur-Zeitung* that he did not even "deserve the name of poet." The review, entitled *Über Bürgers Gedichte* [*On Bürger's Poems*], appeared anonymously; however, word spread quickly that its author was Friedrich Schiller.

II

Schiller's devastating review represents a turning point not only in the fortunes of Bürger's poetry, but also in Schiller's own thought and in the cultural politics of Germany.[19] The young Schiller conceived of literature instrumentally, much as Bürger. In early theoretical writings like his famous essay, "Was kann eine gute stehende Schaubühne eigentlich wirken?" ["What Can a Good Permanent Theater Actually Accomplish?"] (1784), he defends the theater on the grounds of its diverse uses in the lives of its audience. "More than any other public institution," he writes, "the theater is a school of practical wisdom, a guide to bourgeois life, an unfailing key to the secret doors of the human soul."[20] In his review of Bürger, however, Schiller departs from this thoroughly Horatian view of the uses of literature and inaugurates an entirely new poetic program. Drawing on ideas first articulated by Karl Philipp Moritz, as discussed in chapter 1,[21] Schiller derogates the variety of mundane uses to which poetry may be put and assigns it instead a single, more grandiose function: the quasi-metaphysical function that will fall to art in the letters *On the Aesthetic Education of Man*. Near the beginning of the review Schiller writes:

> With the isolation and fragmentation of our mental faculties, necessitated by the expansion of knowledge and the division of labor, it is poetry almost alone that reunites the separate faculties of the soul, that employs head and heart, shrewdness and ingenuity, reason and imagination in a harmonious alliance, that so to speak restores the *whole person* in us.[22]

Here poetry acquires the task of healing the wounds inflicted on man by life in the modern world—specifically, of unifying and reconciling mental powers that the need to specialize has caused to work independently of one another, or not at all. This radical reorientation of poetry's function reads like a prospectus for the *Aesthetic Letters*. There Schiller, having argued in the interest of his larger political project that "wholeness of character" is a necessary condition of freedom (Letter Four), will extend the analysis he initiates here of the devastating effect of "progress" on the individual psyche so as to include its effect on the relations between individuals and among classes (Letters Five–Six). And finding only alienation, dissension, and disintegration all around, he will prescribe aesthetic education. Art alone, he will urge, has the power to restore harmony in all these different spheres— to reverse the debilitating side effects of progress and heal the divisions that tear us apart both individually and socially.

It was not in the interest of furthering any kind of emancipatory political project, however, that Schiller initially put forward these high romantic ideas. His aim in the review of Bürger's volume was rather the much narrower—indeed, as we shall see, counterrevolutionary— one of enhancing the prestige of the craft he wanted to practice. To Schiller, Bürger's program to expand the audience for poetry, far from revitalizing the craft, threatened to render it even more marginal than it had already become in modern society. Having remarked the relative "indifference" of "our philosophizing age" (p. 245) to literature in general, he notes that although drama is in some measure protected by the central role that theaters play in the social life of our communities, and its freer form enables prose fiction to incorporate change easily and thus keep up with changing times, poetry is being sustained only by "yearly almanacs, social singing, the love of music among our ladies" (p. 245). To Schiller such organs of mass dissemination[23] are but "a weak dam against the decline of lyric poetry" (p. 245) because the vast audiences they deliver may be had only by poets willing to cater to them. It is with such opportunism that Schiller charges Bürger.

Bürger himself had supplied the cue. So successful had been his call for the renewal of German poetry that in the preface to the new edition of his *Poems*, which Schiller reviewed, he had felt obliged to dissociate himself from the host of imitators who had heeded it so energetically. And chiding them for mistaking the chaff for the wheat, he had protested: "If I am really the popular poet [*Volksdichter*] they are saying I am, I scarcely owe it to my *Hopp Hopp, Hurre Hurre, Huhu*, etc., scarcely to this or that forceful expression that I may have snatched up by mistake, scarcely to the fact that I put a few popular tales into verse and rhyme" (p. 352). But his protestations were wasted on Schiller.

As Schiller sees it, the effects in which Bürger indulges, far from being an occasional lapse, are an essential feature of his verse and the inevitable consequence of his poetic program. Bürger has been obliged to take such extraordinary measures in order to capture, and hold, the attention of a wide audience. What he fails to recognize, according to Schiller, is that in doing so he has rendered his verse irrelevant to more sophisticated readers.

> The cultivated man cannot possibly seek refreshment for the heart and spirit in an immature youth, cannot possibly want to find in poems those prejudices and common manners, that emptiness of spirit, that repel him in real life. It is his right to demand from the poet who is to be the kind of cherished companion through life that Horace was to the Romans that he be his intellectual and moral *equal,* because even in hours of recreation he does not want to sink beneath himself. Hence it is not enough to depict feeling in heightened colors; one must also feel in a heightened way. Enthusiasm *alone* is not enough; one demands the enthusiasm of a cultivated spirit. (p. 246)

In his examination of Bürger's verse Schiller will simply expand the catalog of failings he begins here. The immaturity, the deficiency of spirit, the enthusiasm, and the vulgarity that endear Bürger's verse to common readers cannot but "repel" the elite.

Without expressly contesting the worthiness of Bürger's goal of reaching all classes, then, Schiller takes strong issue with his strategy. In ancient times it might have been possible to locate the material with which to fashion verse of universal appeal by eavesdropping, as Bürger had put it, "under the village linden trees, in the bleach-yard, and in the spinning rooms" (p. 319). But times have changed, Schiller writes.

> Our world is no longer Homer's world, where all members of society were at roughly *the same* stage with respect to sensibility and opinion and therefore could easily recognize themselves in the same descriptions and encounter themselves in the same feelings. There is now a great gulf between the *elect* of a nation and the *masses.* (p. 247)

Riven into distinct classes by "the expansion of knowledge and the division of labor," the entity Bürger purports to be addressing, *the people*, no longer exists as such, Schiller argues, and thus can no longer be addressed by the poet in a single poem—not at any rate in poems fashioned from the language and sentiments of the uneducated. For, according to Schiller, such poetry cannot hold the interest of the elite. If the gulf separating these classes is to be bridged and a common culture reestablished, some other means will need to be found, Schiller urges—some means of "satisfying the fastidious taste of the connoisseur without thereby becoming unpalatable to the masses, accommodating the childish understanding of the people without sacrificing any of the dignity of art" (p. 248). To Bürger's populist program for poetry Schiller thus opposes an "art of the ideal."

It does not take extensive familiarity with the theory and practice of Bürger or independent evidence of his popularity to discern that Schiller's disparaging remarks shed more light on the genesis of his own aesthetic than on their target. Indeed, were it not for such invective the "art of the ideal" would cut as ineffable a figure here in the review as it does in the *Aesthetic Letters*. Having introduced it in the later work as the only kind of art that will concern him, Schiller goes on to explain only that "this kind of art must abandon actuality and soar with becoming boldness above our wants and needs, for art is a daughter of freedom and takes her orders from the necessity inherent in minds, not from the exigencies of matter" (p. 7). It is not easy for the reader to visualize this crucial player in the treatise about to unfold.

The "art of the ideal" is also subject to handwaving in the review, but here the reader's efforts are facilitated by the very substantiality of its other: the emancipatory and egalitarian orientation of Bürger. The "art of the ideal" evolves *in reaction* to this orientation. This is especially noteworthy inasmuch as in December 1790, when Schiller composed the review, the aspirations expressed by Bürger seemed to progressive intellectuals everywhere to be on the verge of becoming reality. The revolution under way in France was in its most inspiring phase. The violence that was to alienate so many intellectuals and that, as we have noted, provides the rationale for the *Aesthetic Letters*, was still many months away (Louis XIV was executed in January 1793, Marie Antoinette in October of that year). At a historical moment when so much discursive activity was being carried on in the name of the people, Schiller sought to write them out of his model of poetry.[24]

To reach all readers irrespective of differences of background and education, "the poet should choose his subject matter only from situations and feelings that pertain to the human being as a human being," Schiller writes (p. 248). In the interest of universality of appeal he must strive to exclude from his representations, whether they be of "a form, a feeling, or an action *within* himself or *outside* himself," everything that is merely local or idiosyncratic—"everything arising from experiences, conclusions, and accomplishments come by in specific and artificial circumstances" (p. 253). In what do these consist then? When Schiller descends from the heights of pure speculation to spell out the implications of his exhortation for poetic practice, the referent of the merely local and accidental, and hence the target of what sounds like a rather conventional neoclassical exhortation to "idealize," turns out to be the very features supposed to enthrall the broad-gauge audience while (allegedly) offending the elite.

At issue is whether Bürger has succeeded in "elevating the particular and local to the universal" (p. 253). Having complained that this "art of idealization is most notably absent in Herr B. when he depicts feelings" (p. 255), Schiller "wonder[s] how it was possible" for the critics who praised the great beauty of Bürger's poem "Das hohe Lied von der Einzigen" ["The Song of Songs to My Beloved] "to forgive so many sins against good taste" and

> overlook the fact that the poet's enthusiasm not infrequently borders on *madness,* that his fire often becomes *fury,* that for just this reason the emotional state in which one lays down the poem is not the beneficent, harmonious state in which we want to see the poet put us. (p. 256)

And again, as evidence of "how sloppily Herr B. idealizes," Schiller discusses the following stanza from Bürger's lyric "Die beiden Liebenden" ["The Two Lovers]:

> Im Denken ist sie Pallas ganz
> Und Juno ganz an edelm Gange,
> Terpsichore beim Freudentanz,
> Euterpe neidet sie im Sange;
> Ihr weicht Aglaja, wenn sie lacht,
> Melpomene bei sanfter Klage,
> Die Wollust ist sie in der Nacht,
> Die holde Sittsamkeit bei Tage.

[She is Pallas in her thoughts
And Juno in her noble gait,
Terpsichore in her dance,
Euterpe envies her in song;
She bests Aglaia when she laughs,
Melpomene in soft complaint.
At night she's pleasure, straight and true,
And blessed virtue once it's day.]

This opulent play of colors cannot fail to charm and dazzle us at first sight, especially those readers who are susceptible only to the sensuous and who, like children, admire only what is *gaudy*. But how little do portraits of this kind have to offer the more refined artistic sense, which is satisfied not by richness but by wise economy, not by the material but only by the beauty of form, not by the ingredients but only by the skill with which they are blended! (pp. 253–54)

Such practical applications of the principle of idealization tell us more about Schiller than about the verse he is criticizing, for they show not that this verse is especially private or particular, but simply that it is emotive and sensuous. And far from preventing readers from recognizing themselves in the poet's representations, these features evidently cause them to recognize themselves all too readily, to respond, that is, all too powerfully and immediately—the vast majority of readers, at any rate.

To "idealize" with Schiller, then, means to purge one's verse of all such affective qualities. He would have the poet

supply a purer and intellectually richer text for the outpouring of affects that seek expression in language—whether of love, joy, reverence, sorrow, or hope. By giving them expression he would become master of these affects and make their rough, shapeless, often bestial eruption more noble while they are still on the lips of the people. (p. 249)

Schiller himself designates the process of idealization he is advocating *Veredlung* [ennoblement or refinement] (p. 253) in order to suggest the power of verse that is above all *cerebral* to elevate its users socially and distinguish them from the multitude of "vulgar" readers.[25] He notes that by contrast Bürger "frequently mingles with the people, to whom he ought merely to condescend, and instead of elevating them to himself jokingly and playfully, he is often pleased to make himself their equal" (p. 250).

The review exhibits, then, none of the sympathy for revolutionary ideals that one might have expected so early in the progress of the revolution from a poet who two years later in 1792 was to be named an honorary citizen of the French republic for his services to the people. Instead, Schiller disenfranchises them: they enter his model of poetry only as minors—"children," for whom all of the important decisions are made by others. The people have no vote in Schiller's poetic in the sense that although their needs and desires matter, it is for the poet alone to determine what these are, or ought to be, as well as how best to satisfy them. Whether or not he has succeeded in a given poem, moreover, is for the poet alone to decide, and in thus deciding he determines his work's value.

> Herr B. thus by no means exaggerates when he declares the "popularity of a poem the seal of its perfection." But when he makes this claim he tacitly assumes what many a reader might completely overlook: that the first, essential condition for the perfection of a poem is that it possess an absolute intrinsic value that is entirely independent of the powers of comprehension of its readers. (pp. 249–50)

Thus does Schiller rule the response of readers irrelevant to a poem's value. Deliberately misreading Bürger in order to enlist his support for a theoretical departure Bürger would never have agreed to, Schiller notes that if it is merely the *seal* of perfection, popularity could not be of any essential relevance to a work's value.

Having assigned poetry so high-minded a purpose, having sketched a poetic so very much at odds with the expectations of the vast majority of actual readers, it has become critical for Schiller to devise a means of measuring poetic value that does not require that a poem actually be appreciated. In the place of the response of readers, therefore, whom debased taste renders unreliable judges, Schiller proposes that we take only the poem's "intrinsic," or strictly poetic, properties into consideration.

The impetus for this momentous departure from instrumentalist principles appears to have been existential: Schiller is apprehensive about the "decline" in prestige of his chosen craft of verse. Anticipating Hegel's more famous statement of art's supersession by philosophy, Schiller suggests that poetry was once in the vanguard: the vehicle of important, often sacred ideas, it resided near the center of power before it was displaced by "philosophy," both natural and speculative (p. 245). Viewed in this light, Bürger's conquest of new audiences for verse can hardly have seemed a contribution, for, as Schiller sees it, these new readers were being acquired at the expense of the powerful. Anticipating today's conservative culture critics confronted by blues, jazz, or rock and roll, Schiller refuses to see in the resources tapped by Bürger a source of significant new vitality rather than a symptom of decline. This "revival from below" notwithstanding, therefore, he imagines that the genre is in danger of becoming extinct unless it is "possible to define a worthy task" for it. "Perhaps it could be shown," he thus continues, "that if poetry has to take second place to higher intellectual occupations on the one hand, it has become all the more necessary on the other"; and he thereupon tenders the proposition, which will play so essential a role in the *Aesthetic Letters*, that "poetry almost alone" is capable of restoring human wholeness (p. 245). It was in the interest of rescuing the art of poetry, then, in the sense of restoring it to prestige, that Schiller first set out down the high romantic road. In treating Bürger so critically he presents himself as "taking up the *cause of art*" (p. 258).

III

Schiller's deep existential investment in this cause is evident in his correspondence. His essay in defense of the theater was conceived in 1784, several years after the prodigious success of *The Robbers* induced him to give up his medical studies and make a career of writing, and its idealism reflects the young playwright's confidence that he will find a public sufficiently large and well educated to support the kind of dramatic work from which the essay promises so many benefits.

By 1791, however, when the review of Bürger's collected poems appeared, everything looked very different to Schiller. His next two dramas, *Fiesko* and *Kabale und Liebe*, although they did not create anything like the stir *The Robbers* had, were read and performed throughout Germany, and both were translated into French and English. However, in the absence of the protections that would eventually be provided by copyright laws, Schiller was not able to realize any substantial income from them.[26] To prosper in so unregulated a market he would have had to produce as rapidly as Iffland (1759–1814), who had been with the Mannheim theater for four years when

Schiller received a one-year contract as resident dramatist there in 1783. A master of the sentimental drama, Iffland could turn out a successful play in a few weeks (he wrote some sixty-five in all). But Schiller found it impossible to make the concessions that this kind of productivity requires. His contract called for three plays: *Fiesko* and *Kabale und Liebe*, which were nearly finished when Schiller accepted the post, and one entirely new play. But by the end of the year he had barely begun the new play, the ambitious *Don Carlos*—it would not be completed for three more years—and his contract was not renewed. Unemployed and in deep financial debt, Schiller would have to seek more lucrative avenues of expression.

"It may surprise you to learn that I propose to play *this* role in the world," Schiller wrote friends of his plan to found a miscellany, but "the German public forces its writers to choose according to commercial calculations rather than the dictates of genius. I shall devote all my energies to this *Thalia*, but I won't deny that I would have employed them in another sphere if my condition placed me beyond business considerations."[27] Conceived in the fall of 1784, a few months after the termination of his contract with the Mannheim theater, the plan attests to Schiller's recognition that he will have to increase his productivity and pay greater heed to the market if he aims to live by the pen. Schiller makes an energetic effort to do so, but judging from his correspondence, rarely without the reluctance—the element of resentment—he exhibits here, and with scant success financially.

His grasp of the literary market and of the measures required to break into it is demonstrated in this analysis of what it would take to revitalize the *Thalia*. That "*your* plan is too earnest, too respectable—how should I say? too *refined* to be the basis of a journal intended to reach *many* hands," he writes his friend Körner, who was contemplating becoming coeditor, "is evident from the response to our philosophical letters in the *Thalia*. In terms of *your* plan they are exceedingly appropriate and beautiful—but how many readers found them so?"

> Cagliostros and Starks, Flamels, ghostseers, secret chronicles, travel narratives, in any event, piquant stories, *casual* strolls through the current political and the ancient historical worlds—these are subjects for miscellanies. Above all, we would have to make it a rule to choose our material either from what is current—that is,

from the latest things in circulation in the reading world—or from the most remote pastures, where we could count on the bizarre and the strange to interest readers.

He does not mean to discourage Körner, Schiller hastens to add, from eventually inserting more demanding material, but first one has to get the organ off the ground:

> Interesting—light and elegantly treated situations, characters, etc. from history, didactic stories, portraits of manners, dramatic performances, in all events, popular and yet pleasing expositions of philosophical, preferably moral, matter, art criticism, satirical sketches, Meißnerian dialogues and the like must be our *debut*. But above all else 1) the bookseller must do his part to ensure circulation; 2) issues must follow one another rapidly and regularly; 3) the price should not be too high; 4) it should include writers with names to recommend it. My name counts certainly, but not exactly with *all* classes whose money we're after; to get these we'd have to parade, for example, a Garve, Engel, Gotter, or Biester and his ilk (I don't mean the people but the types).[28]

In this survey of the market in which he was attempting to secure a foothold, Schiller counsels compromise: meet readers on their own ground initially in the hope that, once hooked, they may be coaxed into accepting more demanding fare.

It is in such terms, Rudolf Dau observes, that Schiller's diverse activities of the eighties and nineties must be understood.[29] In addition to launching the *Thalia*, which he managed to keep alive under varying fortunes until 1795, Schiller undertook numerous other editorial projects, he threw himself into historical writing, and with his novel *Der Geisterseher* [*The Ghostseer*] he even made a foray into popular fiction. In the last project, which tells the story of a German prince in Venice who falls victim to the machinations of a secret society, the marketing principles Schiller urges on Körner are executed to the letter. In addition to exploiting for its theme the popular interest in the occult that had been aroused by the escapades of the charlatan Cagliostro, the novel combines secret report and travel narrative, it contains a touch of the piquant and the political, "the bizarre and the strange," and a dose of popular philosophy. Response to the novel was correspondingly positive. It had been conceived to improve the circulation of the *Thalia,* in which it appeared serially in 1787–89, and the first installment evidently struck a sufficiently sympathetic chord with readers for Schiller to jest of drawing the project out as long as possible. "I thank the lucky star that led me to the *Ghostseer,*" he writes Körner in the same letter. "Deride me as much as you will, but I intend to work it to death, and it won't get away in less than 30 sheets. I would be an idiot to disregard the praise of wise men and fools. Göschen [Schiller's publisher] can pay me well for it. . . . A time is eventually going to come when I can write something without any ulterior motives at all." [30]

In fact, however, the time did not come until a patron stepped forward to support him. The success of *The Ghostseer* did not improve Schiller's financial situation substantially. Göschen may have paid handsome honoraria,[31] but as one may surmise from the discussion in chapter 2 of the virtually unregulated state of the German book market, all but a fraction of the profits generated by the novel went to those in the expanding entertainment industry who pirated it, translated it, imitated it, or, indeed, simply continued it. For Schiller was not able to finish the novel himself.[32] He was ill-suited to the task he had set himself, and once assured of a captive audience, he began to try to mold the novel into a weightier, philosophical work.[33] When this proved impossible to accomplish effectively midstream, he tired of the project, and even the prospect of further, much needed honoraria could not persuade him to return to it.[34]

More satisfying to Schiller intellectually was the historical writing to which he also turned during this same period. In history he felt he had found a subject for which there was unquestionable demand as well as a genre sorely in need of the special skills of the playwright. Since "history is a necessity," he wrote Körner early in 1788, "no small thanks will go to the writer who transforms it from an arid discipline into an enticing one and strews *pleasures* where one would have had to put up with finding only *toil.*" Schiller felt himself preeminently qualified to perform this service, for did not his peculiar genius lie in breathing life into ideas, in investing "dry bones with muscles and nerves"?[35] Accordingly he hoped to achieve as a historian the fame and fortune—the "economic fame," as he wryly termed it[36]— that had thus far been denied him as a playwright. In words that betray his mounting bitterness at being thus forever diverted from his calling, he explains to Körner that with a historical work of half the merit

I will achieve more recognition in the so-called learned and bourgeois worlds than with the greatest expense of spirit on the frivolity of a tragedy. Don't think I'm jesting. . . . Isn't *solidity* the criterion by which merit is measured? Isn't the *instructive*, that is, what passes itself off as instructive, of a much higher order than the merely beautiful or entertaining? Thus judges the mob—and thus judge the scholars. If people admire a great poet, they revere a Robertsohn—and if this Robertsohn had written with poetic flair, he would be revered and admired. Who says that *I* won't be able to do that—or, more precisely, that I won't be able to make people think I have?

For my [Don] Carlos, the result of three years of hard work, I was rewarded with aversion. My Dutch history, the work of five, at most six, months, may just make a distinguished man of me.[37]

Schiller had calculated correctly. His work in history did bring him the recognition for which he yearned. He was extremely productive in the five years he devoted to it, between 1787 and 1792, completing in addition to the *Geschichte des Abfalls der vereinigten Niederlande* [*Revolt of the Netherlands*], to which he here alludes, another substantial work, his *Geschichte des dreißigjährigen Krieges* [*Thirty Years' War*], and countless shorter studies, sketches, introductions, and forewords in conjunction with the various editorial projects he took on. His industry also paid off in the sense that the recognition it earned him in the learned world led to his appointment in 1789 as professor of history in Jena. The post was unfortunately unsalaried, however, making him entirely dependent on student fees, so it did not ensure him a livelihood. Schiller's correspondence at the end of the decade is thus even more haunted by financial worries than it had been at the beginning, and early in 1791 he became critically ill.

It is understandable, therefore, that he was so grateful for the patronage extended him later that year by the Danish duke of Augustenburg. In Schiller's view the German reading public, whose enthusiastic reception of his first play had given him the courage to flee the grasp of the duke of Württemberg and seek his fortune as a writer, had proved as indifferent to his "genius" as had that petty tyrant. Now, however, through the largesse of another nobleman he was to be liberated from the tyranny of the public. He was to receive 1,000 thalers a year for three years with no conditions whatsoever and then, if he chose to settle in Copenhagen, a government sinecure of some kind. The gift struck Schiller as a miraculous reversal of fortune, as he explains to the Danish poet Jens Baggesen, who had been instrumental in securing it for him:

> From the time of my intellectual birth I have struggled with fortune, and since learning to appreciate intellectual freedom I have been condemned to do without it. A rash step ten years ago deprived me forever of the means of supporting myself by anything other than writing. I chose this vocation before I had assayed its demands, surveyed its difficulties. I was overwhelmed by the necessity of practicing it before knowledge and intellectual maturity had made me a match for it. That I sensed this, that I did not allow my ideal of a writer's task to be contained within the same narrow limits in which I myself was confined, I credit to the good will of heaven, which has thereby held out the possibility of progress to me. But under the circumstances this just compounded my misfortune. For I now saw everything I created as immature and vastly beneath the ideal that lived within me. While sensing all this potential for perfection I had to rush before the public prematurely. Myself so in need of instruction, I had to pose against my will as man's teacher. Each product, under such circumstances only tolerably successful, made me feel all the more keenly how much potential fortune was suppressing in me. The masterpieces of other writers saddened me because I lost hope of ever partaking of the happy leisure they enjoyed, in which alone works of genius can ripen. What would I not have given for two or three quiet years off from writing to devote to study—just to developing my ideas, to bringing my ideals to maturity. I now know that it is impossible in the German world of letters to satisfy the strict demands of art and simultaneously procure the minimum of support for one's industry. I have been struggling to reconcile the two for ten years, but to make it even in some measure possible has cost me my health.[38]

Schiller expresses his gratitude for the duke's patronage by denouncing the institution which was replacing patronage.[39] But note that it is not just for failing to support him in pursuing his inclinations as a writer that the literary market comes under his fire. Schiller generalizes and mystifies, casting the "literary life" he relates as an object lesson in the irreconcilability of the demands of the market and what he terms the "strict demands of art."

With the aid of the stipend Schiller expected to be in a position to pay off his debts and, freed of financial worries, to begin to realize his "ideal of the writer's task."[40] The first step in his "self-realization" seems to have involved an effort to recuperate theoretically the experiences he relates in this letter. That is, before returning to the drama to complete in rapid succession his Wallenstein trilogy, *Maria Stuart, Die Jungfrau von Orleans, Die Braut von Messina,* and *Wilhelm Tell,* Schiller first turned his attention to philosophy.[41] The *Aesthetic Letters* and *Naive and Sentimental Poetry* are the most famous products of this period of intense reading and reflection, in which Schiller explores the implications for art *in general* of his experience as a professional writer.

He had already taken a decisive step in this direction a year earlier in his review of Bürger, for the review, as we have seen, promotes as the sole instrument of human salvation poetry produced in studied indifference to the desires, whether for instruction or diversion, of a buying public that is depicted as being so base that it is beneath a serious poet's consideration. Once liberated from dependence on this public, Schiller is free to develop this idea and, above all, to erase the signs of its provenance in his own struggle as a professional writer for the attention of that public. Composed in the courtly setting of Weimar in the form of letters to his noble patron, his aesthetic retains so few such signs that it has been possible even for students of aesthetics as materialist as Terry Eagleton to read it as fundamentally progressive—the product of "the dismal collapse of revolutionary hopes."[42] Still, to more "resisting" readers schooled in Schiller's "occasional" writings, signs of the theory's provenance remain—for example, the unexpected assertion in Letter Two that to qualify for the high metaphysical task assigned to it an art object must be strictly "not for profit." Why is that? we ask. "The verdict of this epoch does not by any means seem to be going in favour of art, at least not the kind of art to which alone [his] inquiry is directed," Schiller writes. The times are increasingly hostile to "the art of the ideal." It is presently "material needs" [*das Bedürfnis*] that "reign supreme, bending

> a degraded humanity beneath their tyrannical yoke. Utility is the great idol of our age, to which all powers are in thrall and to which all talent must pay homage. Weighed in this crude balance, the insubstantial merits of art scarce tip the scale, and,

bereft of all encouragement, she shuns the noisy market-place of our century. (pp. 6–7)

In such patent examples of making a virtue of necessity the generous portion of *ressentiment* that marks Schiller's theorizing is barely disguised. It is a measure of his power as a theorist that such passages of the *Aesthetic Letters* go unnoticed, drowned out by his heroic rhetoric.

We began our discussion by noting the *Letters'* puzzling trajectory, their conflation of two distinct and seemingly incompatible projects: the expressly political project carried by this heroic rhetoric—a project that, for all its idealism, has the transformation of this world as its goal—and a rather narrowly aesthetic project that takes what was at first presented as the instrument of peaceful political change—aesthetic education—and turns this into a goal sufficient unto itself. This second project, which gradually overwhelms the political project to prevail at the end of the *Letters*, is also asserted to have freedom as its goal, but it is strictly psychic—the freedom we experience in a world of semblance, or make-believe, where unrealized and unrealizable desires are fulfilled, if only momentarily and imaginatively.[43] In the aesthetic state, Schiller writes in the penultimate paragraph of the *Letters*, "the fetters of serfdom fall away," making everyone a "free citizen, having equal rights with the noblest," "the ideal of equality [is] fulfilled," and the "individual" is reconciled with the "species" (pp. 217–19). *Liberté, égalité, fraternité.* All of the aspirations of the revolution may be savored in the experience of beautiful art. Read in the light of Schiller's "occasional" writings, this celebration of art for its own sake is hardly surprising. Schiller's first allegiance was to his craft.

4. AESTHETICS AND THE POLICING OF READING

It is rumoured: We have no classical writers, at least not in prose. *Some have said it loudly, though boorishly. Others don't want the common folk to see the face of the cards, and speak softly. If only we had a fair number of* classical readers, *I imagine a few classical writers would turn up. People read voraciously, but how and what? How many readers are there after all who, once the fascination of novelty has worn off, can return again and again to a work that deserves it—not to kill time or to obtain information on this or that subject, but to clarify its impression through repetition and to appropriate completely what is best in it?*

—Friedrich Schlegel, *"Georg Forster. Fragment einer Charakteristik der deutschen Klassiker"*
(1797)

At the beginning of his essay on *The Pleasures of the Imagination* Joseph Addison observes that very few people "know how to be idle and innocent, or have a Relish of any Pleasures that are not Criminal; every Diversion they take is at the Expense of some one Virtue or another, and their very first Step out of Business is into Vice or Folly." Like *The Spectator* as a whole, in which it appeared in eleven installments in 1712, this essay is addressed primarily to a rising class of bankers, merchants, and manufacturers who had so recently achieved a modicum of the leisure enjoyed by the aristocracy that they were still in the process of developing ways to fill it. Addison aimed to influence this process and accordingly set out to instruct them in an "innocent" alternative to the drinking and gambling in which their social superiors were wont to pass their idle time:

Of this Nature are [the pleasures] of the Imagination, which do not require such a Bent of Thought as is necessary to our more serious Employments, nor, at the same time, suffer the Mind to sink into that Negligence and Remissness, which are apt to accompany our more sensual Delights, but, like a gentle Exercise to the Faculties, awaken them from Sloth and Idleness, without putting them upon any Labor or Difficulty.[1]

Specifically, the pleasures Addison thus commends to his readers are those that are afforded by paintings and statues, musical and architectural works, by the "prospects" with which nature has endowed humankind, and above all by polite literature. Addison uses the subsequent installments of the essay to take his readers on a guided tour through one after another of these "several sources" of "innocent recreation," exploring with them in each case the merits of exemplary instances. Accordingly, *The Pleasures of the Imagination* itself exemplifies the new leisure activity Addison recommends: the kind of amateur occupation with objects of "fine" art that would eventually come to be known as connoisseurship.[2]

Germany responded comparatively late to Addison's call to explore the products of the various arts simply for the sake of their inherent interest and pleasurableness. Let us focus on the progress of *reading*, the art he considered best suited "to fill up [Life's] empty Spaces."[3] In 1740, when England and France could already boast of flourishing literary cultures produced by and for the middle classes, the average German family still owned only a Bible, a hymnal and a catechism, perhaps some popular religious book, and a calendar or almanac. By the end of the century, however, the situation had changed dramatically and, as we saw in chapter 1, Germany had become "a nation of readers."[4]

The way was paved by the "moral weeklies" that began appearing in great abundance in the 1740s.[5] Like the English *Spectator* on which they were modeled, these weekly periodicals helped to break down the deep distrust that the pious and hard-working middle classes in Germany still harbored for profane literature by presenting, in an entertaining form, the kind of moral and practical instruction they had come to expect from the few books to which they had access. Their appetites whetted by the stories, dialogues, and letters they found there, the German middle classes leaped headlong into the pleasures of reading. In 1799 the popular philosopher Johann Adam Bergk could exclaim: "Never has there been as much reading in Germany as today!" However, Bergk then goes on to complain:

> But the majority of readers devour the most wretched and taste-less novels with a voracious appetite that spoils head and heart. By reading such worthless material people get used to idleness that only the greatest exertion can overcome again. People say they read to kill time, but what are the consequences of this kind of reading? Since they choose only works that do not require much reflection and that are full of improbabilities and unnatural events and are worthless and tasteless, they forget the laws of nature . . . and fall prey to countless errors and transgressions because they can no longer hear their own inner warnings. They make demands on people that cannot be met; . . . they want positions in life which morality forbids us to aspire to; they kill all desire for activity and work and all love of freedom. They become moody, peevish, presumptuous, impatient. They become extraordinarily susceptible to every impression, which they are unable to muster inner powers to oppose. . . . The consequences of such tasteless and mindless reading are thus sense-less waste, an insurmountable fear of any kind of exertion, a boundless bent for luxury, repression of the voices of conscience, ennui, and an early death.[6]

Addison undoubtedly would have been gratified to learn what a great success his campaign to promote polite reading had been. But it is doubtful whether he would have known what to make of Bergk's statement, so sharply does it diverge from his own estimation of the value of the pastime. For, as described by Bergk, it clearly has none of the innocence he had ascribed to it. Indeed, to Bergk's way of thinking, it is dissipating readers every bit as thoroughly as the "more sensual Delights" of drinking and gambling that Addison had intended reading to replace.

This spirited repudiation of the claims Addison had made for reading is but one of the countless statements that were fired in the veritable war on reading that was waged in Germany in the final decade of the eighteenth century. So alarmed were contemporary observers by the "reading epidemic" [Leseseuche] they perceived to be sweeping their country in the wake of his campaign that they took up their pens in large numbers, and in an effort to come to grips with it, generated a voluminous body of writing about reading. It is this "reading debate" [*Lesedebatte*] that I propose to explore here.[7] I will touch on only a fraction of the wealth of information it contains about contemporary reading practices because I want to concentrate on the light the debate sheds on the evolution of aesthetics. My thesis, briefly, is that by exposing the limitations of the project launched in Addison's essay, the debate helps to explain the direction the philosophy of art took in the hands of his successors in Germany especially, where, with the appearance of Kant's *Critique of Judgment* in 1790, aesthetics achieved the status of a discipline.

Common to all of this writing on reading is the conviction that too many readers were reading too many of the wrong books for the wrong reasons and with altogether the wrong results. But on the specifics of just what was wrong in each instance critics were divided. Certainly all of the critics of reading shared Bergk's alarm at the way readers seemed to be turning from works that demanded a modicum of mental exertion—some minimal reflection and meditation—to ever lighter forms of entertainment and diversion. Instead of reading and rereading the writings of Gellert, Klopstock, Lessing, Goethe, or Wieland, they preferred to "flit like butterflies" from one mindless, new publication to the next—from sentimental love stories and "edifying" family novels to tales of ghost seers and a purely escapist literature of adventure and intrigue.[8] Their reading ranged from titles like *Karl von Kismar, or Love without Lust, Marriage without Jealousy, Parting without Tears*, and *The Sad Consequences of Precipitate Bethrothal, a True Story Told as a Warning to Parents, Young Men and Girls*, to a novel with the promising subtitle, *A Family Novel, Containing Various Seductions and Sea-Fights with Pirates*; from spinoffs of Schiller's *Geisterseher* like *Die Geisterseherin* and *Der Geisterbanner* to adventure literature designed to capitalize on the French Revolution like *Marki von Gebrian, or Tricks and Pranks of a French Emigré*—to name only a few of the more than 500 works of polite literature brought to market in 1800 alone.[9] Nothing so vexed the German ideologues as the habit their contemporaries had supposedly acquired of devouring greedily one after another of these new titles, forgetting the last one the moment they turned to its replacement. In his 546-page *Appell an meine Nation über Aufklärung und Aufklärer* [*Address to the Nation Concerning Enlightenment and Enlighteners*] (1795), the Swiss publicist Johann Georg Heinzmann compares this *extensive* mode of reading[10] to cruising or philandering [*herumschweifendes Bücherlesen*] to distinguish it from the "safer" and, to his mind, ultimately more satisfying kind of intercourse with texts that involves "getting to know a few good books full of healthy principles and tested truths, reading them repeatedly and nourishing one's soul with them."[11]

But if the German ideologues were unanimous in their disapproval of the "whats" and "hows" of contemporary reading, they diverged sharply over the long-term consequences of these new reading practices and over the measures that ought to be taken to counteract them. To the conservative majority, extensive readers represented a threat to the established moral and social order. It is not just that they fall down in their responsibilities in the home and in the workplace, we are told; their passions inflamed and their minds filled with the half-truths dished up by the books they read, avid readers even begin to question the justice of the order that dictates such responsibilities. Thus the archconservative pastor J. R. G. Beyer advocates systematic regulation of reading because he imagines that if

> the reader fills his or her soul with a host of overheated, fanciful, romantic ideas that cannot be realized in this sublunary world, learns about the world not from the world itself but from books, dreams of a world not as it is but as it should be, judges human beings not according to the actual history of humanity but according to the fictional stories of the world of novels—such reading will produce a creature who is always dissatisfied with the creator and his creation; whose exaggerated complaints and reproaches make him intolerable, who criticizes now the authorities and the government, now legislation and law enforcement, now the manners and mores of the country and its citizens, and would like to reform and reshape everything in the world.[12]

Beyer is afraid that readers who have glimpsed another, better world in books will rise up and forcibly attempt to impose their vision on the real world. His fears were widely shared. So alarming was the specter of revolutionary France that, much as in England at this time, many one-time advocates of literacy had begun to have second thoughts.

These defenders of the status quo advocated systematic regulation of *supply*—that is, various forms of state intervention to restrict the flow of literature. In his address to the nation, the reactionary Heinzmann, for example, demonstrates that he is not altogether oblivious to the dangers of censorship. If it were not for the freedom of the press, he writes, Luther and Calvin would not have had the impact they did, and we should still be living under the "scepter of the clerisy." But he does not think this freedom ought to be extended to "scoundrels": "A good police force ought to watch over the spiritual and moral welfare of its constituency no less than their physical well-being." We incarcerate "enthusiasts and simpletons" who disturb the peace," so why should we not ban "wanton" authors?[13] The equally conservative pastor Beyer, on the other hand, though he sympathizes with Heinzmann's goals, does not favor such extreme measures because he thinks they too often backfire. The slogan "Banned in Vienna" had already proved to be an effective form of advertising! Nor does Beyer favor outlawing the reading societies, the circulating and lending libraries that were emerging to make books accessible at modest prices—as did most of his compatriots on the right. Instead he urges that these organs of distribution simply be, as he puts it, "organized and administered" so that they can better look out for the interests of consumers. Among his concrete proposals, therefore, is the suggestion that the chief suppliers of women and the working classes, the lending libraries, which were then in the hands of entrepreneurs, be "nationalized" so that right-thinking civil servants might be placed in charge of acquisitions.[14]

So much for the "supply-side" ideologues of reading. Although they were fewer in number, there were also more progressive contributors to the reading debate like the popular philosopher Bergk, whom I quoted at the outset, and Johann Gottlieb Fichte, who criticized contemporary reading habits on just the opposite grounds from their counterparts on the right. To these critics it was ridiculous to imagine that the kind of illusory escape into a fictional world that the right so feared could ever result in political action. As they saw it, all that the reading maniac desires is to prolong his escape or to repeat it as often as possible. "Anyone who has tasted this sweet oblivion," Fichte writes, "wants to continue enjoying it, and ceases to want to do anything else in life; he begins to read without any regard whatsoever for keeping up with the literature or the times, simply in order to read and in reading to live."[15] Such "pure readers" [reine Leser], as Fichte terms them, far from presenting a threat to the established order, will, in Bergk's words,

> put up with anything as long as they are not disturbed in their inertia. . . . They will bear the most dishonorable fetters of slavery with patience . . . and watch the freedom of thought and the

freedom of the press being murdered without even grumbling or showing the least sign of indignation.[16]

The corrective measures proposed by these left-leaning contributors to the reading debate are more interesting than those advocated by the right, for while no less manipulative, they are considerably more subtle. Targeted at *demand* rather than supply, they are designed to influence the *way* people read. Here I want to focus on one such scheme as set forth by Bergk in *Die Kunst, Bücher zu lesen* [*The Art of Reading Books*] (1799). Though its length makes it doubtful that many of them read it, this 416-page tome is designed to instruct the same, predominantly middle-class readers for whom Addison had written, in an art of literary connoisseurship for the "modern" age—in a craft of reading, that is, which will serve to steer them through the vast sea of literary offerings to the relatively small number of works that, to Bergk's way of thinking, genuinely merit their attention. Accordingly, Bergk's *Kunst* may be regarded as an effort to carry forward Addison's project under the radically altered conditions of literature in Germany at the end of the eighteenth century.

To this end Bergk dips liberally into contemporary art theory, above all, that of Kant, whose *Critique of Judgment* furnishes him with most of his key terms and concepts. On the premise that an art of reading ought to be derived from the function of reading in human life, Bergk begins, with characteristic German thoroughness, "from the beginning" by exploring with his readers the nature of that entity that is at once the source and end of books, the human mind.[17] Drawing on Kant, he divides the mind into a number of distinct faculties and modes of operation—sense, fantasy and imagination, understanding, reason (both speculative and practical), and judgment (teleological and aesthetic). We must strive to cultivate all of these faculties, he writes, "because only through the independent exertion [*Selbstthätigkeit*] of all of one's powers is a person in a position to fulfill his responsibilities as a human being and a citizen" (p. 107). Bergk recognizes the difficulty of achieving such a goal in an age that favors specialization. He gives lively expression to Schiller's ironic comment that the division of labor has so progressed that the various faculties are beginning to appear "as separate in practice as they are distinguished by the psychologist in theory."[18] Nowadays, Bergk observes,

the poet worships the imagination, the philosopher reason, the businessman healthy understanding, and the epicurean sensuality. The merchant looks down on the scholar, who despises the artist; among themselves the scholars wallow in self-pity; and everybody considers himself far above everybody else in rank, dignity, and utility. The mathematician has no taste for poetics, the poet for mathematics, the lawyer for religious ethics, the theologian for jurisprudence; and the guildsmen among the scholars ply their science like a trade and view philosophy and the arts as superfluous. (pp. 105–6)

With the institutionalization of the faculties as distinct ways of life, the fragmentation of the psyche is complete. However, where Schiller had taken the visionary line that only "a higher art" can restore "the totality of our nature which the arts themselves have destroyed,"[19]— and propounded it in a style so abstract and convoluted that few can have received the message, at least not directly—Bergk makes the modest and preeminently readable suggestion that we combat the effects of specialization by undergoing a rigorous course in liberal reading. The arts and sciences offer us a variety of distinct types of writing—historical, philosophical, literary, scientific, and so forth— that, because they are themselves the product of the one or the other faculty, are uniquely equipped to aid us as readers in cultivating these same faculties in ourselves.

For each of the arts and sciences there is a particular human predisposition or faculty, to which the art or science owes its existence and on which it in turn exerts an impact by breathing vitality into and helping to perfect that faculty. However, we must be familiar not only with the human predispositions and powers and the material with which they may be occupied and trained, but also with the function each science is particularly adapted to serve in [the economy of] the human spirit. (p. 74)

Accordingly, Bergk proceeds to examine each of the faculties in turn to determine what kind of writing is best suited to cultivate it. In each instance it seems that while polite literature (or, "fine art" [*die schöne Kunst*], under which he subsumes novels, poems, plays, and speeches) can contribute in important ways to the development of the faculty in question, it is not as well designed to do so as some other type of writing—until, by a process of elimination, he arrives at aesthetic judgment, or taste. And here it turns out that literature is uniquely equipped. "The function of polite literature is thus not to increase our knowledge, for this it would share with the sciences, but to cultivate our taste." And what is taste? It is, he continues, "an ability to judge nature and art so as to become acquainted with these in terms of the feelings they inspire in us. It manifests itself when an object pleases or displeases. To it we owe the feelings of beauty and sublimity" (p. 176).

By assigning literature a specific function in the economy of the human psyche, Bergk narrows significantly the canon of legitimate literature—to writing designed to cultivate taste. Prudently, he does not leave it to his readers to apply this principle of selection, but goes on to spell out the implications for them. It follows, he writes, that we should concentrate on "classical" authors. Read with care and understanding, classical authors initiate in us a "free play" of the imagination and understanding.

> The play of these two faculties produces a pleasure that is distinct not only from the good but from the merely pleasant and useful. If we repeat this occupation frequently and nourish both our imagination and our understanding, we shall achieve a special proficiency of judgment that is termed taste. (p. 156)

It does not, however, appear that the two faculties are brought into this kind of play by the most popular literary forms—by the sundry robber, ghost, and horror novels, the historical and political novels, the edifying moral tales, the sentimental and lascivious novels, and tales of the supernatural in which readers were then indulging with such abandon. This had been Schiller's objection to Bürger's verse, we will recall. Bergk devotes a separate chapter of his *Kunst* to each of these popular forms, attempting to show in each instance how they either stimulate the wrong faculties or stimulate the right faculties in the wrong way. Thus, for example, he indicts moralizing fiction on the grounds that instruction should be left to the sciences, reform to ethics and religion. The task of the poet is to "arouse aesthetic feelings"—not to teach or to preach, but to "dramatize" ideas:

> If he weaves long-winded moral exhortations and reflections into his stories, then he is attempting to clarify concepts and awaken practical reason, not to cultivate sensitivity to beauty and sublimity. He is taking the understanding and heart to school, whereas his vocation dictates that he animate and cultivate aesthetic feelings and, in this way, develop taste. (p. 258)

In his discussion of the political novels spawned by the French Revolution Bergk takes a similar tack, except that he condemns these on the grounds that they

> excite our passions, whereas works of fine art should only set our feelings in motion: the former thus can never give us such pure and disinterested pleasure [*uninteressirtes Vergnügen*] nor such gentle and pleasant instruction as the latter. Political subjects are not appropriate, therefore, for treatment in works of fine art, because they are not capable of arousing unselfish satisfaction [*uneigennüzziges Wohlgefallen*]. (p. 257)

In this passage, so reminiscent of Kant's derogation of oratory for attempting to affect our emotions and actions,[20] Bergk bans the historico-political novel categorically, and in this way approaches the position of the reactionary pastor Beyer, whose anxiety about literature's capacity to disturb the status quo, even to foment revolution, I cited earlier. Except that, armed with a *theory* of literature, the "liberal" Bergk does not need to advocate any such overtly repressive measures as curtailing the freedom of the press. All that is necessary is to "show" that a given work or genre fails to satisfy literature's proper function in the economy of the psyche—either because it brings the wrong faculties into play or, as is here the case, because it stimulates the right faculties too vigorously, producing a satisfaction that is distinctly *interested*. A more concrete interpretation of the *Critique of Judgment* would be hard to come by. Bergk liberates the prescription couched in Kant's ostensibly pure philosophical analysis in order to rule out as illegitimate the better part of contemporary literary output:[21]

> Works that wear the stamp of genius and taste are rare, to be sure, but our literature possesses enough of them to enable us to cultivate our taste and employ our minds pleasantly and instructively. The following passages from Wieland's *Agathon* and Goethe's *Werther* will serve to demonstrate these propositions. (p. 236)

It is fortunate that deductive argument is not Bergk's only instrument of persuasion, for learning that their favorite forms of diversion do not "follow" from the definition of the mind is not likely to have convinced many readers to give them up. More promising, because if successful it would obviate the need for any such argument, is the *approach* to literature he teaches simultaneously. This approach, or reading methodology, set forth most succinctly in a chapter entitled "How Must One Read Literary Works to Cultivate One's Taste?" is designed to influence his readers' choices, indirectly, by reforming the *way* they read.

Bergk presents the ability to read literature as a special application of the ability to read.[22] The art he sketches thus anticipates the handbooks and treatises in which theorists from Cleanth Brooks to Roland Barthes, E. D. Hirsch, and Robert Scholes have endeavored to make explicit the interpretive operations and strategies that give literary texts the meanings they have for "competent" readers like themselves. Bergk terms these strategies the "rules" that anyone who wishes to "master" the craft of reading must learn to deploy appropriately (pp. 72–73). The super-rule of the craft, which the other strategies he discusses serve to articulate, instructs us to become "active" readers. This critical concept derives its meaning by opposition to the state of mind Bergk associates with the readers of novels "who devour one insipid dish after another in an effort to escape an intolerable mental vacuum. They watch events appear and disappear as in a magic mirror, each one more absurd than the last one. . . . All mental activity is stifled by the mass of impressions" (pp. 64–65).[23]

To this "passive" mode of *consumption* Bergk opposes a highly *reflexive* mode of reading that involves several distinct operations. One must first seek to discover the writer's "purpose"—the basic idea presented in the work. Every literary work has "a central subject to which everything in it is related, and all have a guiding idea which animates and maintains the whole" (p. 181). Having discovered this idea, one must next seek to relate to it all of the work's details. More recently known as "taking a poem to pieces," this step in reading involves exploration of the writer's way of handling characterization, description, and tone, his use of language, and so forth. Finally, the reader must attempt to put all of these elements back together:

> Now it is not the individual part that we consider, but instead the whole is the object of our attention. We do not want to see this or that feature of a scene or a character placed in relief but to present to our minds as a single unity everything that before stood isolated. (p. 82)

This final act of synthesis involves recognizing the harmonious interaction of a work's parts. Thus does Bergk translate into a *principle of* (competent) *reading* the totality that Karl Philipp Moritz had postulated of "true" art.[24] This act of synthesis is the most important operation, according to Bergk, because it produces the special "play of the imagination and understanding" characteristic of a legitimate literary experience.

> Through this synthesis of the individual parts into a whole the imagination prevails over the material and can amply nourish the understanding. . . . No image, no remark, no facet of an expression will go unnoticed once we have achieved sovereignty over the whole. What we now regard is neither the dead letter nor the lifeless thought, but the ever vital breath, the creative spirit that permeates the whole. This comprehension and judgment of the whole results in a pleasure that is a product of taste. (p. 183)

The pleasure he promises is a highly intellectual pleasure, to say the least, for Bergk has transformed reading into a form of explication.[25]

Readers accustomed to devouring one after another new publication are herewith administered what may well be the first course in the kind of "close reading" that would be introduced into classrooms by twentieth-century formalists. Indeed, Brooks and Warren's *Understanding Poetry* (1938), the anthology-cum-commentary that revolutionized the teaching of English literature by displacing literary history and establishing the "New Criticism" as the language of instruction in American classrooms, simply picks up where Bergk left off, refining and elaborating the art of reading he adumbrated. This textbook was able to achieve the tremendous influence it did because, like Bergk's self-help manual, it presupposed little prior knowledge on the part of students and taught a body of transferable skills. It thus proved an efficient means of "broadening and refining the taste"—as Brooks and Warren put it in the sequel, *Understanding Fiction* (1943)—of the multitude of new students of diverse cultural and educational backgrounds whom the GI Bill of Rights (1944) enabled to enter American colleges at the end of World War II. The similarity of their goal to that of Bergk is underscored by Brooks and Warren's observation in the preface to *Understanding Fiction* that as "most students read some kind of fiction of their own free will and for pleasure," the teacher will "not have to 'make' the student read fiction, . . . as he has to 'make' the student read poetry," but instead faces the somewhat "easier problem of persuading the student that some stories or novels which are called 'good' from the literary point of view, or which are important in the history of literature, are also interesting in themselves."[26]

Although he lacks the categories by which to achieve the subtle and detailed analyses Brooks and Warren taught us to expect, Bergk demonstrates how the rules he sets forth are to be applied in model readings of his own—of a poem by Matthisson, a passage from Stern's *Tristram Shandy*, and a scene from Lessing's *Miß Sara Sampson*. He concludes his examination of this last item with the soon-to-be-obligatory bow to the norm of a total unity: "No adjective, no image, no thought is superfluous; everything contributes to increase the effect of the whole; everything intermeshes and intensifies the impression such an unnatural mother [Marwood] makes on us" (p. 199). So that they will be in a better position to survey the whole and to consider the parts in relation to it, Bergk urges his readers to read works more than once (p. 199). But to be able to devote so much time to a single work, he writes, it is necessary to limit ourselves to just a few works:

> We must be extremely selective in our reading and read only works that are distinguished by richness and originality of thought and beauty and liveliness of presentation. . . . It enhances our culture and our learning more to read an original and thoughtful writer several times than to read many common and empty books. (p. 409)

In short, Bergk attacks the problem of literary philandering by teaching an *intensive* mode of reading. In support of his project he enlists the authority of Rousseau, citing on his title page the lines from *La Nouvelle Héloïse:* "To read little and meditate a great deal upon our reading, or what amounts to the same thing, to talk it over extensively with our friends, that is the way to thoroughly digest it."[27]

Bergk's campaign to intensify reading would have been unnecessary at the beginning of the eighteenth century. For to the extent that they read at all, the grandparents and great-grandparents of Bergk's readers had little choice but to return again and again to the handful of sacred and devotional texts available to them, to read and reread these and on each new reading attempt to cull some new food for reflection, some new kernel of wisdom to guide them down the path of life. The goal of Bergk's *Kunst* is to revive these older reading strategies in order to direct them toward a relatively small canon of *secular* texts that he deems capable of playing the same role in the lives of his readers that the sacred texts had once played. Thus, where formerly the reader's aim in poring over the scriptures had been to discern the intentions of God the creator, Bergk specifies that the goal of reading ought to be to penetrate the creative intentions of great authors. If we read a literary "work of art" as he prescribes,

> we come to a point where it places our minds in the same state as that of its creator when he brought the work into being. This is the real purpose of reading and the frame of mind that contributes most to the training and perfection of a faculty. (p. 200)

In this injunction to make reading a kind of creation in reverse, the object of which is to reexperience what an author originally thought and felt, Bergk gathers together the various strategies he seeks to inculcate to oppose the "passive receptivity" [*bloß leidendes Verhalten*] of the new novel readers (p. 64).

Thus do we find domesticated between the covers of a self-help book designed for middle-class readers the principle of reading entailed by the reconceptualization of writing that we investigated in chapter 2—the principle of reading entailed, that is, by the notion, in which Fichte finally grounded the author's claim to legal ownership of his writing, that writing embodies or represents the intellection of its author. Eventually, in the hands of Schleiermacher, this principle was to become a cornerstone of a new "science" of interpretation, or hermeneutics.

Bergk's hope is that readers who have learned to read thus "creatively" will automatically make the "right" choices: too sophisticated to derive much pleasure from the growing literature of sheer diversion, they will demand for their leisure the "classical" authors on whom he draws throughout his book for his illustrations—authors like Lessing, Wieland, Goethe, Schiller, and Klopstock. For only *difficult* authors like these will be able to sustain and reward the reflexive mode of reading he has taught. Indeed, they require it, for as Bergk himself observes, they are virtually inaccessible to readers who have developed the "passive" reading habits he so deplores: "Anyone who does not enjoy thinking for himself . . . [and] who [thus] reads the current novels of Cramer or Spieß with pleasure . . . will not be stimulated by the writings of Wieland and Goethe" (pp. 35, 41–42).

Returning to *The Pleasures of the Imagination*, I believe that we are now in a better position to understand why the philosophy of art developed as it did in the hands of Addison's German successors. As the leisure activity he had commended to his readers in 1712 caught on and polite reading became more and more widespread, the limitations of his propaedeutic became evident. Indeed, it began to look dangerously equivocal. For nowhere in his essay had Addison deemed it necessary to lay down explicit principles to guide his readers in the "hows" and "whats" of literary connoisseurship. He had simply taken it for granted that they would emulate his own procedure, selecting for their leisure works like the classics to which he recurred for illustration—Homer, Virgil, Ovid, and Shakespeare—rather than the kind of fare that would later so vex the German ideologues.[28] Moreover, as part of his strategy to promote polite reading among them, Addison had singled out advantages of the activity that the popular fare could ensure far more readily than these classics. First, in addition to pointing out how much more "refined" the pleasures of the imagination are than "those of sense," it will be recalled that Addison drew on Locke's theory of cognition to emphasize the extreme *ease* with which they could be acquired:

> It is but opening the Eye, and the Scene enters. The Colours paint themselves on the Fancy, with very little Attention of Thought or Application of Mind in the Beholder. We are struck, we know not how, with the Symmetry of any thing we see, and immediately assent to the Beauty of an Object, without enquiring into the particular Causes and Occasions of it.[29]

Not only is it easy to perform because it requires very little mental exertion, connoisseurship also results in highly pleasing sensations. Indeed, it is equally on the grounds of the myriad of sensations it ensures participants that Addison had promoted this new form of recreation among his readers. Thus, for example, when he came to recommend *"the Fairie way of Writing,"* in which *"Shakespear* has incomparably excelled all others," it was in terms of the "pleasing kind of Horrour" such writing "raise[s] ... in the Mind of the Reader."[30] But if all that is required is "opening the Eye" to receive such effects, how much easier to receive the effects contained in the Gothic fantasies that were appearing in such abundance in the 1790s! Addison could not have intended latter-day readers to waste their idle hours on the likes of these, but nowhere did he lay down clear principles that would discourage them. By the end of the eighteenth century this type of light reading matter had so proliferated that some such principles seemed urgently called for. They were provided by the intense philosophizing about the arts on which Bergk drew in order to elaborate a reading propaedeutic that would drive his middle-class readers to classical authors by turning them into classical readers.

Disciplinary history presents the *Critique of Judgment* as the fruit of a century of pure philosophical reflection on the arts. While such purely internal, philosophical factors undoubtedly played an important role in the evolution of aesthetics, the German reading debate calls our attention to some of the broader, cultural-political impulses that fostered it. It remains for a new history of aesthetics to carry the investigation initiated here back to Britain in order both to reread Addison's "legitimate" heirs and to recover the voices like Bergk's that have been repressed by disciplinary history. In chapter 6 we will take a first step by examining the reception of Kant there.

5. ENGENDERING ART

Thus far women have made only a casual appearance—as a chief target of the array of efforts to regulate reading practices that gave the modern philosophy of art so many of its key concepts. This accurately reflects the position women occupy in this formation, for it is strictly as (more and less "competent") recipients of work by men—unless as muses—that they entered it. But it ignores the real historical acts of exclusion by which they ended up in this supporting position, and accordingly also a defining feature of the modern concept of art. For it is not as if women were not painting, writing, and composing during the eighteenth century. Growing recognition over the past two decades of the extent of their productive involvement in, and subsequent effacement from, the arts has put "art" and its subconcepts back into the center of debates every bit as heated as the culture wars we have been examining. A look at one of the primal acts of exclusion, that of Germany's first acclaimed woman novelist, Sophie von La Roche (1730–1807), underscores the relevance of these first, German culture wars to our current situation.

Best remembered until recently as the "muse" of Christoph Martin Wieland (1733–1813), one of the giants of the German literary canon to whom she was briefly engaged and became a lifelong friend, La Roche began her career at the age of forty with the publication of *Geschichte des Fräuleins von Sternheim* (1771), Germany's first epistolary novel.[1] Although it appeared anonymously under the "editorship" of Wieland, who advised and encouraged La Roche during its composition and assisted her in getting it published, the identity of its author did not remain a secret for long, for the novel was an instant best-seller. In addition to requiring three printings in its first year (and four more within the next fifteen years), it was translated into Dutch, French, and Russian, as well as English, and evidently also pirated, making La Roche famous throughout Europe.[2]

Inspired especially by La Roche's reading in Richardson, Sterne, and Rousseau, *Fräulein von Sternheim* recounts the story of a sentimental heroine who survives seduction and betrayal and struggles successfully to vindicate herself not just in marriage but in the kind of charitable activity Clarissa had envisioned. What most struck contemporary readers was the psychological complexity of its title character. Its epistolary form enables the heroine Sophie to tell her own story, offering the reader an unprecedented glimpse into the thoughts and feelings of a sensitive, or "beautiful soul" in an attractive body—a Werther *avant la lettre*.

Germany's first sentimental heroine earned her creator the admiration, even adulation, of the younger generation especially—aspiring writers of Germany's Sturm und Drang such as Herder, Lenz, and Goethe, the Stolbergs, and the Jacobis, as well as a host of women whose names are just beginning to be recovered—making her the center of a succession of literary salons and the source of a rich tradition in sentimental romance.[3] In her thirty-six-year career as a writer, pursued all the more earnestly beginning in the eighties when the collapse of her husband's diplomatic career and then his death caused real financial need, La Roche produced four more novels, many more stories and essays, and an anthology. She founded a journal, *Pomona für Teutschlands Töchter* (1783–84), the first such by a woman in Germany, which she used in part to promote the work of other women writers. It covered such topics as women's education as well as art, literature, music, and travel, and contained a regular advice column, "Letters to Lina." She also published accounts of her travels through Germany and to England, Switzerland, Holland, and France, which she infused with domestic detail uncommon in travel literature by men, opening this genre up to other women writers.[4]

In the light of such achievements, one might expect to find La Roche in the pantheon of authors included in the textbooks and handbooks in aesthetics that began appearing in abundance in the 1770s. But we search for her in vain—even in progressive works like Bergk's *Art of Reading* that devote considerable attention to the still relatively new genre of the novel. In a chapter entitled "Observations on a Few Novelists" Bergk discusses at varying length some thirty German writers, but La Roche is not among them. We find only male writers like Kotzebue and Lafontaine whom she inspired.[5] She is also absent from the list of thirty-three in Karl Heinrich Pölitz's *Aesthetik für gebildete Leser* [*Aesthetics for Educated Readers*]—conspicuously so because his readership, much as Bergk's, is likely to have been predominantly female.

La Roche's disappearance from the pantheon of authors and enshrinement instead as Wieland's muse occurred during her own lifetime—indeed, seems to have been prepared in her first appearance on the literary scene with *Fräulein von Sternheim*. I noted that the work appeared anonymously, in keeping with prevailing norms of feminine modesty. In fact, its title page effaces its author completely, shifting credit for the work's appearance to the already well-established and much-admired Wieland. It reads: *"The Story of Fräulein von Sternheim. As Extrapolated by a Lady Friend from Original Papers and Other Reliable Sources. Edited by C. M. Wieland."*

The implication conveyed by the title that La Roche does not lay claim to the mantle of "authorship" in the modern sense is confirmed in Wieland's preface. Wieland casts his remarks as an open apology to the lady friend of the title for taking the liberty of seeing her manuscript into print without her permission. He realizes she never intended it to be published, he writes, and then quotes at length her description of the manuscript's origins. She began it, we learn, as a form of "recreation" [*Gemüts-Erholung*] in the "idle hours that were left to [her] after discharging essential duties" (p. 9). She was sharing the results with him now, she explains, only because she was interested in his opinion of her "sensibility, the particular angle from which [she] has become accustomed to judge human experience, the reflections which tend to well up in [her] soul when moved [*gerührt*]."

> You know that the ideas I've attempted to realize in the character and actions of Fräulein von Sternheim and her parents have always been dear to my heart. And what is more satisfying than working on something one loves? There were times when it became almost a spiritual necessity. . . . And thus originated unnoticed this little work, which I began and continued without knowing whether I would be able to complete it. (p. 9)

Hence the work's "imperfections" [*Unvollkommenheiten*], she explains, but they should not matter, for it will never be seen by anyone but herself and him—and, if he approves of "the thoughts and deeds of this daughter of [her] mind," perhaps their respective children. If *they* were to be "strengthened in virtuous convictions, in true, impartial, active goodness and uprightness" by the work, she would be overjoyed (pp. 9–10).

In its amateur origins and rather narrowly defined utilitarian purpose the novel would seem to lack the earmarks of literary "art." The product of idle hours, it is intended not for sale to a reading public, but strictly for domestic use: the author's own and that of her close acquaintances. It is ascribed the therapeutic utility of other women's "pastimes," from needlework to the keeping of a journal, the communicative utility of a correspondence designed to bring her closer to Wieland, and the pedagogic utility of reinforcing the moral lessons being taught to their children.

It is noteworthy that Wieland does not contest the modesty of this description of his friend's ambitions, but instead expands upon it in such a way as to drive home the narrowness of her achievement. Whether he does this in the interest of promoting the novel with a reading audience already deeply prejudiced against scribbling women, as Bovenschen and Becker-Cantarino have suggested, or rather with an eye to extending and deepening such prejudice has still to be determined.[6] Certainly he does nothing to dispel this kind of prejudice. The cumulative effect of the preface is to minimize La Roche's accomplishment.

As noted above, Wieland himself assumes responsibility for the novel's publication. Since she was not averse to sharing the work with the children, he trusts she will forgive him for it. He could not "resist the urge to present to all the virtuous mothers and charming young daughters of our nation" a work that seemed to him so well designed to foster wisdom and virtue "among [their] sex, and even among [his] own" (p. 10). Wieland conspicuously delimits the work's audience—it will chiefly be of interest to women readers, he suggests. And by emphasizing its pedagogical value to them, he assimilates the work to the already large, and growing body of nonfiction that was appearing on the market to instruct women in all aspects of running a household and rearing children. The work's great utility is certain to make up for its shortcomings, Wieland writes—for "dear as she is, considered as a work of intellect, as a literary composition, indeed, even as just an ordinary German composition, your Sternheim has defects which will not go unnoticed by detractors" (13).

Wieland's ostensible motive in calling attention to the work's "defects"—its violations of standard usage, its stylistic infelicities, etc.—is to preempt these detractors, but he so warms to the task that even some contemporary male readers became suspicious.[7] Critics with objections to the work's form or style should direct their objections to him, he writes, for you, its author,

> never intended to write for the world or to create a work of art. In all of your reading in the best writers in diverse languages which one can read without an education, it was always your wont to pay less attention to the beauty of form than the value of the content. (p. 13)

Her lack of any professional, "artistic" ambition along with her keen concern for "moral utility" excuse the amateurishness of her execution. In short, while the novel contains the material for a work of art, to aspire to such status, it would need to be invested with aesthetic form—that is, severed from the nexus of everyday means and ends in which it is embedded, shaped, and, as Schiller will later put it, "refined." But it is not as if Wieland were urging the author to undertake such revisions. Indeed, he does not appear to consider her capable of it. Rather, he urges critics to keep an open mind: on reflection, he writes, they may find that the author's deviations from good usage, her little stylistic quirks, and the like actually enhance the work, for are they not in some measure responsible for the "extraordinary individuation of the character of our heroine," which constitutes one of the novel's chief strengths? She is "something that art never could have achieved as effectively as here where nature was at work" (p. 15).

In short, even as he absolves the work's author of responsibility for its defects, Wieland denies her credit for its excellencies.

By thus minimizing La Roche's accomplishment in the preface of her first novel, Wieland may have smoothed its acceptance by readers resistant to the idea of women writing professionally, but he simultaneously removed it from the class of texts worthy of the particular kind of reading and rereading we have identified with the then just evolving category of literary art. Wieland's considerations here played a critical part in giving definition to this new category, even as they authorized an *other*, entirely separate and inferior one—a second, "women's" literature.[8]

The prediction of her friend Julie Bondeli (to whom Wieland was also engaged briefly), proved doubly correct, then. Pondering the likely response to *Fräulein von Sternheim*, Bondeli wrote La Roche early in 1772:

> Perhaps they will say: *that* is no genius because—because you are a woman, and a woman—with your permission—could not have genius. . . . Let them talk. Let us just preserve our tact, our sensibility, our keen perceptiveness, and let them be. The one who runs fastest often overshoots the goal, and the point is but to attain it. There can be little doubt that you have a woman's genius: a sad composite of tact, sensibility, truth, perceptiveness, finesse, and accuracy in our views and observations. There can be no doubt that your style has a feminine elegance, and only God knows why it is so beautiful, so moving. . . . Sophie, Sophie, let them talk, and just keep writing.[9]

Bondeli not only predicts that La Roche will be denied the essential ingredient of modern "authorship," she urges her to make a virtue of necessity and go her separate way. La Roche did just that, too, although not necessarily by choice. For once it had been appropriated by male writers such as Goethe, whose *Werther* (1774) draws heavily from that sphere of "feminine" genius that Bondeli identifies, La Roche's pioneering work in it could be relegated to "women's literature."[10] Indeed, toward the end of their lives Wieland, as if announcing the success of the program of containment he had initiated in the preface to *Fräulein von Sternheim*, describes La Roche as "the oldest and most venerable of Germany's women writers . . . who for thirty-five years has been doing so much good among our German women, mothers, and daughters, through the beautiful effusions of her mind, heart, and example."[11]

It is not surprising, then, that we do not find La Roche in Bergk's pantheon of novelists. Her work and that of the many women writers she inspired served by negation to give content to the notion of literary "art" that his handbook was designed to disseminate. In a chapter entitled "How Must Novels Be Constructed to Count as Models of Taste" Bergk writes that

> any novel which expects to satisfy all of the requirements we place on a beautiful work of art must be a product both of genius and of taste. But what do we mean by this? It must not only be rich in new ideas and contain a wealth of experiences and ingenious reflections, but its way of presenting the ideas and their connection with one another must be beautiful and characteristic. . . . What do we mean by a beautiful presentation? . . . Everywhere cohesion, nowhere a gap, everwhere completeness, nowhere deficiencies and defects. (pp. 234–36)

Bergk concludes with the observation, quoted in chapter 4, that while novels "that wear the stamp of genius and taste are rare," German literature nevertheless "possesses enough of them to enable us to cultivate our taste and employ our minds pleasantly and instructively" (p. 236). In support of the proposition he takes the reader through passages from Goethe's *Werther* and Wieland's *Agathon*.

A Magazine Reader by Paul
Malvieux. From *Leipziger Tas-
chenbuch für Frauenzimmer zum
Nutzen und Vergnügen auf das
Jahr 1792* (Leipzig bey Adam
Friedrich Böhme, 1792), fac-
ing p. 242. Courtesy of Spe-
cial Collections, Northwestern
University Library.

6. THE USES OF
KANT IN ENGLAND

The love of Reading, as a
refined pleasure weaning the
mind from grosser
enjoyments, which it was
one of the Spectator's chief
Objects to awaken, has by
that work, & those that
followed but still more, by
Newspapers, Magazines,
and Novels, been carried
into excess: and the
Spectator itself has
innocently contributed to the •
general taste for
unconnected writing—just
as if "Reading made easy"
should act to give men an
aversion to words of more
than two syllables, instead
of drawing them thro' *those*
words into the power of
reading Books in general.

—*Coleridge, letter to*
Thomas Poole,
January 28, 1810

I

Gottfried August Bürger precipitated quite a different development in England than in Germany. We noted previously that the appearance there in the mid-1790s of several of his ballads, including *Lenore,* helped to inspire Wordsworth and Coleridge to undertake the experimentation that led to the *Lyrical Ballads.*[1] Echoes of Bürger may be heard not only in a number of the poems collected in this revolutionary volume[2] but in the theory of poetry that informs it. When we read in the *Advertisement* that Wordsworth prefixed to the first edition, published jointly with Coleridge in 1798, that the majority of the poems contained therein are "to be considered as experiments" to determine "how far the language of conversation in the middle and lower classes of society is adapted to the purposes of poetic pleasure,"[3] we are reminded of the terms in which William Taylor had described Bürger's "extraordinary" power in the notice that accompanied his translation of *Lenore*. It derives, Taylor had written, from his "rejection of the conventional phraseology of regular poetry, in favour of popular forms of expression, caught by the listening artist from the voice of agitated nature."[4]

On his trip to Germany with Coleridge in the fall of 1798, just after the *Lyrical Ballads* had gone to press, Wordsworth purchased an edition of Bürger's *Gedichte*[5] and within several months was corresponding with his friend about the poet's merits. Coleridge seems to have taken to Bürger from the start. "Bürger of all the German Poets pleases me the most," he wrote his wife in November of that year.[6] But Wordsworth was more reserved, and later that month he wrote Coleridge:

> As to Bürger, I am yet far from that admiration of him which he has excited in you; but I am by nature slow to admire; and I am not yet sufficiently master of the language to understand him perfectly. In one point I entirely coincide with you, in your feeling concerning his versification. In "Lenore" the concluding double rhymes of the stanza have both a delicious and *pathetic* effect—
>
> > "Ach! aber für Lenoren
> > War Gruss und Kuss verloren."
>
> I accede too to your opinion that Bürger is always the poet; he is never the mobbist, one of those dim drivellers with which our island has teemed for so many years.

Wordsworth then goes on to complain that however much delight he gave, Bürger nevertheless left little permanent impression:

> Bürger is one of those authors whose book I like to have in my hand, but when I have laid the book down I do not think about him. I remember a hurry of pleasure, but I have few distinct forms that people my mind, nor any recollection of delicate or minute feelings which he has either communicated to me, or taught me to recognise.

Bürger is not a poet who demands to be *re*read, and the reason for this, Wordsworth suggests, lies in his inability to create convincing characters:

I do not perceive the presence of character in his personages. I see everywhere the character of Bürger himself; and even this, I agree with you, is no mean merit. But yet I wish him sometimes at least to make me forget himself in his creations. It seems to me, that in poems descriptive of human nature, however short they may be, character is absolutely necessary, &c.: incidents are among the lowest allurements of poetry.

Wordsworth goes on to praise Bürger's "manner of relating," which he finds "almost always spirited and lively, and stamped and peculiarized with genius." Nevertheless, he concludes, "I do not find those higher beauties which can entitle him to the name of a *great* poet." And he sums up Bürger as "the poet of the animal spirits." "I love his '*Tra ra la*' dearly; but less of the horn and more of the lute—and far, far more of the pencil." [7]

Although much more appreciative than Schiller, Wordsworth registers familiar reservations:[8] Schiller's contempt for Bürger's sensationalism may be heard in his objection to the poet's exploitation of incident; and Schiller too had been offended by Bürger's extreme subjectivity—by the frequency with which "we are reminded of *him*, of the author himself in these songs."[9] Where Wordsworth attributes the defect to Bürger's inability to create convincing characters, Schiller had complained that the states of mind he depicts are not

> merely *portraits* of [such] state[s] of mind; they are obviously *born* of them. The poet's sensitivity, his anger, his melancholy are not merely the *subject* of his song; they are also, unfortunately, often the *Apollo* who inspires him. (p. 255)

However, by the time Wordsworth began the *Preface* to the second edition of the *Lyrical Ballads* in 1800, the defects that here serve merely to qualify his appreciation of Bürger had acquired something of the significance they held for Schiller. And in the *Preface* he casts them as the defining features of a rapidly proliferating literature of pure entertainment that, like Schiller, he views as at once a cause and a symptom of the malaise into which contemporary civilization has sunk.

> For a multitude of causes, unknown to former times, are now acting with a combined force to blunt the discriminating powers of the mind, and unfitting it for all voluntary exertion to reduce it to a state of almost savage torpor. The most effective of these

causes are the great national events which are daily taking place [such as the war with France], and the encreasing accumulation of men in cities, where the uniformity of their occupations produces a craving for extraordinary incident which the rapid communication of intelligence hourly gratifies. To this tendency of life and manners the literature and theatrical exhibitions of the country have conformed themselves. The invaluable works of our elder writers, I had almost said the works of Shakespear and Milton, are driven into neglect by frantic novels, sickly and stupid German Tragedies, and deluges of idle and extravagant stories in verse. (p. 21)

Like Schiller, Wordsworth is committed to oppose this tendency. Indeed, he presents the *Lyrical Ballads* as an endeavor to counteract it. But in contrast to Schiller he does not perceive this mission as cause to abandon completely the theoretical principles on which the literature of entertainment was based. To the contrary, he adopts all of the key principles of the instrumentalist poetic of Bürger, and refining them in such a way as better to adapt them to this mission, he promotes these principles to the end and test of all good poetry.

I have described Wordsworth as *refining* the poetic of Bürger because I believe that the theory of poetry he develops in the *Preface* subjects Bürger's poetic to much the same kind of modification that Schiller was advocating in his revealingly ambiguous pronouncement on Bürger: "One of the first requirements of the poet is idealization, refinement, without which he ceases to deserve the name of poet" (p. 253).[10] It is no idle task, for Wordsworth had come under the fire of "readers of superior judgment" in the reviews of the first edition of the *Lyrical Ballad*. To these readers, whose literary standards and expectations derived from the precept and practice of Dryden, Pope, and Johnson, Wordsworth's attempt to approximate the spoken idiom amounted to willful vulgarity.[11] And the meanness of his subjects identified him with the "dim drivellers" who were deluging readers in the magazines; for the children and bereaved mothers, the insane, the destitute, the aged, and the outcast individuals who peopled their verse all had their counterparts in his poetry. In short, from the standpoint of the literary establishment the *Lyrical Ballads* were indistinguishable from the popular verse of the day—that literature of "outrageous stimulation" that Wordsworth is denouncing in the *Preface*.[12] It is to distinguish his project from this phenomenon that he undertakes to refine the instrumentalist model of poetry. Here, briefly, is the form his refinements take.

Wordsworth takes the subjective turn that he had observed in Bürger's verse. "All good poetry," he writes "is the spontaneous overflow of powerful feelings." But wary of the frequency with which this virtue had been abused in the magazines, he hastens to add:

> But though this be true, Poems to which any *value* can be attached, were never produced on any variety of subjects but by a man who being possessed of more than usual organic sensibility had also *thought* long and deeply. (p. 19; emphasis added)

The force of his qualification, designed to distinguish the *Lyrical Ballads* from the sentimental poetry popular in the 1790s, is to intellectualize the concept of composition—that is, to render it more reflective or contemplative. Schiller, we will recall, had advocated much the same thing in his review of Bürger's poetry. Disturbed by the "large role that the poet's own *self* plays" in many of the songs in his collection (p. 257), Schiller had cautioned the poet:

> Let him write from more gentle, more distant memory, and then the more he has experienced of what he sings, the better for him; but never under the sway of the emotion he is attempting to render beautifully concrete for us. Even in poems of which it is said that love, friendship, etc., itself guided the poet's brush, he had to begin by becoming a stranger to himself, by disentangling the object of his enthusiasm from his own individuality, by contemplating his passion from a mitigating distance. (p. 256)

Echoes of the corrective here prescribed by Schiller to poets who *feel* too deeply may be heard in the psychology of composition that Wordsworth develops out of his observation that poetry is a "spontaneous overflow of powerful feelings":

> It takes its origin from emotion recollected in tranquility: the emotion is contemplated till by a species of reaction the tranquility gradually disappears, and an emotion, similar to that which was before the subject of contemplation, is gradually produced, and does itself actually exist in the mind. (p. 27)

In terms remarkably similar to Schiller's, Wordsworth endeavors to stem the flow of powerful feeling, or *Herzens-Ausguss*, of the popular poets in favor of a concept of composition that is more "objective," reflexive, intellectual.[13]

His effort to refine the activity of the reader takes a comparable form. Like Bürger, he is committed to the proposition that poetry ought to move us profoundly: "The end of Poetry is to produce excitement in coexistence with an overbalance of pleasure" (p. 26). Wordsworth rings numerous variations on this idea in the *Preface*—indeed, few terms recur with greater frequency than the *pleasures* of poetry—but not, significantly, without the qualification that "the understanding" of the reader "must necessarily be in some degree enlightened . . . and his affections ameliorated" (p. 19). In short, Wordsworth seeks to transform the pleasure of stimulation, in which the rapidly growing entertainment industry traded, into a pleasure that is more contemplative.[14] To this end he urges subordination of incident—that "low allurement" that he charged Bürger with exploiting too freely—to the emotions incidents arouse in characters.[15] The feeling developed in a poem, he writes, should give

> importance to the action and situation and not the action and situation to the feeling. . . . For the human mind is capable of excitement without the application of gross and violent stimulants. (pp. 20–21)

It is the endeavor he has made to "enlarge this capability," Wordsworth explains, that "distinguishes" the *Lyrical Ballads* "from the popular Poetry of the day" (pp. 20–21).

In working this refinement on popular notions of how poetry ought to affect readers, Wordsworth follows as closely in the steps of Schiller as he does in his treatment of composition. But he stops short of Schiller and, with the popular poet Bürger, makes it his *readers'* responsibility to decide whether he has attained his object of effecting "a purer, more lasting, and more exquisite" variety of excitement "and, what is a much more important question, whether it be worth attaining." "Upon the decision of these two questions," he concludes, "will rest my claim to the approbation of the public" (p. 32). For Wordsworth, in short, unlike Schiller, it proves possible to oppose the public's "degrading thirst after outrageous stimulation" without abandoning instrumentalist principles of poetry. In the *Preface* the value of a poem remains inextricably linked to the appreciation of its readers.

I would be leaving my own readers with a distorted picture of the fortunes of the instrumentalist model in England, however, if I were to conclude this discussion with the *Preface*. For after the publication of the second edition of the *Lyrical Ballads* this link between value and reception began to weaken perceptibly. And in the *Essay, Supplementary to the Preface* to his *Miscellaneous Poems* of 1815 it is strained to the breaking point. The *Essay* is almost entirely devoted to the question of the relation between a work's reception and its value. Musing over the "unremitting hostility" with which the *Lyrical Ballads* had been "opposed" during the seventeen years since their publication, Wordsworth tells a reassuring history of English poetry in which it turns out that all of the great poets from Spenser to Percy met with similar fates during their lifetimes while lesser talents flourished. The lesson of his history, Wordsworth writes, is that "every Author, as far as he is great and at the same time *original*, has had the task of *creating* the taste by which he is to be enjoyed" (p. 182). In the *Essay*, in short, the approbation of contemporary readers is dismissed as a measure of a poem's merit in favor of posterity. Continuity with instrumentalist principles of poetry is attenuated.

Wordsworth's temporal deferral of the identity of value with reception has its counterpart in the vision of their reconvergence with which Schiller consoles the aspiring *Volksdichter* in his review of Bürger's *Poems*. If he follows Schiller's advice and writes over the heads of the multitude directly to the educated, Schiller urges, the sheer magnitude of his accomplishment will bridge, or cancel [*aufheben*] the monstrous gulf that separates the classes (p. 248). This vision of plenitude would perhaps rescue Schiller's poetic theory from aestheticism and restore to it a kind of attenuated continuity with instrumentalist tradition were it not for the fact that, should it come to pass, such an event would be merely contingent—of no bearing whatsoever on the value of a work, which, later in the review, as we have seen, Schiller pronounces absolute, intrinsic, and totally distinct from its reception (p. 250).

The much strained link between poetic value and the appreciation of readers is *re*inforced at the end of Wordsworth's *Essay* of 1815 by means of a similar sleight of hand—by a redefinition of the relevant audience for (significant) poetry. In an effort to establish communication with the contemporary audience he has just written off in favor of posterity, Wordsworth distinguishes between the approbation of the *public*, which he deems irrelevant to a poem's value, and the *voice of the people*.

Lamentable is his error, who can believe that there is any thing of divine infallibility in the clamour of that small though loud portion of the community, ever governed by factitious influence, which, under the name of the PUBLIC, passes itself, upon the unthinking for the PEOPLE. Towards the Public, the Writer hopes that he feels as much deference as it is intitled to: but to the People, philosophically characterized, and to the embodied spirit of their knowledge, so far as it exists and moves, at the present, faithfully supported by its two wings, the past and the future, his devout respect, his reverence, is due. (p. 187)

Thus does Wordsworth seek to preserve continuity with the tradition of Horace under the radically altered conditions of poetry at the beginning of the nineteenth century.

II

The various prefaces to the *Lyrical Ballads* reflect a mounting crisis in the relation of serious writers to the reading public. By 1815 we can observe an erosion of the confidence Wordsworth had displayed in 1800 that he would be able to compete effectively with an ever-growing literature of diversion. Having lost hope of reforming the reading habits of the middle-class audience of his day, Wordsworth follows in the footsteps of Schiller, who, in his attack on the popular poet Bürger in 1791, had consoled himself and other floundering poets of the ideal by proposing a new way of measuring the merit of their writing that did not require that they achieve the veneration of the multitude of contemporary readers enjoyed by Bürger. It is in much the same spirit that Wordsworth contemns the voice of "the Public" at the end of the *Essay* of 1815; but instead of eliminating the reader in favor of purely internal criteria of value, as had Schiller, Wordsworth seeks to dehistoricize the reader. Appealing to "the People, philosophically characterized," he makes the measure of literary merit the kind of veneration a (transhistorical) people, or nation, extends to its classics. More systematic articulation of this dehistoricizing strategy fell to Coleridge.

No English writer of the period grappled with the relation of writer and reader as intensively as Coleridge.[16] Concern with this relation pervades his prose—his essays no less than his correspondence, lectures, and notebooks. Nurtured by lifelong struggle to earn a livelihood by his writing, this concern manifests itself stylistically in repeated appeals to the "reflective reader" and baroque apologies for method; but it may also be explicitly thematized, as in his essays *On the Principles of Genial Criticism Concerning the Fine Arts, More Especially Those of Statuary and Painting, Deduced from the Laws and Impulses Which Guide the True Artist in the Production of His Works*, making this work surely one of the most self-reflexive contributions to aesthetic theory in English.[17] In these essays, which constitute the only substantial foray into general aesthetics that he saw into print, Coleridge goes to battle against the growing taste for diversion by challenging the theory of art that sanctioned it. Because he borrows most of his artillery, surreptitiously, from the *Critique of Judgment*, the essays contain much of interest for a new history of aesthetics.

Coleridge's plagiarisms are legendary, and I do not intend to add to, or examine in detail, those that have been identified in *Principles*, but instead will focus on the larger project to which he attempted to assimilate the ideas he found in the third *Critique*.[18] The occasion for the project was an exhibit by the American painter Washington Allston. Allston, whom Coleridge had met in Rome some years before, was exhibiting in Bristol in the summer of 1814, and in order to draw public attention to his works Coleridge, who was living in England's "second city" at the time, agreed to compose a series of essays "on the Principles of *genial* criticism concerning the Fine Arts, especially those of Statuary and Painting" for one of the local newspapers, *Felix Farley's Bristol Journal*.[19] But if this was originally Coleridge's objective, it did not survive in the execution. In correspondence with Daniel Stuart he wrote of extending the project to sixteen or twenty essays—covering "all of the *best* pictures of the great Masters in England, with characteristics of the great Masters from Giotto to Correggio"[20]—but in the three that actually saw the light of day, in five installments in August–September 1814, Allston's paintings figure only incidentally. The scope of the project had evolved since its inception and would continue to evolve, as we shall see.

As it is articulated in the Preliminary Essay, Coleridge's objective is to provide his readers with "practical guidance" in the appreciation of the fine arts. Having "carefully perused all the works on the Fine Arts known to him," Coleridge writes, he has determined that "the works, that have hitherto appeared, have been either technical, and useful only to the Artist himself (if indeed useful at all) or employed in explaining by the laws of association the effects produced on the spectator by such and such impressions" (p. 222). Although they at least approach the arts from the spectator's perspective, this latter group of writings—Coleridge singles out the associationist aesthetics of Archibald Alison—provides little "practical guidance." It is this deficiency that Coleridge hopes to remedy in the essays, and he proposes to accomplish this by instructing his readers in principles of criticism. His project is thus explicitly pedagogical. In this it resembles Bergk's *Art of Reading*. Like Bergk, moreover, Coleridge aims to bring reception into line with artistic production. This is the thrust of the title of the essays. The Preliminary Essay had appeared under the title *On the Principles of Sound Criticism*, but Coleridge substituted the word *Genial* in subsequent installments[21] to indicate, as he explains in the subtitle, that the principles were to be "deduced from the laws and impulses which guide the true artist in the production of his works." In specifying that he will derive his principles from the practice of the "true artist," Coleridge calls attention to a further feature of *Principles* that brings them into close affiliation with the German theories we have examined, and that is that reception is to be attuned not to all who compose or paint, but only to a selection of those who step forward—the great masters. He spells this out in the final clause of his statement in the Preliminary Essay that the "specific object of the present attempt is to enable the spectator to judge in the same spirit in which the Artist produced, or ought to have produced" (p. 222). Intended to create an audience for "true" art out of the readers of the *Bristol Journal*, Coleridge's project presents itself as a concrete program for realizing the conditions that Wordsworth, in commending his poetry to posterity, seems no longer to consider realizable.

Existing conditions seem anything but propitious as Coleridge depicts them. Echoing Wordsworth's description of cultural malaise in the *Preface*, he evokes a world in which commerce is king. The Bristol burghers are indifferent to art. Long years of following the progress of the Napoleonic wars in the newspapers has accustomed them to strong "stimulants," with the result that the writer faces a difficult task. Hostilities having ceased (Coleridge is writing during the brief period of quiet that preceded Napoleon's escape from Elba), he cannot "hope to excite the same keen and promiscuous sensation as when he had to announce events, which by mere bond of interest brought home the movements of monarchs and empires to every individual's counting-house and fire-side" (pp. 219–20). How, then, is he to retain the multitude of readers whom "these troublesome times occasioned ... to acquire a habit, and almost a necessity, of reading"? He could of course substitute a fictional stimulant. But what if he wishes to write about the arts—"the noblest works of peace"?

To engage their interest in his subject Coleridge goes to considerable lengths to meet his Bristol readers on their own ground. Far from contemning the attitudes responsible for their indifference to art, he appeals to these attitudes in defense of his project. Thus, he acknowledges the legitimacy of their desire for diversion, promising them a "stimulant, which though less intense is more permanent, and by its greater divergency no less than duration, even more pleasureable" (p. 220). And appealing to their patriotism and commercial spirit, he further commends the project to them by noting that Britain's artists not only enhance her cultural preeminence; through their influence on design they increase the appeal of her exports in china, textiles, furniture, and the like, thus contributing to her commercial preeminence as well. In a word, the same "bond of interest" that caused his Bristol readers to follow the progress of the war so avidly ought now in peace to devolve on the arts. Coleridge seeks to cement the rapport he has thus attempted to establish with his readers by assuring them that *they* will be the judge of the principles of appreciation he sets forth in the essays:

> The writer therefore concludes this his preparatory Essay by two postulates, the only ones he deems necessary for his complete intelligibility: the first, that the reader would steadily look into his own mind to know whether the principles stated are ideally true; the second, to look at the works or parts of the works mentioned, as illustrating or exemplifying the principle, to judge whether or how far it has been realized. (p. 223)

Having been so painstakingly courted, readers must have been surprised, to say the least, when Coleridge used the subsequent installments to delve into metaphysics—to take them down a path so tortuous that, as he himself suggests when he breaks off the project in the Appendix, it could be followed only by those already familiar with it. That is to say, *Principles* departs sharply from the kind of practical project Coleridge has led his readers to anticipate. Instead of setting forth principles qua guidelines to make Allston's—or any other painter's—work more accessible to them, Coleridge is propelled back to far more *fundamental* principles. In explanation of this regress he writes to Daniel Stuart: "Till it could be determined what *Beauty* was, whether it was Beauty merely because it pleased, or pleased because it was Beauty, it would have been as absurd to talk of general Principles of Taste, as of Tastes."[22] The impulse to pursue this Kantian question displaces the more practical aim he announced at the outset, with the result that the essays turn into an abstract philosophical investigation of the nature of beauty. They become a prolegomena— the groundwork or foundation of some future course in practical criticism.[23]

The problem this regress poses has already been intimated. It is simply that the philosophical project that evolves in Essay Second and Third places demands on readers that the subscribers to the *Bristol Journal* are not equipped to meet. To follow Coleridge down the metaphysical path he pursues there one needs to be versed in philosophy, in particular in the philosophy of art that was being generated in England and on the continent at the beginning of the nineteenth century. That is because Coleridge does so little to facilitate his readers' progress in these essays. They are as convoluted and schematic as the Preliminary Essay is direct and concrete. If they are more readerly today, therefore, it is because unlike the burghers of Bristol we are able to turn to the *Critique of Judgment* for aid. We will return to this problem once we have taken advantage of our posteriority to extrapolate the main outlines of the theory of art contained in the essays.

The regress begins with the definition of art proposed in the Preliminary Essay and recapitulated in Essay Second: "The common essence of all [the fine arts] consists in the excitement of emotion for the purpose of immediate pleasure through the medium of beauty" (p. 221). Instead of employing this idea heuristically to elaborate the practical guidelines he has promised, Coleridge devotes the remaining essays to defending its accuracy. It is in the pleasure they provide that he locates the defining feature of the arts, he explains, because this is what distinguishes them from the sciences, "the immediate object and primary purpose of which is truth and possible utility." The arts "may lead to important truth, and be in various ways useful in the ordinary meaning of the word," he writes, "but these are not the direct and characteristic ends, and we define things by their peculiar, not their common properties" (p. 221). The bulk of the essays is devoted to unpacking the proposition that the arts provide "pleasure through the medium of beauty." This final term assumes such importance because pleasure is the object not only of art appreciation but of many of our other activities as well. Specifying that art has pleasure as its purpose may suffice, therefore, to distinguish the arts from science, but it does not distinguish them from the other activities in which we engage for pleasure, such as eating, drinking, gambling, and love-making. Following well-established tradition, Coleridge figures these as the pleasures of the palate and sets out to show that the pleasures of art differ essentially—in *kind*, not merely in *degree,* as he stresses repeatedly—from such pleasures. It is to convey this difference, he explains, that he has defined art as providing pleasure "through the medium of beauty":

> The term, pleasure, is unfortunately so comprehensive, as frequently to become equivocal: and yet it is hard to discover a substitute. *Complacency,* which would indeed better express the intellectual nature of the enjoyment essentially involved in the sense of the beautiful, yet seems to preclude all emotion: and *delight,* on the other hand, conveys a comparative *degree* of pleasureable emotion, and is therefore unfit for a *general* definition, the object of which is to abstract the *kind.* For this reason, we added the words "through the medium of beauty." (p. 224)

The term "beauty" may not be quite as "comprehensive" as "pleasure," but it does not help much to clarify the nature of the pleasures afforded by art, as Coleridge himself admits. This insufficiency, which he attributes to "promiscuous use of the term, Beauty," dictates his task in the remainder of the essays. He will attempt to define beauty in order to give content to his assertion that the pleasures of art, defined as pleasure through the medium of beauty, are unique—differ essentially from our other pleasures.

To accomplish this Coleridge borrows heavily from the *Critique of Judgment,* drawing in particular on Kant's distinction between the different kinds of satisfaction provided by the beautiful, the pleasant (or agreeable), and the good; but, as we shall see, he articulates the distinction in accordance with local requirements. In Essay Third, for example, he resuscitates the ancient Greek formula to define beauty as "multëity in unity"—"that in which the *many,* still seen as many, becomes one" (p. 232). He offers several illustrations of this notion:

> An old coach-wheel lies in the coachmaker's yard, disfigured with tar and dirt (I purposely take the most trivial instances)—if I turn away my attention from these, and regard the *figure* ab-

stractly, "still," I might say to my companion, "there is beauty in
that wheel, and you yourself would not only admit, but would
feel it, had you never seen a wheel before. See how the rays
proceed from the centre to the circumferences, and how many
different images are distinctly comprehended at one glance, as
forming one whole, and each part in some harmonious relation
to each and to all." But imagine the polished golden wheel of
the chariot of the Sun, as the poets have described it: then the
figure, and the real thing so figured, exactly coincide. There is
nothing heterogeneous, nothing to abstract from: by its perfect
smoothness and circularity in width, each part is (if I may borrow
a metaphor from a sister sense) as perfect a melody, as the whole
is a complete harmony. This, we should say, is beautiful
throughout. (pp. 232–33)

The beauty of both wheels derives from the way in which their
respective parts interact to form harmonious wholes; however, since
all of its parts are perfectly integrated—it contains "nothing heterogeneous"—the golden wheel surpasses the old coach wheel in beauty
and affords the spectator proportionately greater pleasure: "Of all 'the
many,' which I actually see, each and all are really reconciled into
unity: while the effulgence from the whole coincides with, and seems
to represent, the effluence of delight from my own mind in the
intuition of it" (p. 233).

If "beauty is harmony, and subsists only in composition," as
Coleridge concludes from this example, it should follow that to enjoy
the pleasures distinctive of art the spectator need only attend to the
way in which artists have arranged their material. And indeed when
he "offend[s] ... against the laws of method" and, "anticipating
materials which rather belong to a more advanced stage of the disqui-
sition," actually refers his readers to concrete works of art—first to
one of Allston's paintings and then to Raphael's *Galatea*—Coleridge
focuses exclusively on matters of composition. Both artists have arranged their figures in a circular grouping.

In Raphael's admirable Galatea (the print of which is doubtless
familiar to most of my readers) the circle is perceived at first
sight; but with what multiplicity of rays and chords within the
area of the circular group, with what elevations and depressions
of the circumference, with what an endless variety and sportive
wildness in the component figure[s], and in the junctions of the

figures, is the balance, the perfect reconciliation, effected between these two conflicting principles of the FREE LIFE, and of the confining FORM! How entirely is the stiffness that would have resulted from the obvious regularity of the latter, *fused* and (if I may hazard so bold a metaphor) almost *volatilized* by the interpenetration and electrical flashes of the former. (pp. 234–35)

Coleridge's emphasis on the composition of this work suggests the direction a course in practical criticism might have taken had he advanced beyond the "ground-works" of his "edifice" to the "super-structure" (p. 223), instead of becoming mired in "metaphysical Pre-liminaries," as he terms the ground he has covered when he breaks off the project in the Appendix (p. 246): the formalist direction perfected in such latter-day introductions to the pleasures of art appreci-ation as *The Story of Art* where, having noted that in the *Galatea* Raphael chose as his subject a verse from a poem by the Florentine Angelo Poliziano—describing "how the clumsy giant Polyphemus sings a love song to the fair sea-nymph Galatea and how she rides across the waves in a chariot drawn by two dolphins, laughing at his uncouth song, while the gay company of other sea-gods and nymphs is milling round her"—E. H. Gombrich calls readers' attention to this work's rich composition:

Every figure seems to correspond to some other figure, every movement to answer a counter-movement. . . . To start with the small boys with Cupid's bows and arrows who aim at the heart of the nymph: not only do those to right and left echo each other's movements, but the boy swimming beside the chariot corresponds to the one flying at the top of the picture. It is the same with the group of sea-gods which seems to be "wheeling" round the nymph. There are two on the margins, who blow on their sea-shells, and two pairs in front and behind, who are making love to each other. But what is more admirable is that all these diverse movements are somehow reflected and taken up in the figure of Galatea herself. Her chariot had been driving from left to right with her veil blowing backwards, but, hearing the strange love song, she turns round and smiles, and all the lines in the picture, from the love-gods' arrows to the reins she holds, converge on her beautiful face in the very centre of the picture. By these artistic means Raphael has achieved constant movement throughout the picture, without letting it become restless or unbalanced. It is for this supreme mastery of arranging his figures, this consummate skill in composition, that artists have admired Raphael ever since.[24]

For Gombrich, as for Coleridge, the pleasures of beholding the *Galatea* lie in the comparatively cerebral activity of appreciating its form. And Gombrich calls attention to how very closely attuned these pleasures are to those of production—to the concerns, that is, of the practicing artist. That this should be so is self-evident to Gombrich. A product of the institutionalization of the model of art appreciation Coleridge is outlining, *The Story of Art* retains little trace of the struggle of ideas out of which this model emerged.

But it is still wonderfully evident in *Principles*. Coleridge elaborates his *painterly* treatment of the *Galatea* in opposition to the dominant theory of the arts at that time—the very *spectatorly* orientation of associationist aesthetics. Hence it is to this theoretical tradition that we must turn for a fuller understanding of the scope of the formalist model of appreciation Coleridge is proposing. In taking it on, he will draw on Kant's assistance, appropriating key concepts and distinctions from the beginning of the "Analytic of the Beautiful" in order to charge associationists with reducing "the beautiful" to the merely "pleasant," or "agreeable" [*das Angenehme*]. The "regress" to fundamental principles thus set in motion, the essays will spend their remaining energy defining these concepts—to the exasperation of readers, as we shall see.[25]

III

The associationist tradition in British aesthetics has its source in an increasingly empirical philosophy of mind for which Locke laid the foundations when, having postulated a mind composed only of sensations and their faint copies, mental images, he introduced the concept of association to explain all the more complex ideas and trains of thought of which we are capable. By the time of Addison his doctrine of the association of ideas was already exerting an impact on thinking about the arts. In fact, Addison provides one of the most lucid early accounts of this operation of the mind in "The Pleasures of the Imagination." Prefatory to discussing the need for poets to cultivate "the Power of imagining Things strongly," he writes:

We may observe, that any single Circumstance of what we have formerly seen often raises up a whole Scene of Imagery, and awakens numberless Ideas that before slept in the Imagination; such a particular Smell or Colour is able to fill the Mind, on a sudden, with the Picture of the Fields or Gardens where we first met with it, and to bring up into View all the Variety of Images that once attended it. Our Imagination takes the Hint, and leads us unexpectedly into Cities or Theatres, Plains or Meadows.[26]

Addison goes on to explain this phenonomen in terms that anticipate the neurophysiological explanation of David Hartley thirty years later. According to Hartley, who was instrumental in transforming philosophical speculation into an empirical science of the the mind, what Addison is describing is the phenomenon whereby if several stimuli occur simultaneously and produce several corresponding vibrations in different regions of the brain—vibration A arising, say, from an olfactory stimulus and vibration B arising from a visual stimulus—the repetition of only the olfactory stimulus producing vibration A will arouse vibration B *even in the absence* of the original stimulus that produced B.[27]

The doctrine of the association of ideas proved extremely fruitful to theorists of the arts from Addison and Hutcheson to Burke, Hume, and Alison,[28] the last of whose *Essays on the Nature and Principles of Taste* (1790) comes under Coleridge's attack. The most sweeping of the many applications of the principle of association to the arts, Alison's work was on the way to becoming a best-seller when Coleridge wrote *Principles,* owing to Francis Jeffrey's highly favorable essay review of the second edition of 1811 in the influential *Edinburgh Review.* Today Jeffrey is remembered primarily as the poets of the Lake School, and especially Coleridge, wished—as the philistine who had the shortsightedness to challenge their poetic program in sarcastic and sometimes brutal reviews, the most famous of which, a review of Wordsworth's *Excursion,* in 1814, began with the schoolmasterly words, "This will never do."[29] This is unfortunate, for Jeffrey's theory of the arts rings refreshingly current. Jeffrey had long admired Alison's work as "the most rational, original and philosophical" of any that had appeared on the arts, and having himself suggested the changes that needed to be made to remove "the chief obstructions to its popularity," he was well prepared to handle promotion of the new edition.[30] So skillfully and thoroughly does he expound its key ideas in his review—it runs to forty-six pages—that he not only made it into something of a best-seller,[31] he very likely obviated any necessity of reading it. I will thus speak of the ideas of the two interchangeably.

On the associationist model according to Alison the pleasures of the imagination lie not in analyzing a work's composition, but in pursuing the "ideas of emotion"—following out the associations— produced by objects of nature and of art. His aesthetic is a psychology of reception, which is to say that it is devoted to ascertaining and describing what goes on in the mind when we experience an object as beautiful or sublime. What he finds is that a "train of ideas of emotion" is triggered:

> When we feel either the beauty or sublimity of natural scenery— the gay lustre of a morning in spring, or the mild radiance of a summer evening, the savage majesty of a wintry storm, or the wild magnificence of a tempestuous ocean—we are conscious of a variety of images in our minds, very different from those which the objects themselves can present to the eye. Trains of pleasing or of solemn thought arise spontaneously within our minds; our hearts swell with emotions, of which the objects before us seem to afford no adequate cause.[32]

It is only when they are productive of such trains of thought that we experience objects as beautiful or sublime. Thus, to take the simple example adduced by Jeffrey, the sound of thunder is so widely experienced as sublime that we are given to imagine that this effect is produced by the peculiarity of the sound itself. That this is not so, that the sublimity of thunder results rather from the ideas of "prodigious power and undefined danger" we associate with the sound, may be seen from the way we respond if we learn that we were mistaken and that the noise we heard was produced instead by a cart rattling over stones. As soon as we discover our mistake, the effect is destroyed: we cease to experience the sound as sublime and experience it instead only as a "vulgar" disturbance. Since the sound itself has not changed, this can only be because the association "dissolves": realizing our error, we cease to associate the sound with "that vast and uncontrouled Power which is the natural object of awe and veneration."[33] It is in this way, and only in this way, that objects affect us aesthetically, according to Alison: by becoming "the signs or expressions of such qualities [e.g., vast and uncontrolled power] as are fitted, by the constitution of our nature, to produce emotion [e.g., awe and veneration]" (p. 115). Once this original emotion is aroused, ideas "allied" to it awaken spontaneously, creating the succession or "train of ideas of emotion" that distinguishes aesthetic pleasure.

Jeffrey's highly romanticized account of the effect of a "common" English landscape offers a convenient illustration of the drift of such trains of thought. "In what does the beauty consist?" he asks.

> Not certainly in the mere mixture of colours and forms; for colours more pleasing, and lines more graceful, (according to any theory of grace that may be preferred), might be spread upon a board, or a painter's pallet, without engaging the eye to a second glance, or raising the least emotion in the mind;—but, in the picture of human happiness that is presented to our imaginations and affections,—in the visible and unequivocal signs of comfort, and cheerful and peaceful enjoyment,—and of that secure and successful industry that ensures its continuance,—and of the piety by which it is exalted,—and of the simplicity by which it is contrasted with the guilt and the fever of a city life;—in the images of health and temperance and plenty which it exhibits to every eye,—and in the glimpses which it affords to warmer imaginations, of those primitive or fabulous times, when man was uncorrupted by luxury and ambition, and of those humble retreats in which we still delight to imagine that love and philosophy may find an unpolluted asylum. (pp. 13–14)

It is to such trains of thought, according to Jeffrey, that the "green meadows with fat cattle," the "well fenced, well cultivated fields," and "neat, clean, scattered cottages" that characterize the English countryside give rise. In following out the train, which is triggered by the idea of happiness we associate with these objects, we experience the landscape's beauty.

Artworks affect us in much the same way, according to the associationists. It is thus not enough, Alison argues in sharp contrast to Coleridge, that we attend to the "qualities they present to our senses" or to "qualities of their composition." If our attention is thus "confined" to the object, whether it be a landscape by Claude Lorrain, the music of Handel, or the poetry of Milton, the effect will be "feeble," and we will not experience its beauty or sublimity. Our imagination must rather be "kindled by [its] power" (pp. 20–21) so that there passes before it

> a variety of great or pleasing images . . . beyond what the scene or description . . . can, of itself, excite. They seem often, indeed,

to have but a very distant relation to the object that at first excited them; and the object itself appears only to serve as a hint to awaken the imagination, and to lead it through every analogous idea that has place in the memory. It is then, indeed, in this powerless state of revery, when we are carried on by our conceptions, not guiding them, that the deepest emotions of beauty or sublimity are felt; that our hearts swell with feelings which language is too weak to express; and that, in the depth of silence and astonishment, we pay to the charm that enthrals us the most flattering mark of our applause. (p. 51)

This extravagant description of the pleasures of art was inspired by the lines from Book IV of Milton's *Paradise Regained*:

> Either tropic now
> 'Gan thunder, and both ends of heaven; the clouds
> From many a horrid rift abortive, pour'd
> Fierce rain, with lightning mix'd; nor slept the winds
> Within their stony caves, but rush'd abroad
> From the four hinges of the world, and fell
> On the vex'd wilderness, whose tallest pines,
> Though rooted deep as high, and sturdiest oaks
> Bow'd their stiff necks, loaden with stormy blasts
> Or torn up sheer. Ill wast thou shrouded then,
> O patient Son of God! (p. 51)

We experience the sublimity of this passage, according to Alison, much as we would the sublimity of an actual storm—by following out the train of "ideas of emotion" it arouses. The pleasures of art differ from the pleasures of nature only insofar as the artist, by selecting and arranging his material, is able to invest it with expressive "character" (pp. 88–89) and in this way give direction to the train of ideas it arouses in the recipient. To accomplish this the artist must organize his material. But it would be a mistake to conclude with Coleridge that composition is therefore a terminal value. We are continuously surrounded by the union of uniformity and variety. "The greater part of forms, both in art and nature, are possessed of this union," Alison writes, but "the union of such qualities is felt to be beautiful only in those cases where the object . . . has some determinate expression" (pp. 223–24). To take the example of landscape gardening,

if there is no character discernible, no general expression which may afford our imaginations the key of the scene, although we may be pleased with its neatness or cultivation we feel no beauty whatever in its composition. . . . If, on the other hand, the scene is expressive, if the general form is such as to inspire some peculiar emotion, and the different circumstances such as to correspond to this effect, or to increase it, we immediately conclude that the composition is good, and yield ourselves willingly to its influence. (p. 227)

The most noteworthy feature of associationist theory in the present context affiliates it closely with poststructuralist currents in criticism. As our sketch of its bold outlines will already have suggested, associationist theory vests considerable authority in the recipient in aesthetic transactions, and it construes the recipient empirically. Alison believes that the way an object affects us depends heavily on what we bring to it, and that what we bring to it depends in turn on our individual situation. To recur to the simple example of the sound of thunder, he observes that while its sublimity is almost universally

> founded on awe, and some degree of terror; yet how different is the emotion which it gives to the peasant, who sees at last, after a long drought, the consent of Heaven to his prayers for rain— to the philosopher, who from the height of the Alps hears it roll beneath his feet—to the soldier, who, under the impression of ancient superstition, welcomes it, upon the moment of engagement, as the omen of victory! In all these cases, the sound itself is the same; but how different the nature of the sublimity it produces! (p. 124)

Insofar as their situations differ, so too will the ideas individuals associate with a given object, and hence also will its effect, which is to say, its meaning and value to them. There is thus bound to be an individual element in every act of reception. It is, however, the societal features that emerge most clearly in the associationist investigations of reception we are examining. "There is scarcely any class in society," Jeffrey writes,

> which could not be shown to have peculiar associations of interest and emotion with objects which are not so connected in the minds of any other class. The young and the old—the rich and the poor—the artist and the man of science—the inhabitant of the city and the inhabitant of the country—the man of business and the man of pleasure—the domestic and the dissipated,— nay, even the followers of almost every different study or profes-

sion, have perceptions of beauty, because they have associations with external objects, that are peculiar to themselves, and have no existence for any other persons. (p. 21)

Our affiliations of age, income, education, occupation, nationality, and the like disperse us into distinct interpretive communities.[34] By shaping the ideas we associate with objects, they differentiate the way in which we construe, or construct our world. If their modus operandi is only beginning to be explored again today, that is because of the success of the model of appreciation Coleridge is advocating, the chief goal of which, as we shall see, is to enforce rigorous abstraction from all such local affiliations or "interests."

The cost of Coleridge's triumph is suggested by the fruitfulness of Alison's insight into the intertextual element in appreciation. Examining the influence of education on our capacity to experience beauty and sublimity, he observes that it is often due to our reading that we are affected by objects. What else could account for the "emotion of sublime delight" that the spectator feels on first perceiving Rome?

> It is not the scene of destruction which is before him. It is not the Tiber, diminished in his imagination to a paltry stream, flowing amid the ruins of that magnificence which it once adorned. It is not the triumph of superstition over the wreck of human greatness, and its monuments erected upon the very spot where the first honors of humanity have been gained. It is ancient Rome which fills his imagination. It is the country of Caesar, and Cicero, and Virgil which is before him. It is the mistress of the world which he sees, and who seems to him to rise again from her tomb, to give laws to the universe. All that the labors of his youth or the studies of his maturer age have acquired with regard to the history of this great people, open at once before his imagination, and present him with a field of high and solemn imagery, which can never be exhausted. Take from him these associations, conceal from him that it is Rome which he sees, and how different would be his emotion! (p. 41)

Anticipating the poststructuralist insight into the textuality of experience, Alison concludes that if we abstract from the associations mediated by classical literature, all that we will *see* before us are indifferent ruins.

Jeffrey is boldest about drawing the axiological implications of thus privileging the recipient in a model of appreciation. If the perception of beauty is dependent on the opportunities individuals have had to associate "ideas of emotion" with an object, he writes, there is certain to be wide disagreement about the beauty of any given object—the same object "appearing beautiful to those who have been exposed to the influence of such associations and indifferent to those who have not" (p. 17). While the beauty of the bucolic English landscape described above might be universally acknowledged, according to Jeffrey, a highland scene is a different matter. To percipients who share his own background the "lofty mountains, and rocky and lonely recesses" that characterize the highlands will appear beautiful because they will suggest

> romantic seclusion, and primeval simplicity;—lovers sequestered in these blissful solitudes, "from towns and toils remote,"—and rustic poets and philosophers communing with nature, at a distance from the low pursuits and selfish malignity of ordinary mortals;— ... the sublime impression of the Mighty Power which piled the massive cliffs upon each other, and rent the mountains asunder, and scattered their giant fragments at their base;—and all the images connected with the monuments of antient magnificence and extinguished hostility,—the feuds, and the combats, and the triumphs of its wild and primitive inhabitants, contrasted with the stillness and desolation of the scenes where they lye interred;—and the romantic ideas attached to their antient traditions, and the peculiarities of their present life,—their wild and enthusiastic poetry, their gloomy superstitions,—their attachment to their chiefs,—the dangers, and the hardships and enjoyments of their lonely huntings and fishings,—their pastoral shielings on the mountains in summer,— and the tales and the sports that amuse the little groupes that are frozen into their vast and trackless valleys in the winter. (pp. 14–15)

But if these are the thoughts to which a highland landscape can give rise, it may fail to do so in beholders with backgrounds different from Jeffrey's. Jeffrey cites the frank confession of two Cockney tourists, recently returned from an expedition to the highlands, that they were unable to discover any beauty there whatsoever and were astonished how any intelligent person could voluntarily pass his time in the

" 'cold and laborious pastimes' " that the highlands afforded, when he might have devoted it to " 'the gay vivacity of plays, operas, and polite assemblies.' They accordingly post back to London as fast as possible; and after yawning, in a sort of disconsolate terror, along the banks of Lochlomond, enlarge, with much animation, on the beauty and grandeur—of Finsbury Square!" (p. 16). The reactions of Jeffrey and the Cockney tourists to the highlands could not diverge more sharply. How are such divergences of taste to be resolved?

This question brings us to the feature of the associationist model of appreciation that appears to have propelled Coleridge back to *fundamental* principles. For as Jeffrey sees it, such disagreements cannot be resolved, at least not rationally, nor need they be. He could not be more explicit. One of the chief advantages of Alison's book, he writes toward the conclusion of his review, is that it promises to put an end to all questions about "the standard of taste":

> If things are not beautiful in themselves, but only as they serve to suggest interesting conceptions to the mind, then every thing which does in point of fact suggest such a conception to any individual, *is beautiful* to that individual; and it is not only quite true that there is no room for disputing about tastes, but that all tastes are equally just and correct, in so far as each individual speaks only of his own emotion. When a man calls a thing beautiful, he may indeed mean to make two very different assertions:—he may mean that it gives him pleasure, by suggesting to him some interesting emotion; and, in this sense, there can be no doubt that, if he merely speak truth, the thing *is* beautiful; and that it pleases him precisely in the same way that all other things please those to whom they appear beautiful. But if he mean to say that the thing possesses some quality which ought to make it appear beautiful to every other person, and that it is owing to some prejudice or defect in them if it appear otherwise, then he is as unreasonable and absurd as he would think those who should attempt to convince him that he felt no emotion of beauty. (pp. 43–44)

In the disagreement between Jeffrey and the Cockney tourists, then, both parties are correct. No matter that in his remarks on the highland landscape Jeffrey demonstrates qualifications that the Cockney tourists seem to lack. His "expertise" as a native of the region and a reader of romantic literature do not put him in closer touch with the highland landscape as it really is. For on associationist theory the landscape *in itself* is nothing more than a neutral configuration of colors and forms. The meanings with which Jeffrey "invests" these (p. 14) are of his own making, hence no more true of the landscape than the dull dreariness the Cockney tourists ascribe to it. They tell us about Jeffrey and other connoisseurs of the sublime, not about the scenery itself. Because he cannot appeal to the way the landscape really is, Jeffrey believes that he lacks rational grounds for demanding agreement from the Cockney tourists. He can reasonably assert only that the Highland landscape gives him pleasure and that it will give them pleasure too insofar as they resemble him in the relevant respects, not that it *ought* to give them pleasure. Following Alison (pp. 65–66), Jeffrey will allow that his own judgment of the scenery is preferable to that of the Cockney tourists only in the sense that his capacity to be affected by it extends the range of "innocent" pleasures available to him, and in this way enriches his life (p. 44). Those available to the Cockney tourists are narrower by comparison, limited by the boundaries of the City of London. It is for *comprehensiveness* of taste that we should strive.

Convinced that aesthetic disagreement is not rationally resolvable, and entirely comfortable with diversity, Jeffrey concludes the review by criticizing the uniformitarian impulse.

> It is a strange aberration indeed of vanity that makes us despise persons for being happy—for having sources of enjoyment in which we cannot share;—and yet this is the true account of the ridicule we bestow upon individuals who seek only to enjoy their peculiar tastes unmolested;—for, if there be any truth in the theory we have been expounding, no taste is bad for any other reason than because it is peculiar—as the objects in which it delights must actually serve to suggest to the individual those common emotions and universal affections upon which the sense of beauty is every where founded. The misfortune is, however, that we are apt to consider all persons who communicate their tastes, and especially all who create any objects for their gratification, as in some measure dictating to the public, and setting up an idol for general adoration; and hence this intolerant interference with almost all peculiar perceptions of beauty, and the unsparing derision that pursues all deviations from acknowledged standards. This intolerance, we admit, is often provoked

by something of a spirit of *proselytism,* and arrogance in those
who mistake their own casual associations for natural or universal relations; and the consequence is, that mortified vanity dries
up the fountain of their peculiar enjoyment, and disenchants, by
a new association of general contempt or ridicule, the scenes
that had been consecrated by some innocent but accidental
emotion. (pp. 45–46)

This resounding affirmation of diversity bespeaks a confidence in the
free market for culture that Coleridge, like the German ideologues we
have examined, considers naive. On this note of laissez-faire Jeffrey
lends his considerable authority, and that of the *Edinburgh Review*,[35]
to a theory of art that affirms art's complete integration into an
economy in which the value of an object is a function of its utility to
consumers who cannot be wrong—except by consuming too little.
Only slightly revised and expanded, Jeffrey's review entered the sup-
plement to the seventh edition of the *Encyclopedia Britannica* in 1824
as the "Essay on Beauty." It was subsequently incorporated into the
new edition of 1841 and, to quote René Wellek, "continued to figure
there as the authoritative treatment of aesthetics till 1875."[36] In short,
the triumph of the model of appreciation Coleridge is articulating in
Principles occurred much more recently than is often imagined.[37]

IV

The polemic in which the second installment of *Principles* explodes
suggests that it was above all the associationists' joyful affirmation of
diversity that precipitated Coleridge's regress to fundamental principles:[38]

An English critic, who assumes and proceeds on the identity in
kind of the pleasures derived from the palate and from the
intellect, and who literally considers *taste* to mean one and the
same thing, whether it be the taste of venison, or a taste for
Virgil, and who, in strict consistence with his principles, passes
sentence on Milton as a tiresome poet, because he finds nothing
amusing in the Paradise Lost (i.e., damnat Musas, quia animum
a musis non divertunt [he condemns the muses because they do
not divert his mind from the arts])—this taste-meter to the
fashionable world gives a ludicrous portrait of an African belle,

and concludes with a triumphant exclamation, "such is the ideal of beauty in Dahoma!" (pp. 225–26)[39]

Nowhere does Alison or the unrivaled "taste-meter" Francis Jeffrey pass sentence on Milton, that I know of, but such a verdict is fully consistent with the theory of appreciation they set forth. A reader who finds nothing amusing in *Paradise Lost* is as justified in pronouncing Milton "a tiresome poet" as are the Cockney tourists in derogating the highlands. On associationist theory, Coleridge goes on to object, it is

> impossible either to praise or to condemn any man's taste, how-
> ever opposite to our own, and we could be no more justified in
> assigning a corruption or absence of just taste to a man, who
> should prefer Blackmore to Homer or Milton, or the Castle
> Spectre to Othello, than to the same man for preferring a black-
> pudding to a sirloin of beef. (p. 227)

In short, associationist theory pulls the rug out from under the "classics." It exposes as contingent their position at the pinnacle of a hierarchy that includes not only inferior rivals like Blackmore (whose " 'The Creation,' a philosophical poem demonstrating the existence and providence of God" [1712], had been warmly praised by Samuel Johnson), but works that do not even share any of their aims, works like Monk Lewis's play, *Castle Spectre*, which were produced solely and simply to divert their audiences.

That "the noblest productions of human genius"—in addition to the works of Homer, Shakespeare, and Milton, Coleridge mentions "the Pantheon, Raphael's Gallery, and Michael Angelo's Sistine Chapel, the Venus de Medici and the Apollo Belvedere"—should "delight us merely by chance" (pp. 226–27), that their authority should rest on as fragile a foundation as the accidental convergence of idiosyncratic acts of reception by recipients of diverse aims and backgrounds, is unacceptable to Coleridge who, as our examination of the Preliminary Essay has shown, does not share Jeffrey's confidence in the free market for culture. In the interest of shoring up their claim to our veneration—of grounding their authority more firmly—he turns to Kant's inquiry into the conditions of the possibility of arguing about taste in the *Critique of Judgment.*

Of the many ideas that Coleridge appropriates, the key one is Kant's distinction at the beginning of the "Analytic of the Beautiful" between the different kinds of satisfaction provided by the beautiful, the pleasant or agreeable [*das Angenehme*], and the good, respectively. "Of these three kinds of satisfaction, that of taste in the beautiful is alone a disinterested and *free* satisfaction," Kant had written, "for no interest, either of sense or of reason, here forces our assent" (p. 44). And he suggests that insofar as we judge an object thus *disinterestedly*—without regard, that is, for its ability to satisfy our own desires, be they of the senses or the intellect—we are justified in "demanding" (which does not mean that we will necessarily get) universal agreement (p. 47). In practice this means that we must restrict judgment to the object's formal structure.

Coleridge spells out this idea when he identifies the pleasures of art with the apprehension of multeity in unity, and he puts it into practice in his observations on the *Galatea*. Devoted entirely to matters of composition, as we have seen, they do not relate the work to anything else, least of all to the desires of the percipient. In the lingo of the times, they refrain from pursuing *associations*. Indeed, Coleridge stipulates as *Principle the First* of the "genial" criticism about to be that an object's "connection or association" with things "separate or separable from it," is irrelevant to appreciation of it *as art:*

> That which has become, or which has been *made* agreeable to us, from causes not contained in its own nature, or in its original conformity to the human organs and faculties; that which is not pleasing for its own sake, but by connection or association with some other thing, separate or separable from it, is neither beautiful, nor capable of being a component part of Beauty: though it may greatly increase the sum of our pleasure, when it does not interfere with the beauty of the object, nay, even when it detracts from it. (p. 236)

However much they may increase the spectator's pleasure, a work's associations with things external to it have no bearing on its beauty, according to Coleridge. Thus does he render the "disinterestedness" that Kant had asserted to distinguish judgments of beauty, and indeed in summarizing he relies on Kant even more closely, promulgating as *Principle the Third* that

> *The sense of beauty subsists in simultaneous intuition of the relation of parts, each to each, and of all to a whole: exciting an immediate and absolute complacency, without intervenence, therefore, of any interest, sensual or intellectual.* (p. 239) [40]

Lacking any bearing on its beauty, a work's associations with things external to it cannot be relevant to appreciation of it as art, for it is the function of art, as Coleridge defines it, to provide *"immediate* pleasure, through the medium of beauty" (p. 224). He is outlining a model of appreciation, in short, which suppresses all of the "associative" activity that, on the prevailing model championed by Alison and Jeffrey, had been thought to be responsible for art's whole meaning and value to us. The pleasures to be anticipated from focusing our attention in this way would seem to be austere indeed.

Coleridge makes his case against associationism by activating the potential for social discrimination contained in Kant's isolation of a special "disinterested" form of satisfaction (from those that are "bound up with interest"). He attempts to discredit the practice of allowing associations to affect one's judgment of a work by depicting this as a kind of category error that only the vulgar would commit: a case of conflating mind and body, confusing Taste with taste, reducing Milton to meat—in a word, a brutish practice that merits our contempt.

> If a man, upon questioning his own experience, can detect no difference in *kind* between the enjoyment derived from the eating of turtle, and that from the perception of a new truth; if in *his* feelings a taste *for* Milton is essentially the same as the taste *of* mutton, he may still be a sensible and a valuable member of society; but it would be desecration to argue with him on the Fine Arts; and should he himself dispute on them, or even publish a book (and such books *have* been perpetrated within the memory of man) we can answer him only by silence, or a courteous waiving of the subject. (p. 225)

The ridicule does not stop here. In the continuation, quoted earlier, Coleridge derides the critic we identified as Jeffrey for the tastelessness of allowing the way *Paradise Lost* had affected him to influence his judgment of the work: evidently he can't tell the difference between the pleasures of the palate and the intellect! By thus inflecting it with social import, Coleridge seeks to discredit the practice that from Joseph Addison to Francis Jeffrey had seemed both natural and rational of treating all of our pleasures as *continuous* in the sense at least that, whether they derive from the palate or the intellect, we deem their effect—their satisfaction of our desires and needs—a relevant consideration in deciding their value.

Coleridge anticipates two related benefits from the suppression of associations: the possibility not only of universally valid judgments but of judgments that are "genial" in the sense specified in the subtitle of the essays. He suggests, that is, that by abstracting from the diverse aims and experiences that differentiate us and thus also our responses to art—by surrendering our *selves*, as it were—we not only create the conditions for universal agreement, we open ourselves to being guided in our response by—entering into a kind of collaboration with—the artist. Coleridge aims, in a word, to eradicate the *empirical* recipient so prominent in the prevailing associationist model to make room for the production of a recipient who, to quote the Preliminary Essay, will "judge in the same spirit in which the Artist produced, or ought to have produced." In contemporary criticism we term this construct a *competent*, an *implied*, sometimes an *ideal* recipient.

Coleridge's deep investment in the triumph of this Kantian model of appreciation is apparent from his relationship to his own recipients—the readers of *Felix Farley's Bristol Journal*.[41] At the outset of our discussion we noted the great care with which he attempts to engage their interest in his project. But he dissipates the good will he has cultivated when he succumbs to the call of metaphysics in the second installment and defers the course in practical criticism that he has promised. The resulting "analytic of the beautiful" makes its methodical Kantian prototype seem readerly, if colorless, by comparison. The readers of the *Bristol Journal* could not follow Coleridge. A letter to the editor of a competing weekly attests to the breakdown in communication. "I have read with much attention two Essays upon the *Fine Arts*, lately published in *Felix Farley's Bristol Journal*," a reader who signs himself "Cosmo" writes,

> and really much attention is required to understand the abstract sense, the singularity of style, the various subtleties with which the composition is carried on. I should be ambitious to know whom the Author intends to address? If the Public in general, I confess it to be my humble opinion, that scarcely the tenth part of his readers will be able to understand him: but if it be principally intended to instruct that class of society, who, as Professors, are particularly devoted to the fine arts, assuredly few will read beyond a single paragraph without nausea and weariness.

Following several only slightly more substantive objections, "Cosmo" confesses that Coleridge is just "too sublime for my common and limited comprehension. His second and third Essays are framed in a style of lecturing Philosophy, so profound, so high, so mysterious, that you entirely forget that the *simplicity* of the Fine Arts was the proposed argument."[42]

Such external evidence of a breakdown in communication just serves to confirm the evidence of the essays themselves. For Coleridge internalizes the uncomprehending reader—brings the "Cosmos" into his text. "And let not these distinctions be charged on the writer, as obscurity and needless subtlety," he explodes after his first, impenetrable stab at defining the unique pleasures of art, and then he goes on to hurl the charge back at his (uncomprehending) readers. If his exposition seems obscure, it is not his fault, but rather that they are obtuse,

> for it is in the nature of all disquisitions on matters of taste, that the reasoner must appeal for his very premises to facts of feeling and of inner sense, which all men do not possess, and which many, who do possess and even act upon them, yet have never reflectively adverted to, have never made them objects of a full and distinct consciousness. (p. 225)

The obtuse readers here addressed so condescendingly haunt the remaining installments of *Principles* to be alternatingly solicited, insulted, and cajoled before Coleridge finally breaks off the project in order to await "a more appropriate audience."

At the end of Essay Second he suggests that his "candid" readers' patience is about to be rewarded—that having suffered the laying of the "ground-works" of the "edifice," they may now at long last look forward to the "superstructure," the practical guidance in art appreciation that he promised them. But, alas, it is not yet to be. Instead of proceeding expeditiously to the promised goal, the third essay opens with an extended defense against the charge of pedantry—a charge, readers learn (if they persist), that Coleridge anticipates not for past commissions, but for the pedantry he still has in store for them, for he intends to introduce yet another series of specialized terms and distinctions. In a kind of preemptive strike, Coleridge again turns the charge back on his accusers, this time by redefining pedantry. Insofar as it "consists in the use of words unsuitable to the time, place, and company," readers are being at least as pedantic as he when they insist that he employ ordinary language:

> The language of the market would be as pedantic in the schools as that of the schools in the market. The mere man of the world,

who insists that in a philosophic investigation of principles and general laws, no other terms should be used, than occur in common conversation, and with no greater definiteness, is at least as much a *pedant* as the man of learning, who, perhaps overrating the acquirements of his auditors, or deceived by his own familiarity with technical phrases, talks at the wine-table with his eye fixed on his study or laboratory. . . . If (to use the old metaphor) both smell of the shop, yet the odour from the Russia-leather bindings of the good old *authentic-looking* folios and quartos is less annoying than the steams from the tavern or tallow-vat. (pp. 228–29)

Since the *Bristol Journal* was not, after all, an organ of the schools, Coleridge cannot have convinced many readers, but he will have richly diverted them before subjecting them to another barrage of specialized terms.

In short, once he launches into his analytic of the beautiful Coleridge does not expect to be understood. While this prospect weighs heavily on him, it does not cause him to simplify or clarify his exposition in order to accommodate his readers, but only to tender increasingly baroque apologies that retard the exposition, further deferring the "practical criticism" that readers anticipate, thus exacerbating their alienation.[43] It would be interesting to know how many of the good burghers of Bristol remained to experience the ultimate deferral. For, finding only what he considers *resisting* readers, Coleridge abruptly breaks off the whole project without even having completed his "metaphysical Preliminaries." He "close[s]" them, he explains, having covered only

the Beauty of the Senses, and by the Good hav[ing] chiefly referred to the relatively good. Of the supersensual Beauty, the Beauty of Virtue and Holiness, and of its relation to the ABSO-LUTELY GOOD, distinguishable, not separable, . . . I discourse not now, waiting for a loftier mood, a nobler subject, a more appropriate audience, warned from within and from without, that it is profanation to speak of these mysteries . . . [and there follows *in ancient Greek* the passage from Plotinus] to those to whose imagination it has never been presented, how beautiful is the countenance of justice and wisdom; and that neither the morning nor the evening star are so fair. For in order to direct the view aright, it behoves that the beholder should have made himself congenerous and similar to the object beheld. Never could the eye have beheld the sun, had not its own essence been soliform, neither can a soul not beautiful attain to an intuition of beauty. (p. 246)[44]

To go on, Coleridge explains, he would need "a more appropriate audience"—an audience, he intimates, that, like the beholder of the sun in the example of Plotinus, is *already* in possession of the truths he is attempting to communicate. With such "genial" readers, however, it would not even be necessary for him to go on because, having collaborated with—"judged in the same spirit as"—the author from the start, they would already have intuited what he is driving at.

Principles is characteristic of Coleridge's way of relating to his readers: painfully aware of what they require, substantively and stylistically, he nevertheless resists accomodating them, even his most privileged readers—the doctors, lawyers, lords, professors, clergymen, and landowners who constituted the intended audience of his ill-fated periodical of 1809–10, *The Friend.*[45] To do so, he reasons, not disinterestedly, would be to contribute to the dissipation of readers that began with the entirely "innocent" efforts of Addison and Steele to extend the "love of Reading, as a refined pleasure weaning the mind from grosser enjoyments," by writing in a style as well as of a subject matter that was suited to the particular situation—to the restricted preparation and leisure—of a predominantly middle-class audience. Thus, he suggests, was conceived the "unconnected" style—the magic formula that subsequent enterprising purveyors of the word like Francis Jeffrey would deploy so opportunistically in newspapers, novels, and magazines that, as Coleridge sees it, the reading public had become unwilling and unable to process "words of more than two syllables."[46]

This streamlined history of the rise and fall of the reading public, which appears as a motto at the beginning of this chapter, is constructed by Coleridge to justify the all but certain failure of *The Friend.* Urging him to try to make it more accessible to readers, an acquaintance had suggested that he take the *Spectator* as a model. Coleridge apparently complied (even though *The Friend* had been conceived in express opposition to "this great founder of the race"),[47] for soon thereafter he wrote Thomas Poole of having "*studied* the Spectator—& with increasing pleasure & admiration." But then he continues:

Yet it must be evident to you, that there is a class of Thoughts & Feelings, and these too the most important, even practicably, which it would be impossible to convey in the manner of Addison: and which if Addison had possessed, he would not have been Addison. Read for instance Milton's prose tracts, and only *try* to conceive them translated into the style of the Spectator— or the finest parts of Wordsworth's pamphlet. It would be less absurd to wish, that the serious Odes of Horace had been written in the same style, as his Satires & Epistles.— Consider too the very different Objects of the Friend & of the Spectator: & above all, do not forget, that these are AWEFUL TIMES![48]

So difficult is what he has to say, Coleridge rationalizes, that it cannot possibly be conveyed in the style of *The Spectator* or, significantly, the *Edinburgh Review*, which he considered its direct heir.[49]

In the *Critique of Judgment* Coleridge had clearly found the principles he needed to "solve" the problems with his readers that his essays on the subject enact so colorfully—principles by means of which to transform the heterogeneous readers of the *Bristol Journal*, or "PUBLIC," as Wordsworth terms them, into the "more appropriate audience," or "PEOPLE," for which both authors yearned.

To get the message across, however, he would have had to stoop to adopt the "unconnected" style of the many middlebrow authors who had come forward in the quarter-century since the publication of Kant's work in 1790 to satisfy this public's desire for detailed guidance in connoisseurship. For, as our examination of Bergk's manual in chapter 4 will have indicated, not all of Germany's impressive output in aesthetics was as inaccessible as the *Critique of Judgment*. There had also evolved a spectrum of more readerly aesthetics from the handbook in which in 1799 Benediktus Joseph von Koller surveys the *Geschichte und Literatur der Aesthetik, von Baumgarten bis auf die neueste Zeit* [*History and Literature of Aesthetics from Baumgarten to the Present*] for beginning university students to the comprehensive textbook of 1807, *Die Aesthetik für gebildete Leser* [*Aesthetics for Educated Readers*], in which Karl Heinrich Ludwig Pölitz articulates and applies to all of the fine arts principles he derives from the *Critique*, in a form that is patently designed for the libraries of aspiring middle-class readers. So vivid an illustration as the latter of the reformatory milieu in which the *Critique* was hatched invites us to inquire into the "interests" or investments that have led subsequent philosophers of art, in denial of their history, to present Kant's achievement as a hard-won triumph of pure philosophical reason operating on timeless and universal facts of art.

V

> *The [Copyright] Bill has for its main object, to relieve*
> *men of letters from the thraldom of being forced to court*
> *the living generation, to aid them in rising above de-*
> *graded taste and slavish prejudice, and to encourage them*
> *to rely upon their own impulses, or to leave them with*
> *less excuse if they should fail to do so.*
> —*Wordsworth, Petition to Parliament (1839)*

At about the time Wordsworth and Coleridge were grappling theoretically with the reading public's relative indifference to their writing, a law was enacted by Parliament extending an author's copyright in his work to twenty-eight years from the date of publication, or for the remainder of the author's life if he outlived that term. This was the Copyright Act of 1814. Wordworth had taken an interest in the bill from the beginning. In anticipation of its discussion in Parliament he had complained in a letter to Richard Sharp that the proposed extension was much too short:

> It requires much more than that length of time to establish the reputation of original productions, both in Philosophy and Poetry, and to bring them consequently into such circulation that the authors, in the Persons of their Heirs or posterity, can in any degree be benefited, I mean in a pecuniary point of view, for the trouble they must have taken to produce the works.[50]

To benefit writers the "originality" of whose work forces them to look to posterity for recognition—Wordsworth mentions the slow growth of Collins's fame and the long neglect of Milton's minor poems—copyright would need to extend well beyond the term being contemplated. Only writers who cater to popular taste can be certain of realizing a profit from their investment within twenty-eight years, as Wordsworth sees it: "The useful drudges in Literature, or . . . flimsy and shallow writers, whose works are upon a level with the taste and knowledge of the age; while men of real power, who go before their age, are deprived of all hope of their families being benefited by their exertions."[51]

Wordsworth did not actively seek to influence legislation until much later, but when he did it was to implement the project suggested in these remarks of 1808: to enlist the law in support of *difficult* authors by getting legal protection of their property in their writing extended—in perpetuity. When a new Copyright Bill was finally introduced in 1837, it contained no mention of perpetuity, but it proposed the generous term of sixty years following the author's death. Serjeant Thomas Noon Talfourd had introduced the bill at Wordsworth's urging, and Wordsworth worked energetically for more than five years to get it through Parliament, supplying Talfourd with material for his speeches, personally lobbying Members of Parliament and other influential people, drafting petitions, and firing off anonymous letters to newspapers.[52] In one of these, a letter "To the Editor of the Kendal Mercury," Wordsworth attempted a point-by-point rebuttal of a petition by members of the publishing trade opposing the bill. "Objections against the proposed bill," he concludes the letter, "rest upon the presumption that it would tend to check the circulation of literature, and by so doing would prove injurious to the public." He has attempted to show that such fears are "groundless," he continues, but even if they were not, it would hardly matter, for

> what we want in these times, and are likely to want still more, is not the circulation of books, but of good books, and above all, the production of works, the authors of which look beyond the passing day, and are desirous of pleasing and instructing future generations. Now there cannot be a question that the proposed bill would greatly strengthen such desire. A conscientious author, who had a family to maintain, and a prospect of descendants, would regard the additional labour bestowed upon any considerable work he might have in hand, in the light of an insurance of money upon his own life for the benefit of his issue; and he would be animated in his efforts accordingly, and would cheerfully undergo present privations for such future recompense. Deny it to him, and you unfeelingly leave a weight upon his spirits, which must deaden his exertions; or you force him to turn his faculties . . . to inferior employments.[53]

In proposing that the law foster writing produced in relative indifference to the desires of the buying public, Wordsworth obviously seeks to operationalize the theory advanced in his *Essay* of 1815 that the value of a work is decided by posterity not by contemporary readers. What he and difficult authors like him stood to gain from the legislation is suggested by the statement in his petition to Parliament in 1839 that "within the last four years" his works have brought him "a larger pecuniary emolument than during the whole of the preceding years in which they have been before the public"—an income, he adds, that under current law will cease the moment he dies.[54] Wordsworth was sixty-nine at the time.

Opposition to the bill was sustained and fierce, but Parliament eventually came around to Wordsworth's way of thinking. He did not get perpetual copyright, or even the sixty years Talfourd had proposed, but in 1842 a new copyright law was enacted extending protection to forty-two years or, if the author survived that period, life plus seven years—which it remained until 1911. By designating the new law an act "to afford greater Encouragement to the Production of Literary Works of lasting Benefit to the World" and specifying that it was to supersede all previous copyright legislation, including the "Act for the Encouragement of Learning" (1709), the "Act for the further Encouragement of Learning" (1801), and the "Act to amend the several Acts for the Encouragement of Learning" (1814),[55] Parliament, in evident agreement with Wordsworth's reasoning, placed the law in the service of art. The decisions that have been handed down in the wake of the Copyright Act of 1842 wear the stamp of this provenience.

Introduction: Rereading the History of Aesthetics

1. Paul Oskar Kristeller, "The Modern System of the Arts," in Morris Weitz, ed., *Problems in Aesthetics,* 2d ed. (New York: Macmillan, 1970), pp. 160–61. The essay first appeared in the *Journal of the History of Ideas* 12 (1951):496–527, and 13 (1952):17–46.

2. Kristeller, "The Modern System of the Arts," pp. 161ff.

3. Weitz, ed., *Problems in Aesthetics,* p. 3.

4. This dehistoricizing strategy has the pedagogical advantage, of course, of bringing these great dead philosophers into dialogue with us—of inviting them to contribute to the contemporary debate which it is the object of anthologies like Weitz's to stimulate. But at what cost? For, as I suggest below, among the bizarre side effects of this strategy is that it turns these philosophers into bunglers. That is, if their object was "to state the defining properties of art" (in the modern sense), as Weitz maintains, why did they perform so poorly? For reflections on these and related issues, see Richard Rorty, J. B. Schneewind, and Quentin Skinner, eds., *Philosophy in History* (Cambridge: Cambridge University Press, 1984).

5. "The Historicity of Aesthetics," *British Journal of Aesthetics* 26(1986):101. Cf. Daniel Shaw's statement that "aesthetic theories, like scientific theories, are proposed to explain a certain set of phenomena" in "A Kuhnian Metatheory for Aesthetics," *Journal of Aesthetics and Art Criticism* 45 (1986):29.

6. "Recent Scholarship and the British Tradition: A Logic of Taste—

the First Fifty Years," in George Dickie and R. J. Sclafani, eds., *Aesthetics: A Critical Anthology* (New York: St. Martin's Press, 1977) p. 627.

7. "On the Origins of 'Aesthetic Disinterestedness,'" *Journal of Aesthetics and Art Criticism* 20 (1961):143.

8. Ibid., p. 139.

9. *Aesthetics from Classical Greece to the Present: A Short History* (University, Alabama: University of Alabama Press, 1966), pp. 183–85.

10. A convenient overview of the scope and accomplishments of the "analytic" philosophy of art may be found in a special issue of the *Journal of Aesthetics and Art Criticism* edited by Richard Shusterman (46 [1987]). Some interesting illustrations of its pathological relationship to the historicity of its subject matter may be found in the issue edited by John Hospers and Anita Silvers that *The Monist* recently devoted to "Aesthetics and the Histories of the Arts" (71[2] [April 1988]).

11. *The Ideology of the Aesthetic* (Oxford: Basil Blackwell, 1990), p. 1. Subsequent references are given in the text.

12. Cf. Robert C. Holub's complaint against the histories of Ernst Cassirer, Georg Lukács, and Odo Marquard that "theories concerning the reason for the rise of aesthetics [so often] retain the abstract and idealistic nature of the science itself" ("The Rise of Aesthetics in the Eighteenth Century," *Comparative Literature Studies* 15 [1978]:277). See also Peter Uwe Hohendahl, "Prolegomena to a History of Literary Criticism," in *The Institution of Criticism* (Ithaca: Cornell University Press, 1982), pp. 224–41. Instructive inquiries into the problems historians of aesthetics and criticism face clarifying their historical relationship to their subject matter may be found in Jonathan Arac, *Critical Genealogies: Historical Situations for Postmodern Literary Studies* (New York: Columbia University Press, 1987); Dominick La Capra, "Writing the History of Criticism Now?" in *History and Criticism* (Ithaca: Cornell University Press, 1985), pp. 95–114; Clifford Siskin, "Introduction: A New Literary History," in *The Historicity of Romantic Discourse* (New York: Oxford University Press, 1988), pp. 3–14; and James J. Sosnoski, "Literary Study in a Post-Modern Era: Rereading Its History," *Works and Days* 5 (1987):7–33.

1. The Interests in Disinterestedness

1. Moritz's most important writings on the arts are collected in *Schriften zur Ästhetik und Poetik,* edited by Hans Joachim Schrimpf (Tübingen: Max Niemeyer, 1962), and in volume II of the three-volume *Werke,* edited by Horst Günther (Frankfurt am Main: Insel, 1981).

2. They mark out, for example, the area of agreement among critical movements and schools as divergent in other respects as the phenomenology of Roman Ingarden; Anglo-American philosophical aesthetics as professed by Monroe Beardsley, Jerome Stolnitz, or Paul Ziff; linguistic criticism, from the formalism of Roman Jakobson to the many applications of John Austin's theory of speech acts; the mythopoeic criticism of Northrop Frye; as well as the New Criticism of Warren, Brooks, and Wimsatt; and they are retained as conventions of reading in much poststructuralist criticism.

3. "Versuch einer Vereinigung aller schönen Künste und Wissenschaften unter dem Begriff des in sich selbst Vollendeten," *Schriften zur Ästhetik und Poetik*, p. 3. Subsequent page references in the text are to this edition.

4. There can be little doubt that the *Versuch* came to Kant's attention, for Kant published regularly in the *Berlinische Monatsschrift*. In 1784 this influential periodical had carried his "Idee zu einer allgemeinen Geschichte in weltbürgerlicher Absicht" ["Idea for a Universal History from a Cosmopolitan Point of View"] and "Beantwortung der Frage: Was ist Aufklärung?" ["What Is Enlightenment?"]; and the issue in which the *Versuch* appeared, that of March 1785, contained a piece by Kant, "Über die Vulkane im Monde" ["On the Volcanoes of the Moon"]. Moritz even sent him a copy of the first two issues of his own journal, *Magazin zur Erfahrungsseelenkunde* (see below, p. 30), in the hope, expressed in an accompanying letter dated October 4, 1783, that Kant would review it in the Königsberg newspaper and possibly contribute something to it. He does not appear to have done either (*Kant's Briefwechsel*, I [Berlin and Leipzig: Vereinigung wissenschaftlicher Verleger, 1922], p. 355). On Kant's position in the theoretical shift under investigation, see esp. E. D. Hirsch, "Two Traditions of Literary Evaluation," in *Literary Theory and Criticism: Festschrift in Honor of René Wellek* (Bern: Peter Lang, 1984), pp. 283–98, and Barbara Herrnstein Smith, "Axiologic Logic," in *Contingencies of Value* (Cambridge, Mass.: Harvard University Press, 1988), pp. 54–84.

5. "Les beaux arts réduits à un même principe," in *Principes de la littérature*, vol. 1 (Göttingen and Leyden, 1764), pp. 11–12. Subsequent page references in the text are to this edition.

6. Charles Batteux, "Author's preface," in *A Course of Belles Lettres; or, The Principles of Literature*, translated by John Miller (London: B. Law, 1761), p. vii.

7. Leading the way were *Die schönen Künste aus einem Grunde hergeleitet; aus dem Französischen übersetzt von P. E. B[ertram]* (Gotha: J. P. Mevius, 1751) and *Batteux' Einschränkung der schönen Künste auf einen einzigen Grundsatz; aus dem Französischen übersetzt und mit einem Anhange einiger Abhandlungen versehen* by Johann Adolf Schlegel (Leipzig: Weidmann, 1751). On the reception of Batteux in Germany, see Manfred Schenker, *Charles Batteux und seine Nachahmungstheorie in Deutschland* (Leipzig: H. Haessel, 1909), esp. pp. 61ff.

8. First announced in 1735 on the final page of his master's thesis, *Meditationes philosophicae de nonnullis ad poema pertinentibus* (English translation by Karl Aschenbrenner and William B. Holther, *Reflections on Poetry* [Berkeley: University of California Press, 1954]), and developed 1750–58 in his unfinished work, *Aesthetica*.

9. See Schenker, *Charles Batteux*, pp. 61ff.

10. Mark Boulby, *Karl Philipp Moritz: At the Fringe of Genius* (Toronto: University of Toronto Press, 1979), p. 74.

11. *Gesammelte Schriften*, edited by F. Bamberger et al., continued by Alexander Altmann, vol. I (Stuttgart: Fr. Frommann, 1972), p. 167. Subsequent page references in the text are to this edition.

12. The development that Moritz describes in his opening sentence was

summed up in one of the lectures on the fine arts given by August Wilhelm Schlegel at the beginning of the nineteenth century. "A few people finally noticed," he observes, that the principle that art should imitate nature "was much too vague, and feared that if one were to give art this latitude it might lose itself in the irrelevant and offensive, and thus said: art should imitate beautiful nature. . . . This is just to refer us from Pontius to Pilate. For one either imitates nature as one finds it, in which case things may not turn out beautiful, or one makes [*bildet*] it beautiful and we no longer have an imitation. Why don't they say right from the start: art should represent [*darstellen*] beauty, and leave nature out of it completely." Mendelssohn had done just that, as we have seen. In the same lecture Schlegel goes on to credit Moritz with having been the one to spell out the implications of this new concept of art according to which, to adopt Arthur Danto's terms, the artist is to be understood "not as unsuccessfully imitating real forms, but as successfully creating new ones" (Schlegel, *Kritische Schriften und Briefe, II: Die Kunstlehre,* edited by Edgar Lohner [Stuttgart: W. Kohlhammer, 1963], pp. 84ff., 91f.). Cf. Tzvetan Todorov's discussion of the "Misfortunes of Imitation" theory in *Theories of the Symbol,* translated by Catherine Porter (Ithaca: Cornell University Press, 1982), pp. 111–28. For Danto's explanation of the erosion of imitation theory, see "The Artworld," *Journal of Philosophy* 61 (1964):572–74; and see my critique in "Deconstructing Deconstruction: Toward a History of Modern Criticism," in *Erkennen und Deuten,* edited by Martha Woodmansee and Walter F. W. Lohnes (Berlin: Erich Schmidt, 1983), pp. 23–29.

13. Moritz's elaboration of the principle of perfection is treated by Todorov, *Theories of the Symbol,* pp. 147–64. Relying too heavily on the lectures of Schlegel (see n. 12 above), Todorov obscures the fact that Moritz's dispute in the *Versuch* is not with neoclassical imitation theory—which, as we have seen, had already been superseded by the principle of perfection—but with pragmatic theory, that is, with the emphasis placed by his immediate precursors on the need of a work of art to achieve effects on an audience.

14. Like the moral philosophers of the period, Moritz uses "uneigennützig" and "uninteressiert" interchangeably to designate the absence of selfish motives, or interests, denoted by the English term "disinterested." On the clash of these opposing attitudes in the seventeenth and eighteenth centuries, see Albert O. Hirschman, *The Passions and the Interests: Political Arguments for Capitalism before Its Triumph* (Princeton: Princeton University Press, 1977). The concept of "disinterested" appreciation had already been imported into discussion of the arts by Shaftesbury in the essays collected in *Characteristics* (1711). See Jerome Stolnitz, "On the Significance of Lord Shaftesbury in Modern Aesthetic Theory," *Philological Quarterly* 11 (1961):97–113; and "On the Origins of 'Aesthetic Disinterestedness,'" *Journal of Aesthetics and Art Criticism* 20 (1961):131–43. As M. H. Abrams has pointed out, however, Shaftesbury introduced the concept "only as ancillary to his ethical and religious philosophy." It was left to Shaftesbury's successors in Germany to specialize the concept in order "specifically to differentiate aesthetic experience from religious and moral, as well as practical experience" ("Kant and the Theology of Art," *Notre Dame English Journal* 13 [1981]:91). Although

Moritz may be presumed to have had at least second-hand knowledge of Shaftesbury from Mendelssohn, it is not known whether he ever read the *Characteristics*. However, as I show below, his own religious background provided fertile enough soil for the germination of these same ideas.

15. In its origins in the late seventeenth century, as Boulby notes, Pietism proper was "an introverted, emotional modification of Lutheranism" that sought "the realization of the Kingdom of God on earth by the mystical transformation of the individual soul." There were some sects, however, that rejected the devotion to feeling practiced by the Pietists, and one of these was the Separatist sect of a nobleman named Fleischbein (1700–1774) under whose influence Moritz's father had fallen shortly before his son's birth in 1756. Followers of the teachings of Madame Guyon, the Catholic mystic and close friend of Fénelon, the Fleischbein Separatists "taught an extreme form of quietism" (Boulby, *Karl Philipp Moritz*, p. 6). For the influence of German mysticism on Moritz's writings, see also Robert Minder, *Glaube, Skepsis und Rationalismus. Dargestellt aufgrund der autobiographischen Schriften von Karl Philipp Moritz* (Frankfurt am Main: Suhrkamp, 1974). Minder, however, gives no sense of the systematic use to which this body of ideas is put in Moritz's writings on the arts (see pp. 246–56).

16. *Werke*, I, p. 38. *Anton Reiser* documents Moritz's emancipation from the quietist creed and simultaneous initiation into rationalist philosophy. It makes the following observation about these two incompatible habits of mind. Shortly after his discovery of Wolff and Gottsched (key disseminators of the ideas of Leibniz), the protagonist pays a visit to his family, and we are told that by this time he had

> collected so much material for mystical discussions with his father that they often talked on into the night. Reiser attempted to give a metaphysical explanation of all the mystical ideas his father had drawn from the writings of Madame Guyon—of "All and One," of "Perfection in the One," and so on. It was easy for him because mysticism and metaphysics actually coincide inasmuch as the former has often revealed *accidentally*, by means of the imagination, what in the latter is the work of reflective reason. (p. 281)

If Leibnizian metaphysics seemed to confirm the quietist creed, it is because of their common Platonic heritage. On Moritz's assimilation of this tradition, see Thomas P. Saine's study, *Die ästhetische Theodizee. Karl Philipp Moritz und die Philosophie des 18. Jahrhunderts* (Munich: Fink, 1971), the final two chapters of which treat Moritz's writings on art.

17. For one of the most comprehensive of such histories, see M. H. Abrams, *Natural Supernaturalism* (New York: W. W. Norton, 1971). Abrams pursues his study of art's theological provenience in "Kant and the Theology of Art," pp. 75–106.

18. These intrusions of contingency upon Moritz's argument are not taken into account by his commentators. Saine is sufficiently disturbed by them to caution us against taking Moritz "too literally" (p. 129). However, more often they are simply repressed. See, for example, Todorov, *Theories of*

the Symbol, pp. 148–64; the fifth lecture in Peter Szondi's "Antike und Moderne in der Ästhetik der Goethezeit," *Poetik und Geschichtsphilosophie* (Frankfurt am Main: Suhrkamp, 1974), I, pp. 82–98; and Erdmann Waniek, "Karl Philipp Moritz's Concept of the Whole in His 'Versuch einer Vereinigung . . .' (1785)," *Studies in Eighteenth-Century Culture* 12 (1983):213–22. Exceptions to the rule may be found in Jochen Schulte-Sasse's pioneering study, *Die Kritik an der Trivialliteratur seit der Aufklärung* (Munich: Fink, 1971), pp. 63–73; Martin Fontius, "Produktivkraftentfaltung und Autonomie der Kunst: Zur Ablösung ständischer Voraussetzungen in der Literaturtheorie," in *Literatur im Epochenumbruch*, edited by Günther Klotz, Winfried Schröder, and Peter Weber (Berlin: Aufbau, 1977), pp. 489–520; and Hartmut Scheible, *Wahrheit und Subjekt. Ästhetik im bürgerlichen Zeitalter* (Bern: Francke, 1984), pp. 206ff.

19. W. H. Bruford, *Germany in the Eighteenth Century: The Social Background of the Literary Revival* (Cambridge: Cambridge University Press, 1935), pp. 271ff. For the most comprehensive treatment in English of the whole range of issues I am exploring, see Albert Ward, *Book Production, Fiction, and the German Reading Public, 1740–1800* (Oxford: Clarendon Press, 1974). See also Arnold Hauser, *The Social History of Art*, vol. 3 (New York: Random House, n.d.). For the evolution of the professional writer in Germany, see chapter 2, below, including the sources listed in n. 12.

20. J. G. F. Schulz, *Firlifimini*, edited by Ludwig Geiger (Berlin, 1885), pp. 73f.

21. In anticipation of his responsibilities with the *Bibliothek*, Mendelssohn writes somewhat wistfully to Lessing that it is going to mean "depriving the venerable matron [metaphysics] of some of my love in order to share it with the fine arts" (Letter to Lessing, August 2, 1756, in Moses Mendelssohn, *Gesammelte Schriften*, IV (Stuttgart: Fr. Frommann, 1977), p. xxiii.

22. Ibid., p. xxxvii.

23. See esp. Lessing's correspondence with Nicolai and Mendelssohn on tragedy, in *Briefwechsel über das Trauerspiel*, edited by Jochen Schulte-Sasse (Munich: Winkler, 1972). These considerations also underlie his position in *Laokoön* and the *Hamburgische Dramaturgie*.

24. Quoted in Wolfgang Martens, *Die Botschaft der Tugend. Die Aufklärung im Spiegel der deutschen moralischen Wochenschriften* (Stuttgart: J. B. Metzler, 1968), pp. 406–7. Rudolf Zacharias Becker's *Noth- und Hülfsbüchlein*, an 800-page compendium of knowledge written expressly for the peasant, was one of the period's greatest commercial successes. According to Bruford, 30,000 copies were printed for the first edition in 1787—it took two years to print them—and by 1791 eleven more authorized and four unauthorized editions had been published (*Germany in the Eighteenth Century*, p. 280).

25. The figures are Rudolf Schenda's in *Volk ohne Buch. Studien zur Sozialgeschichte der populären Lesestoffe. 1770–1910* (Frankfurt am Main: Vittorio Klostermann, 1970), p. 444. Schenda estimates literacy at around 15 percent of the population in 1770. In addition to the sources cited below on the "reading revolution," see chapter 4, n. 4.

26. Quoted by Ward, *Book Production*, p. 88.

27. Ibid., p. 61.

28. In *Das gelehrte Teutschland; oder, Lexikon der jetzt lebenden teutschen Schriftsteller,* for example, Johann Georg Meusel places the number of writers in 1800 at around 10,650, up dramatically from some 3,000 in 1771, 5,200 in 1784, and 7,000 in 1791 (quoted in Helmuth Kiesel and Paul Münch, *Gesellschaft und Literatur im 18. Jahrhundert* [Munich: C. H. Beck, 1977], p. 90). See also Ward (*Book Production,* p. 88), who deduces from Meusel's figures that in 1790 there would have been one writer to every 4,000 of the German population.

29. Johann Georg Heinzmann, *Appell an meine Nation über Aufklärung und Aufklärer; über Gelehrsamkeit und Schriftsteller; über Büchermanufakturisten, Rezensenten, Buchhändler; über moderne Philosophen und Menschenerzieher; auch über mancherley anderes, was Menschenfreyheit und Menschenrechte betrifft* (Bern: Auf Kosten des Verfassers, 1795), p. 421. Alarm over this proliferation of writers produced its own body of writing. See, for example, the discussions, "Ursachen der jetzigen Vielschreiberey in Deutschland," in *Journal von und für Deutschland* 6 (1789):139–43, and 7 (1790):498–502.

30. *Reichsbote,* June 20, 1805. Ward's translation, *Book Production,* p. 187, n. 45. On the secularization of the book market, see his comparative analysis of the contents of the catalogs for the Leipzig book fairs of 1740, 1770, and 1800 (pp. 29–58). See also Rolf Engelsing, "Die Perioden der Lesergeschichte in der Neuzeit," *Archiv für Geschichte des Buchwesens* 10 (1970), cols. 945–1002.

31. *Faust,* translated by Walter Arndt, edited by Cyrus Hamlin (New York: W. W. Norton, 1976), p. 3, lines 89–116; I have made minor changes in the translation.

32. See Ward, *Book Production,* p. 56. The spin-offs he cites of the greatest commercial success of the last decade of the century, Karoline von Wobeser's sentimental novel, *Elisa, or Woman as she ought to be* (1795), give an idea of this trend: *Elisa, not the Woman she ought to be; Louise, a Woman as I would wish her to be; Elisa, the Girl from the Moon; Maria, or the Misfortune of being a Woman; Family as it ought to be; Petticoat as it ought to be, a few Words in Private.* Ward notes that writers were still exploiting Elisa's success as late as 1800, for the Easter book fair catalog for that year offers eleven spin-offs, including spin-offs of spin-offs like *Robert, or Man as he ought to be* and *Robert, or Man as he ought not to be* (pp. 137–38).

33. *Sämtliche Werke und Briefe,* 2d ed., edited by Helmut Sembdner (Munich: Carl Hanser, 1961), II, 562–63; Ward's translation, *Book Production,* pp. 186–87, n. 43.

34. On the evolution of two separate cultures in the perception of eighteenth-century elites, see Harry C. Payne, "Elite versus Popular Mentality in the Eighteenth Century," *Studies in Eighteenth-Century Culture* 8 (1979):3–32; the essays collected in Christa Bürger, Peter Bürger, and Jochen Schulte-Sasse, eds., *Zur Dichotomisierung von hoher und niederer Literatur* (Frankfurt am Main: Suhrkamp, 1982); and Peter Stallybrass and Allon White, *The Politics and Poetics of Transgression* (Ithaca: Cornell University Press, 1986), pp. 27–124. Patrick Brantlinger pursues this theme into the nineteenth and

twentieth centuries in *Bread and Circuses: Theories of Mass Culture as Social Decay* (Ithaca: Cornell University Press, 1983). For the relation of this development to the transformation of the bourgeois public sphere as traced by Jürgen Habermas (*The Structural Transformation of the Public Sphere*, translated by Thomas Burger [Cambridge, Mass.: MIT Press, 1989]), see the essays collected in Christa Bürger, Peter Bürger, and Jochen Schulte-Sasse, eds., *Aufklärung und literarische Öffentlichkeit* (Frankfurt am Main: Suhrkamp, 1980); Peter Weber, "Politik und Poesie. Literarische Öffentlichkeit im Übergang zur Kunstperiode," in Peter Weber et al., *Kunstperiode. Studien zur deutschen Literatur des ausgehenden 18. Jahrhunderts* (Berlin: Akademie, 1982); Peter Uwe Hohendahl, "Literary Criticism and the Public Sphere," in *The Institution of Criticism*, pp. 52ff.; and Terry Eagleton, *The Function of Criticism: From the Spectator to Post-Structuralism* (London: Verso, 1984), pp. 1–43. For the situation in the United States, see Lawrence W. Levine, *Highbrow/Lowbrow: The Emergence of Cultural Hierarchy in America* (Cambridge, Mass.: Harvard University Press, 1988). Postmodern critiques of this high/low opposition are examined in Andreas Huyssen, *After the Great Divide: Modernism, Mass Culture, Postmodernism* (Bloomington: Indiana University Press, 1986); and Jim Collins, *Uncommon Cultures: Popular Culture and Post-Modernism* (New York: Routledge, 1989).

35. Friedrich Nicolai, *Das Leben und die Meinungen des Herrn Magister Sebaldus Nothanker,* edited by Fritz Brüggemann (Leipzig: Reclam, 1938), p. 72. The *Insel Felsenburg* to which Nicolai refers is Johann Gottfried Schnabel's 2,300-page novel published 1731–43 and modeled on *Robinson Crusoe.*

36. Johann Adam Bergk, *Die Kunst, Bücher zu lesen. Nebst Bemerkungen über Schriften und Schriftsteller* (Jena: In der Hempelschen Buchhandlung, 1799), p. 407. Cf. Helmut Kreuzer, "Gefährliche Lesesucht? Bemerkungen zu politischer Lektürekritik im ausgehenden 18. Jahrhundert," in *Leser und Lesen im 18. Jahrhundert,* edited by Rainer Gruenter (Heidelberg: Carl Winter Universitätsverlag, 1977), pp. 62–75.

37. "Merkwürdige Rechtsfälle als ein Beitrag zur Geschichte der Menschheit" (1792), in *Sämtliche Werke,* V, edited by Gerhard Fricke and Herbert G. Göpfert (Munich: Carl Hanser, 1959), p. 864. Cf. also "Ursachen der jetzigen Vielschreiberey in Deutschland" (n. 29, above).

38. The disenchantment of English writers begins somewhat later and is expressed with less intensity. See the investigation in chapter 6 of the relation of Wordsworth and Coleridge to their readers.

39. Letter to Goethe, June 25, 1799, in *Schillers Briefe,* VI, edited by Fritz Jonas (Stuttgart: Deutsche Verlags-Anstalt, n.d.), p. 49.

40. *Reisen eines Deutschen in England im Jahre 1782* (1783) and *Reisen eines Deutschen in Italien in den Jahren 1786 bis 1788* (1792–93). The former appeared in England under the title *Travels, chiefly on foot, through several parts of England, in 1782 . . . by Charles P. Moritz, a literary gentleman of Berlin, translated by a lady* (London: For G. G. and J. Robinson, 1795).

41. *Magazin zur Erfahrungsseelenkunde. Als ein Lesebuch für Gelehrte und Ungelehrte* (1783–93).

42. On Moritz's influence, see Boulby, *Karl Philipp Moritz,* chaps. 5–6.

43. August 22, 1795. Reprinted in Hugo Eybisch, *Anton Reiser. Untersuchungen zur Lebensgeschichte von K. Ph. Moritz und zur Kritik seiner Autobiographie* (Leipzig: R. Voigtländer, 1909), p. 272.

44. *Erinnerungen aus den zehn letzten Lebensjahren meines Freundes Anton Reiser. Als ein Beitrag zur Lebensgeschichte des Herrn Hofrath Moritz von Karl Friedrich Klischnig* (Berlin, 1794), pp. 248–49.

45. Joachim Heinrich Campe, *Moritz. Ein abgenöthigter trauriger Beitrag zur Erfahrungsseelenkunde* (Braunschweig: Im Verlage der Schulbuchhandlung, 1789), pp. 6, 20. Cf. Saine, *Die Ästhetische Theodizee*, pp. 182–83.

46. Letter to Campe, July 5, 1788, as reprinted in Eybisch, *Anton Reiser*, p. 234. See also Campe, *Moritz*, p. 20.

47. Ibid., p. 21. For the resulting quill war between Moritz and Campe, see Gerhard Sauder, "Ein deutscher Streit 1789. Campes Versuch 'moralischen Totschlags' und Moritz' Verteidigung der Rechte des Schriftstellers," in *Akten des VII. internationalen Germanisten-Kongresses*, edited by Albrecht Schöne (Tübingen: Max Niemeyer, 1986), pp. 91–97. Even a "competent reader" like Schiller registered the similar complaint that Moritz's masterpiece was "hard to understand because it has no consistent terminology, and half way down the path of philosophical abstraction, loses its way in figurative language. But it is packed full of ideas—and packed only too full, for without a commentary he will not be understood" (Letter to Caroline von Beulwitz, January 3, 1789, in *Schillers Briefe*, II, 199–200).

2. Genius and the Copyright

1. "What Is an Author?" in Josué V. Harari, ed., *Textual Strategies: Perspectives in Post-Structuralist Criticism* (Ithaca: Cornell University Press, 1979), p. 141. See also Roland Barthes, "The Death of the Author," *Image-Music-Text*, edited and translated by Stephen Heath (New York: Hill and Wang, 1977), pp. 142–48, which originally appeared in 1968, about a year before the more penetrating as well as comprehensive piece by Foucault. Twenty-one articles stemming from a conference organized by the Society for Critical Exchange to remedy the dearth of interdisciplinary discussion of the subject are collected in Martha Woodmansee and Peter Jaszi, eds., *The Construction of Authorship: Textual Appropriation in Law and Literature* (Durham: Duke University Press, 1993).

2. As in the case of the "artist," I have retained the masculine pronoun in my discussion of the "author" in order not to obscure the exclusion of "scribbling women" (and simultaneous colonization and appropriation of their "feminine" attributes) in which the concept is rooted. See, in addition to chapter 5 below, Sandra M. Gilbert and Susan Gubar, *The Madwoman in the Attic* (New Haven: Yale University Press, 1979), esp. chap. 1; Nancy K. Miller, "Changing the Subject: Authorship, Writing, and the Reader," in *Subject to Change* (New York: Columbia University Press, 1988), pp. 102–21; Marlon B. Ross, *The Contours of Masculine Desire* (New York: Oxford University Press, 1989), esp. chap. 1; Carla Hesse, "Reading Signatures: Female Authorship and Revolutionary Law in France, 1750–1850," *Eighteenth-Cen-*

tury Studies 22 (1989):469–87; and Christine Battersby, *Gender and Genius* (Bloomington: Indiana University Press, 1989). On the gendering of the visual arts, see also Rozsika Parker and Griselda Pollock, *Old Mistresses. Women, Art and Ideology* (New York: Pantheon, 1981).

3. Of course not every writer who invoked the muses did so with the passion and conviction, say, of Milton. The important thing, in the present context, is that writers continued to employ the convention of ascribing the creative energy of a poem to an external force right through the Renaissance and into the eighteenth century.

4. This tendency to turn over to the writer's own genius what had long been the function of the muses is neatly documented in Johann Georg Sulzer's entry for *Dichter* [*Poet*] in his dictionary of aesthetic terms, *Allgemeine Theorie der schönen Künste*, first issued in 1771–74. After citing with favor Horace's willingness to extend the honorific term "poet" only to the writer "ingenium cui sit, cui mens divinior atque os magna sonaturum," Sulzer observes that on occasion verse, i.e., "the customary language of the poet, contains something so extraordinary and enthusiastic that it has been called the language of the gods—for which reason it must have an extraordinary cause that undoubtedly is to be sought in the genius and character of the poet" ([Frankfurt and Leipzig, 1798], I, p. 659).

5. Hazard Adams, ed., *Critical Theory since Plato* (New York: Harcourt, Brace, Jovanovich, 1971), p. 281.

6. Ibid., pp. 279–80.

7. "Essay, Supplementary to the Preface," in Paul M. Zall, ed., *Literary Criticism of William Wordsworth* (Lincoln: University of Nebraska Press, 1966), p. 182.

8. Ibid., p. 184.

9. See the documentation collected in the facsimile edition of H. E. von Teubern's translation, *Gedanken über die Original-Werke* (1760), edited by Gerhard Sauder (Heidelberg: Verlag Lambert Schneider, 1977).

10. For some of the other reasons for German thinkers' peculiar receptiveness to Young's ideas, see M. H. Abrams, *The Mirror and the Lamp* (Oxford: Oxford University Press, 1953), pp. 201ff.

11. *Conjectures on Original Composition in a Letter to the Author of Sir Charles Grandison*, in Edmund D. Jones, ed., *English Critical Essays. Sixteenth, Seventeenth and Eighteenth Centuries* (London: Oxford University Press, 1975), p. 189. For some of the issues Young's *Conjectures* brings into focus, see Joel Weinsheimer, "Conjectures on Unoriginal Composition," *The Eighteenth Century: Theory and Interpretation* 22 (1981):58–73; and Thomas McFarland, "The Originality Paradox," *Originality and Imagination* (Baltimore: Johns Hopkins University Press, 1985), pp. 1–30. See also Edward W. Said, "On Originality," in *The World, the Text, and the Critic* (Cambridge, Mass.: Harvard University Press, 1983), pp. 126–39.

12. Bruford offers the best brief English treatment of the evolution of the professional writer in Germany in *Germany in the Eighteenth Century*, pp. 271–327. See also Hans Jürgen Haferkorn (on whose spadework all of the more recent treatments draw heavily), "Der freie Schriftsteller," *Archiv für Ge-*

schichte des Buchwesens 5 (1964): cols. 523–712; Helmuth Kiesel and Paul Münch, *Gesellschaft und Literatur im 18. Jahrhundert* (Munich: C. H. Beck, 1977), pp. 77–104; and Wolfgang von Ungern-Sternberg, "Schriftsteller und literarischer Markt," in Rolf Grimminger, ed., *Deutsche Aufklärung bis zur Französischen Revolution, 1680–1789* (Munich: DTV, 1980), pp. 133–85; and the essays edited by Helmut Kreuzer in the issue that *LiLi* devoted to authorship in 1981 (42). For the evolution of the professional writer in England and America, see J. W. Saunders, *The Profession of English Letters* (London: Routledge and Kegan Paul, 1964); Alvin Kernan, *Printing Technology, Letters, and Samuel Johnson* (Princeton: Princeton University Press, 1987); Nigel Cross, *The Common Writer: Life in Nineteenth-Century Grub Street* (Cambridge: Cambridge University Press, 1985); Cathy N. Davidson, *Revolution and the Word: The Rise of the Novel in America* (New York: Oxford University Press, 1986; R. Jackson Wilson, *Figures of Speech: American Writers and the Literary Marketplace, from Benjamin Franklin to Emily Dickinson* (Baltimore: Johns Hopkins University Press, 1989); Kenneth Dauber, *The Idea of Authorship in America: Democratic Poetics from Franklin to Melville* (Madison: University of Wisconsin Press, 1990).

13. Gotthold Ephraim Lessing, *Gesammelte Werke*, edited by Paul Rilla (Berlin: Aufbau, 1968), IX, p. 277.

14. Kiesel and Münch, *Gesellschaft und Literatur im 18. Jahrhundert*, p. 79.

15. Friedrich Schiller, *Schillers Werke*. XXII, edited by Herbert Meyer (Weimar: Hermann Böhlaus Nachfolger, 1958), pp. 94–95.

16. Letter to Baggesen, December 16, 1791, in *Schillers Briefe*, 3, p. 179.

17. On the dramatic increase in the number of would-be writers in the last quarter of the century, see n. 28 in chapter 1.

18. For the contribution of legal theory to the evolution of this idea in relation to authorship, I am especially indebted to Martin Vogel, "Der literarische Markt und die Entstehung des Verlags- und Urheberrechts bis zum Jahre 1800," in *Rhetorik, Ästhetik, Ideologie. Aspekte einer kritischen Kulturwissenschaft* (Stuttgart: J. B. Metzler, 1973), pp. 117–36; and Heinrich Bosse, *Autorschaft ist Werkherrschaft* (Paderborn: Ferdinand Schöningh, 1981). See also Gerhard Plumpe, "Der Autor als Rechtssubjekt," in Helmut Brackert and Jörn Stöckrath, eds., *Literaturwissenschaft* (Reinbek bei Hamburg: Rowohlt, 1981), pp. 179–93.

19. Luther's famous statement, "Ich habs umsonst empfangen, umsonst hab ichs gegeben und begehre auch nichts dafür [Freely have I received, freely given, and I want nothing in return]," occurs in his "Vorrhede und Vermanunge" ["Warning to Printers"] in the *Fastenpostille* (1525). On Luther's evident lack of any concept of intellectual property and his position on book piracy, see Ludwig Gieseke, *Die geschichtliche Entwicklung des deutschen Urheberrechts* (Göttingen: Verlag Otto Schwartz, 1957), pp. 38–40.

20. Johann Heinrich Zedler, *Grosses vollständiges Universal-Lexikon aller Wissenschaften und Künste* (Leipzig and Halle: Zedler, 1735).

21. Johann Wolfgang von Goethe, *Werke* (Hamburg: Christian Wegner, 1955), IX, p. 517.

22. Ibid., pp. 517–18.

23. Kiesel and Münch, *Gesellschaft und Literatur im 18. Jahrhundert,* pp. 147–48.

24. As quoted by Carsten Schlingmann, *Gellert. Eine literar-historische Revision* (Bad Homburg: Gehlen, 1967), p. 36.

25. Gotthold Ephraim Lessing, *Werke,* edited by Herbert G. Göpfert (Munich: Carl Hanser, 1973), V, p. 781. This proposal was never completed and was not published until after Lessing's death, in 1800.

26. For the history of Anglo-American copyright, see Benjamin Kaplan, *An Unhurried View of Copyright* (New York: Columbia University Press, 1967), esp. pp. 6ff.; Lyman Ray Patterson, *Copyright in Historical Perspective* (Nashville: Vanderbilt University Press, 1968), esp. pp. 143–50. A briefer account may be found in Marjorie Plant, *The English Book Trade: An Economic History of the Making and Sale of Books* (London: George Allen and Unwin, 1939), pp. 98–121, 420–44. For a fuller treatment of the privilege and of copyright law in Germany, see Martin Vogel, "Der literarische Markt und die Entstehung des Verlags- und Urheberrechts bis zum Jahre 1800"; Ludwig Gieseke, *Die geschichtliche Entwicklung des deutschen Urheberrechts;* and Ch. F. M. Eisenlohr, *Das literarisch-artistische Eigenthum und Verlagsrecht mit Rücksicht auf die Gesetzgebungen* (Schwerin: F. W. Bärensprung, 1855).

27. Johann Gottlieb Fichte, "Beweis der Unrechtmässigkeit des Büchernachdrucks. Ein Räsonnement und eine Parabel," *Sämtliche Werke,* edited by J. H. Fichte (Leipzig: Mayer and Müller, n.d.), pt. III, vol. III, p. 237.

28. Such was the case in Vienna, for example, whence Johann Trattner, one of the most successful pirate publishers of the later eighteenth century, terrorized the German book trade for over three decades. Trattner's activities were apparently sanctioned as late as 1781 by royal decree (Gieseke, *Die geschichtliche Entwicklung,* pp. 105ff). Ward reports that the otherwise strict Viennese censorship "was not even averse to pirate editions of otherwise forbidden books as long as they were 'local products' which thus brought more profits to the capitol" (*Book Production,* p. 93). See also Hellmut Rosenfeld, "Zur Geschichte von Nachdruck und Plagiat," *Archiv für Geschichte des Buchwesens* 11 (1971): cols. 337–72; Reinhard Wittmann, "Der gerechtfertigte Nachdrucker?" *Buchmarkt und Lektüre im 18. und 19. Jahrhundert* (Tübingen: Max Niemeyer, 1982), pp. 69–90. A mercantilist defense of piracy is quoted below, pp. 49–50.

29. *Memoirs of Frederick Perthes,* 3d ed. (London and Edinburgh, 1857), vol. I, p. 295ff.

30. As quoted by Ward, *Book Production,* p. 98 (translation Ward's). The dramatic increase in the demand for light entertainment in the last quarter of the century is the focus of chapter 4.

31. Philipp Erasmus Reich (edited and translated Linguet's *Betrachtungen über die Rechte des Schriftstellers und seines Verlegers* [Leipzig, 1778]); Joachim Heinrich Campe ("An Joseph den Einzigen," *Deutsches Museum* [February 1784]:101–4); Johann Stephan Pütter (*Der Büchernachdruck nach ächten Grundsätzen des Rechts geprüft* [Göttingen: Vanderhoeck, 1774]); Johann Jakob Cella ("Vom Büchernachdruck," *Freymüthige Aufsätze,* I [Anspach: Haueisen, 1784]); Rudolf Zacharias Becker (*Das Eigenthumsrecht an Geisteswerken, mit*

einer dreyfachen Beschwerde über das Bischöflich-Augsburgische Vikariat wegen Nachdruck, Verstümmelung und Verfälschung des Noth- und Hülfsbüchleins [Frankfurt and Leipzig, 1789]), Gottfried August Bürger ("Vorschlag dem Büchernachdrucke zu steuern," *Deutsches Museum* 2 [1777]:435–55); J. G. Müller von Itzehoe (chapter 20 of his novels, *Siegfried von Lindenberg* [1779] and chapter 61 of *Komische Romane aus den Papieren des braunen Mannes und des Verfassers des Siegfried von Lindenberg* [1784–91]); von Knigge (*Über den Büchernachdruck. An den Herrn Johann Gottwerth Müller, Doktor der Weltweisheit in Itzehoe* [Hamburg: Hoffmann, 1792]); Kant ("Von der Unrechtmäßigkeit des Büchernachdrucks," *Berlinische Monatsschrift* 5 [May 1785]:403–17); Johann Georg Feder ("Versuch einer einleuchtenden Darstellung der Gründe für das Eigenthum des Bücherverlags, nach Grundsätzen des natürlichen Rechts und der Staatsklugheit," *Göttingisches Magazin der Wissenschaften und Litteratur* 1[1780]1–37, 220–42, 459–66]); Martin Ehlers (*Ueber die Unzulässigkeit des Büchernachdrucks nach dem natürlichen Zwangsrecht* [Dessau and Leipzig, 1784]); and Fichte (n. 27 above). The intense involvement of *Dichter und Denker* would seem to distinguish the debate from the slightly earlier English struggle over copyright that Mark Rose examines ("The Author as Proprietor: *Donaldson v. Becket* and the Genealogy of Modern Authorship," *Representations* 23 [1988]:51–85). For the situation in France, see Carla Hesse, "Enlightenment Epistemology and the Laws of Authorship in Revolutionary France, 1777–1793," *Representations* 30 (1990):109–37; and more generally, see Peter Jaszi, "Toward a Theory of Copyright: The Metamorphoses of 'Authorship,'" *Duke Law Journal* (1991):455–502; and Susan Stewart, *Crimes of Writing* (New York: Oxford University Press, 1991), esp. pp. 3–30.

32. Leipzig: In Kommission bey den Gebrüdern Gräff, 1794, 382 pp.

33. As quoted in Helmut Pape, "Klopstocks Autorenhonorare und Selbstverlagsgewinne," *Archiv für Geschichte des Buchwesens* 10 (1969): cols. 103f. Cf. Philipp Erasmus Reich, *Zufällige Gedanken eines Buchhändlers über Herrn Klopstocks Anzeige einer gelehrten Republik* (Leipzig, 1773).

34. Kiesel and Münch, *Gesellschaft und Literatur im 18. Jahrhundert*, p. 152.

35. Goethe, *Werke*, IX, p. 398.

36. In this encyclopedia (*Celestial Emporium of Benevolent Knowledge*), Borges writes, "animals are divided into a) those that belong to the Emperor, b) embalmed ones, c) those that are trained, d) suckling pigs, e) mermaids, f) fabulous ones, g) stray dogs, h) those that are included in this classification, i) those that tremble as if they were mad, j) innumerable ones, k) those drawn with a very fine camel's hair brush, l) others, m) those that have just broken a flower vase, n) those that resemble flies from a distance" (Jorge Luis Borges, "The Analytical Language of John Wilkins," in *Other Inquisitions, 1937–1952* [New York: Simon and Schuster, 1964], p. 103).

37. As quoted by Bosse, *Autorschaft*, p. 13.

38. "Über den Büchernachdruck," *Deutsches Museum* (May 1783): 415–17.

39. Fichte, *Beweis der Unrechtmässigkeit des Büchernachdrucks*, p. 225.

40. Ibid., p. 225.

41. Ibid., pp. 227–28 (final two emphases added).

42. On the grounding of an author's property [*Eigentum*] in his writing in its uniqueness or originality [*Eigentümlichkeit*], see Gerhard Plumpe, "Eigentum - Eigentümlichkeit," *Archiv für Begriffsgeschichte* 23 (1979):175–96. See also Alois Troller, "Originalität und Neuheit der Werke der Literatur und Kunst und der Geschmacksmuster," in Fritz Hodeige, ed., *Das Recht am Geistesgut. Studien zum Urheber-, Verlags- und Presserecht* (Freiburg i. B.: Rombach, 1964), pp. 269–70.

43. Ch. F. M. Eisenlohr, ed., *Sammlung der Gesetze und internationalen Verträge zum Schutze des literarisch-artistischen Eigenthums in Deutschland, Frankreich und England* (Heidelberg: Bangel and Schmitt, 1856), p. 51.

44. Gieseke believes that this is how the law's framer, Carl Gottlieb Suarez, viewed the matter (*Die geschichtliche Entwicklung*, pp. 112ff.).

45. Johann Nikolaus Friedrich Brauer, *Erläuterungen über den Code Napoléon und die Großherzoglich Badische bürgerliche Gesetzgebung* (Karlsruhe, 1809), vol. 1, pp. 466f.

46. Eisenlohr, ed., *Sammlung der Gesetze*, p. 11. The extent of the Baden law's debt to the close identification between author and text postulated by Fichte may be seen in the reasoning that led its framers to limit an author's rights in his work to his own lifetime. Just as in the natural world, Brauer argues,

> the body becomes a corpse as soon as the personality that animated it has departed the world, so too did literary property have to lose its vital and effective character in the civil constitution as soon as that person ceased to exist through whom alone it exerted an effect and was able to exert an effect.

Brauer sums up his reasoning in the pithy phrase: "If the head falls, its writing goes free" (Gieseke, *Die geschichtliche Entwicklung*, pp. 118–19).

47. Quoted in ibid., p. 122.

48. Eisenlohr, ed., *Sammlung der Gesetze*, p. 54; Gieseke, *Die geschichtliche Entwicklung*, pp. 151–54.

49. Young, *Conjectures on Original Composition*, p. 274.

50. Ibid., p. 273.

51. See Abrams, *The Mirror and the Lamp*, pp. 198ff.

52. Orientations to the extensive literature on genius may be found in Joachim Ritter, "Genie," in *Historisches Wörterbuch der Philosophie*, edited by Joachim Ritter (Basel: Schwabe, n.d.), III, cols. 279–309; and Rudolf Wittkower, "Genius: Individualism in Art and Artists," in Philip P. Wiener, ed., *Dictionary of the History of Ideas* (New York: Scribner's, 1973), II, pp. 297–312. The best comprehensive study of the cult of genius remains Edgar Zilsel, *Die Geniereligion. Ein kritischer Versuch über das moderne Persönlichkeitsideal mit einer historischen Begründung* (Vienna and Leipzig: Wilhelm Braumüller, 1918). See also his *Die Entstehung des Geniebegriffs. Ein Beitrag zur Ideengeschichte der Antike und des Frühkapitalismus* (Tübingen: Mohr, 1926); and Oskar Walzel, "Das Prometheussymbol von Shaftesbury zu Goethe," *Neue Jahrbücher für das klassische Altertum* 13 (1910):40–71, 133–65. For a recent investigation of the

evolution and manifold reverberations of the idea in German politics as well as in literature and philosophy, see Jochen Schmidt, *Die Geschichte des Genie- gedankens in der deutschen Literatur, Philosophie und Politik 1750–1945.* (Darmstadt: Wissenschaftliche Buchgesellschaft, 1985). And for the ways in which the rhetoric of genius has been deployed to marginalize the productions of women, see Battersby, *Gender and Genius.*

53. *Herders Sämmtliche Werke,* edited by Bernhard Suphan (Berlin: Weid- mann, 1892), VIII, pp. 175–76.

54. Letter to Jacobi, August 21, 1774, in *Goethes Briefe.* (Hamburg: Chris- tian Wegner, 1962), vol. 1, p. 116. Cf. Johann Georg Sulzer's elaboration of this view of the creative process in his entries on *Genie* and especially *Origi- nalgeist* and *Originalwerk* in *Allgemeine Theorie der schönen Künste.*

55. *Vom Erkennen und Empfinden der menschlichen Seele,* p. 208.

56. Ibid., pp. 208–9.

3. Aesthetic Autonomy as a Weapon in Cultural Politics: Rereading Schiller's "Aesthetic Letters"

1. *On the Aesthetic Education of Man in a Series of Letters,* edited and translated by Elizabeth M. Wilkinson and L. A. Willoughby (Oxford: Claren- don Press, 1967), p. 9. Subsequent references are to this edition and will be given in the text. I have made minor changes in their translations.

2. The deep ambivalence in Schiller's aesthetic theory is noted, for example, by Reginald Snell in his introduction to what is still the most widely used English translation (*On the Aesthetic Education of Man in a Series of Letters,* translated by Reginald Snell [New York: Frederick Ungar, 1965], pp. 14–16) and by Käte Hamburger in her afterword to what is undoubtedly the most widely used German edition (*Über die ästhetische Erziehung* [Stuttgart: Reclam, 1965], p. 149). It was first analyzed in detail by Hans Lutz in *Schillers Anschauungen von Kultur und Natur* (Berlin: E. Ebering, 1928), pp. 169–233. In their dual-language edition Wilkinson and Willoughby mount a herculean effort to refute Lutz's conclusion that the *Letters* contain "two completely unreconciled, and irreconcilable, strata of thought" (*On the Aesthetic Education of Man in a Series of Letters,* p. xliii). Although—or perhaps because—their defense of Schiller's argument runs a dense 90 pages, doubts about its coherence continue to be raised. See, for example, Dieter Borchmeyer's lucid treatment of the *Letters* in *Die Weimarer Klassik* (Königstein/Ts.: Athenäum, 1980), pp. 203–11, esp. 209–10; and Terry Eagleton, *The Ideology of the Aesthetic,* pp. 110ff.

3. Stephen Maxfield Parrish, *The Art of the "Lyrical Ballads"* (Cambridge, Mass.: Harvard University Press, 1973), p. 86. For *Lenore*'s reception in England, see Evelyn B. Jolles, *G. A. Bürgers Ballade "Lenore" in England* (Regensburg: Hans Carl, 1974).

4. *Monthly Magazine* i (March 1796): 118. Quoted in Mary Jacobus, *Tradition and Experiment in Wordsworth's "Lyrical Ballads"* (Oxford: Clarendon, 1976), p. 218.

5. The *Confessions* appeared as part II of a slightly longer, fragmentary

work entitled *Aus Daniel Wunderlichs Buch*. For Herder's influence, see Bürger's letter to Boie, June 18, 1773, in *Briefe von und an Gottfried August Bürger*, edited by Adolf Strodtmann (Berlin: Gebrüder Paetel, 1874), vol. 1, p. 122. The influence both direct and indirect, through Herder, of James Macpherson and Thomas Percy is also audible in Bürger's ideas.

6. *Werke in einem Band*, edited by Lore Kaim and Siegfried Streller (Weimar: Volks-Verlag, 1962), p. 316. Subsequent references to Bürger's theoretical writings are to this edition and will be given in the text.

7. Klaus L. Berghahn, "Volkstümlichkeit ohne Volk?," in *Popularität und Trivialität*, edited by Reinhold Grimm and Jost Hermand (Frankfurt am Main: Athenäum, 1974), pp. 6off. See also Helga Geyer-Ryan, *Der andere Roman. Versuch über die verdrängte Ästhetik des Populären* (Wilhelmshaven: Heinrichshofen, 1983), pp. 91–98; and Hans-Jürgen Ketzer, " 'Ihr letztes Ziel ist es, daß sie Vergnügen verursachen sollen,' " *Weimarer Beiträge* 33 (1987):1145–58.

8. See Bürger's reiteration of this goal in the preface to the second edition of *Gedichte* (1789), where he discusses how the poet can ensure that everything he wants the reader to see will "spring into the eye of his imagination," that everything he wants the reader to feel will "strike the right chord of his sensibility" (*Werke*, p. 352).

9. "LENORA. A Ballad, from Bürger," translated by William Taylor, *Monthly Magazine* i (March 1796):135–37. Quoted in Jacobus, *Tradition and Experiment in Wordsworth's "Lyrical Ballads,"* pp. 277–83.

10. J. G. Robertson, *A History of German Literature*, 6th ed., edited by Dorothy Reich (Elmsford, N.Y.: London House and Maxwell, 1970), p. 247. According to Bürger's German editors *Lenore* produced a play, a novel, an opera, and an operetta as well as many a painting and illustration; it was set to music by no less than 16 composers, including Franz Liszt; and it was translated into French, Italian, Portuguese, Dutch, Polish, Bulgarian, Russian, and Latin, as well as English, which alone produced at least 30 different translations (Gottfried August Bürger, *Sämtliche Werke*, edited by Günter Häntzschel and Hiltrud Häntzschel [Munich: Carl Hanser, 1987], p. 1214). See also Evelyn B. Jolles, *G. A. Bürgers Ballade "Lenore" in England*.

11. Letter to Boie, May 27, 1773, in *Briefe*, 1, p. 120.

12. Letter to Boie, August 12, 1773, in *Briefe*, 1, p. 132.

13. Letter to Christian Gottlob Heyne, November 1773. Quoted in William Little, *Gottfried August Bürger* (New York: Twayne, 1974), p. 106. Translation Little's.

14. Translation Little's (*Gottfried August Bürger*, p. 72). I have made minor changes.

15. *Schillers Werke*, Nationalausgabe, vol. 22, edited by Herbert Meyer (Weimar: Hermann Böhlaus Nachfolger, 1958), pp. 257–58. Schiller may not have been the first to use the term "occasional poem" [*Gelegenheitsgedicht*] to disparage verse written to accomplish a specific purpose, but he was surely the first to extend the abuse to poems designed to accomplish *any* purpose narrower and more mundane than harmonizing the faculties. See Wulf Segebrecht, *Das Gelegenheitsgedicht: Ein Beitrag zur Geschichte und Poetik der deutschen Lyrik* (Stuttgart: J. B. Metzler, 1977), esp. pp. 283–86.

16. Wolfgang von Wurzbach, *Gottfried August Bürger. Sein Leben und seine Werke* (Leipzig: Dieterich, 1900), pp. 148–49. Cf. Bürger, *Sämtliche Werke*, pp. 1042ff.

17. *Der teutsche Mercur* (July 1778):92f.; quoted in Bürger, *Sämtliche Werke*, pp. 1071–72.

18. Wurzbach, *Gottfried August Bürger*, p. 153. Cf. Bürger, *Sämtliche Werke*, p. 1074.

19. See Hohendahl, *The Institution of Criticism*, pp. 54ff. Of the substantial literature on this decisive moment in German cultural politics, I am indebted especially to Klaus Berghahn, "Volkstümlichkeit ohne Volk?"; Christa Bürger, *Der Ursprung der bürgerlichen Institution Kunst* (Frankfurt am Main: Suhrkamp, 1977), pp. 119–39; Rudolf Dau, "Friedrich Schiller und die Trivialliteratur," *Weimarer Beiträge* 16(9) (1970):162–89; Geyer-Ryan, *Der andere Roman*, pp. 79–98; and Jochen Schulte-Sasse, *Die Kritik an der Trivialliteratur*, esp. pp. 73–81; and for its survey of the literature, Walter Muller-Seidel, "Schillers Kontroverse mit Bürger und ihr geschichtlicher Sinn," *Formenwandel. Festschrift für Paul Böckmann* (Hamburg: Hoffmann und Campe, 1964), pp. 294–318. On the bifurcation of culture that this moment signals, see the works listed above, chapter 1, n. 34.

20. *Schillers Werke*, Nationalausgabe, vol. 20, pt. 1, edited by Benno von Wiese (Weimar: Hermann Böhlaus Nachfolger, 1962), p. 95.

21. Although he at first expressed objections to Moritz—see his letter to Caroline, January 3, 1789 (quoted in part in chapter 1, n. 47)—Schiller appears to have been won over quickly, for within a month of having read Moritz's elaboration in *Über die bildende Nachahmung des Schönen* of the ideas contained in *Versuch*, he writes of Moritz approvingly, calling him "a deep thinker" who "seine Materie scharf anfaßt und tief heraufholt" (Letter to Körner, February 2, 1789, in *Schillers Briefe*, 2, pp. 217–18).

22. *Schillers Werke*, Nationalausgabe, vol. 22, p. 245. Subsequent page references will be given in the text.

23. For the evolution of the almanac, or anthology, the most crucial medium of mass dissemination not only of poetry, but also of stories and essays, see Maria Lanckorónska and Arthur Rümann, *Geschichte der deutschen Taschenbücher und Almanache aus der klassisch-romantischen Zeit* (Munich: E. Heimeran, 1954).

24. For an overview of Schiller's ideas on the revolution, see Karol Sauerland, "Goethes, Schillers, Fr. Schlegels und Novalis' Reaktionen auf die neuen politischen, konstitutionellen und sozialphilosophischen Fragen, die die französische Revolution aufwarf," *Daß eine Nation die ander verstehen möge. Festschrift für Marian Szyrocki*, edited by Norbert Honsza (Amsterdam: Rodopi, 1988), pp. 621–35.

25. For the grammar underlying Schiller's distinctions, see Pierre Bourdieu, *Distinction: A Social Critique of the Judgement of Taste*, translated by Richard Nice (Cambridge, Mass.: Harvard University Press, 1984); and Stallybrass and White, *The Politics and Poetics of Transgression*, pp. 27–124. For their articulation in concrete reading pedagogies, see chapter 4 below.

26. See chapter 2 above.

27. Letter to Huber, December 7, 1784, in *Schillers Briefe*, 1, p. 223.

28. Letter to Körner, June 12, 1788, in *Schillers Briefe*, 2, pp. 76–77. Cagliostro, an Italian swindler who specialized in spiritualism and alchemy, was famous for the scandal he precipitated in 1785 at the French court. Johann August Starck (1741–1816), head preacher at the court of Darmstadt, secretly converted to Catholicism. Nicolas Flamel, a fourteenth-century French alchemist, was reported to have lived until the beginning of the eighteenth century. August Gottlieb Meißner, Christian Garve, Johann Jacob Engel, Friedrich Wilhelm Gotter, and Johann Erich Biester were all respected, middlebrow men of letters in Schiller's day.

29. Rudolf Dau, "Friedrich Schiller und die Trivialliteratur," p. 175.

30. Letter to Körner, June 12, 1788, in *Schillers Briefe*, 2, p. 74. See also his letter to Körner, May 15, 1788, pp. 61–63.

31. Letters to Göschen, November 25, 1792 and April 26, 1799, in *Schillers Briefe*, 3, pp. 229–30; 6, pp. 27–28.

32. It was thus as a fragment that *The Ghostseer* finally appeared in book form in 1789. Having devoted five issues of the *Thalia* to it, Schiller held back the final "farewell" installment to prevent the pirates from beating Göschen to press and depriving him of a profit (Letter to Göschen, June 19, 1788, in *Schillers Briefe*, 2, pp. 79–80).

33. Letter to Körner, January 22, 1789, in *Schillers Briefe*, 2, p. 211. See also pp. 214–15.

34. Letter to Friedrich Unger, July 26, 1800, in *Schillers Briefe*, 6, pp. 178–79.

35. Letter to Körner, January 7, 1788, in *Schillers Briefe*, 2, pp. 2–3.

36. Letter to Körner, March 17, 1788, in *Schillers Briefe*, 2, p. 30.

37. Letter to Körner, January 7, 1788, in *Schillers Briefe*, 2, pp. 2–3.

38. Letter to Baggesen, December 16, 1791, in *Schillers Briefe*, 3, pp. 178–79.

39. For the details, especially the posturing on both sides to avoid the appearance of patronage extended or received, see Klaus-Detlef Müller, "Schiller und das Mäzenat. Zu den Entstehungsbedingungen der 'Briefe über die ästhetische Erziehung des Menschen,'" *Unser Commercium. Goethes und Schillers Literaturpolitik*, edited by Wilfried Barner, Eberhard Lämmert, and Norbert Oellers (Stuttgart: J. G. Cotta, 1984), pp. 151–67, esp. pp. 155ff.

40. "What I have yearned for so ardently all my life is about to come to pass," Schiller writes Körner upon learning of the stipend. "I will [soon] be able to do just as I please, to pay off my debts, and, free of worry about where my next meal will come from, live entirely according to my own mental schemes. For once I will finally have the leisure to learn and to gather and to work for eternity" (December 13, 1791, in *Schillers Briefe*, 3, pp. 174–75).

41. It is at this time that he finally delved into Kant, tackling the *Critique of Judgment* just after he completed the review of Bürger, in the winter of 1791, before daring to attempt the first *Critique* at the end of the year. The *Aesthetic Letters* reflect Kant's influence—indeed, Schiller mentions Kant explicitly at the beginning of them—but the review suggests that he developed the key categories of his aesthetic independently of Kant, finding in the latter the corroboration he needed to efface their material existential foundation.

42. Eagleton, *Ideology of the Aesthetic*, p. 106.

43. Borchmeyer, *Die Weimarer Klassik*, pp. 209–10.

4. Aesthetics and the Policing of Reading

1. *The Spectator* (no. 411), edited by Donald F. Bond (Oxford: Clarendon Press, 1965), vol. 3, pp. 538–39.

2. More specialized guides to connoisseurship like Jonathan Richardson's *Discourse on the Dignity, Certainty, Pleasure and Advantage of the Science of a Connoisseur* (London, 1719) began appearing simultaneously. Such writing belongs to the vast literature of conduct explored in John E. Mason, *Gentlefolk in the Making: Studies in the History of English Courtesy Literature and Related Topics from 1531 to 1774* (Philadelphia: University of Pennsylvania Press, 1935); and Nancy Armstrong and Leonard Tennenhouse, eds., *The Ideology of Conduct* (New York: Methuen, 1987). Some of the literature of connoisseurship is explored in Iain Pears, *The Discovery of Painting. The Growth of Interest in the Arts in England 1680–1768* (New Haven: Yale University Press, 1988). See also Joseph Alsop, *The Rare Art Traditions: The History of Art Collecting and Its Linked Phenomena Wherever These Have Appeared* (Princeton: Princeton University Press, 1982). M. H. Abrams explores its theorization in "Art-as-Such: The Sociology of Modern Aesthetics," *Bulletin of the American Academy of Arts and Sciences* 38(6) (1985):8–33, as does Lawrence Lipking in *The Ordering of the Arts in Eighteenth-Century England* (Princeton: Princeton University Press, 1970). On the organization of leisure time in general, see J. H. Plumb, "The Commercialization of Leisure in Eighteenth-century England," in Neil McKendrick, John Brewer, and J. H. Plumb, *The Birth of a Consumer Society: The Commercialization of Eighteenth-Century England* (Bloomington: Indiana University Press, 1982), pp. 265–85.

3. *The Spectator* (no. 93), vol. 1, p. 397.

4. So, at least, it seemed to contemporary observers; in reality reading was not all that widespread (see chapter 1, p. 24, and p. 154, n. 25). On the reading revolution in Germany, see especially Ward, *Book Production*; Engelsing, "Die Perioden der Lesergeschichte"; and Rolf Engelsing, *Der Bürger als Leser. Lesergeschichte in Deutschland. 1500–1800* (Stuttgart: J. B. Metzler, 1974). Of particular relevance to the present problematic is John A. McCarthy, "The Art of Reading and the Goals of the German Enlightenment," *Lessing Yearbook* 16 (1984):79–94. For the situation in England and America, see Richard D. Altick, *The English Common Reader. A Social History of the Mass Reading Public 1800–1900* (Chicago: University of Chicago Press, 1957), esp. pp. 15–77; Davidson, *Revolution and the Word*, pp. 55–79; and Cathy N. Davidson, ed., *Reading in America* (Baltimore: Johns Hopkins University Press, 1989).

5. For a comprehensive study of the German moral weeklies, see Wolfgang Martens, *Die Botschaft der Tugend. Die Aufklärung im Spiegel der deutschen moralischen Wochenschriften* (Stuttgart: J. B. Metzler, 1968).

6. *Die Kunst, Bücher zu lesen*, pp. 411–12.

7. Of the growing number of studies of this body of writing about

reading, I have profited most from Kreuzer, "Gefährliche Lesesucht?" pp. 62–75. See also Dominik von König, "Lesesucht und Lesewut," in Herbert G. Göpfert, ed., *Buch und Leser* (Hamburg: Ernst Hauswedell, 1977), pp. 89–112; Schulte-Sasse, *Die Kritik an der Trivialliteratur*, pp. 52ff; and Schenda, *Volk ohne Buch*, pp. 40ff.

8. Johann Rudolph Gottlieb Beyer, *Ueber das Bücherlesen, in so fern es zum Luxus unsrer Zeiten gehört.* (Erfurt: Sumtibus Georg. Adam. Keyser, 1796), p. 5. See also Johann Gottfried Hoche, *Vertraute Briefe über die jetzige abentheuerliche Lesesucht und über den Einfluß derselben auf die Verminderung des häuslichen und öffentlichen Glücks* (Hannover: In Commission bei Chr. Ritscher, 1794).

9. In his pioneering study of the catalogs of books to be traded at the semiannual fairs in Leipzig, Rudolf Jentzsch estimates that by 1800 polite literature had captured 21.45 percent of the book market, up from 16.43 percent in 1770 and a mere 5.83 percent in 1740 (*Der deutsch-lateinische Büchermarkt nach den Leipziger Ostermeß-Katalogen von 1740, 1770 und 1800 in seiner Gliederung und Wandlung* [Leipzig: R. Voigtländer, 1912], pp. 241ff. and tables). Cf. Ward, *Book Production*, pp. 29–58, 163–65. On the popular fiction of the period, see Marion Beaujean, *Der Trivialroman in der zweiten Hälfte des 18. Jahrhunderts* (Bonn: H. Bouvier, 1969).

10. The term is Engelsing's. See his distinction between *extensive* and *intensive* modes of reading in "Die Perioden der Lesergeschichte."

11. *Appell an meine Nation über Aufklärung und Aufklärer*, p. 397.

12. Beyer, *Ueber das Bücherlesen*, p. 16. For a fanatical expression of the same ideas, see Heinzmann's chapter on "Folgen aus der heutigen Schriftstellerey" (*Appell an meine Nation über Aufklärung und Aufklärer*, pp. 441–62).

13. Ibid., pp. 296ff.

14. *Ueber das Bücherlesen*, pp. 24ff.

15. *Die Grundzüge des gegenwärtigen Zeitalters* (1804–5), edited by Fritz Medicus (Leipzig: Fritz Meiner, 1908), pp. 99–100.

16. *Die Kunst, Bücher zu lesen*, p. 413. See also Bergk's essay, "Bewirkt die Aufklärung Revolutionen?" in Zwi Batscha, ed., *Aufklärung und Gedankenfreiheit. Fünfzehn Anregungen, aus der Geschichte zu lernen* (Frankfurt am Main: Suhrkamp, 1977), pp. 206–14.

17. *Die Kunst, Bücher zu lesen*, p. 73. Subsequent page references will be given in the text.

18. *On the Aesthetic Education of Man*, p. 33.

19. Ibid., p. 43.

20. It is in opposition to the "treacherous art" of oratory that Kant elaborates his definition of (genuine) poetry as discourse in which

> everything proceeds with honesty and candor. It declares itself to be a mere entertaining play of the imagination, which wishes to proceed as regards form in harmony with the laws of the understanding; and it does not desire to steal upon and ensnare the understanding by the aid of sensible presentation.

Critique of Judgment, translated by J. H. Bernard (New York: Macmillan, 1951), p. 172.

21. For some of the ways in which "philosophical" method is deployed in the *Critique of Judgment* to empower these same aesthetic preferences, and a penetrating analysis of their social implications, see Bourdieu, *Distinction,* pp. 485–500.

22. Bergk associates distinct reading strategies with each different type of writing. See, for example, the strategies of "resistance" he recommends to readers of philosophical works (pp. 338ff.). The term was coined by Mortimer Adler, whose best-seller, *How to Read a Book* (1940, rev. 1967 and 1972) reads like an update of Bergk's *Kunst.*

23. Cf. Fichte's extended analogy between reading and taking narcotics ("Die Grundzüge des gegenwärtigen Zeitalters," pp. 99–100).

24. See chapter 1 above.

25. On the growing effort at this time to impose a reflexive mode of reception on readers, see Schulte-Sasse, "Das Konzept bürgerlich-literarischer Öffentlichkeit und die historischen Gründe seines Zerfalls," in Bürger, Bürger, and Schulte-Sasse, eds., *Aufklärung und literarische Öffentlichkeit,* pp. 108ff.; and Aleida Assmann, "Die Domestikation des Lesens. Drei historische Beispiele," *LiLi* 57/58 (1985):95–110. A penetrating short history of the rise of reading qua interpretation, which focuses on England, is provided by Jane P. Tompkins, "The Reader in History: The Changing Shape of Literary Response," in Jane P. Tompkins, ed., *Reader-Response Criticism: From Formalism to Post-Structuralism* (Baltimore: Johns Hopkins University Press, 1980), pp. 201–32.

26. *Understanding Fiction* (New York: Appleton-Century-Crofts, 1943), p. vii.

27. If the "intensive" mode of reading that Rousseau is advocating had still been as entrenched at the end of the eighteenth century as Robert Darnton has argued (*The Great Cat Massacre* [New York: Basic Books, 1984], esp. pp. 249ff.), then it would be difficult to understand why people like Bergk would have felt compelled to write so vehemently in its defense.

28. In his essay on taste Addison exhibits equal confidence that his readers will make the "right" choices (*The Spectator* [no. 409], vol. 3, pp. 527–31).

29. *The Spectator* (no. 411), vol. 3, p. 538.

30. *The Spectator* (no. 419), vol. 3, pp. 570–73.

5. *Engendering Art*

1. *Geschichte des Fräuleins von Sternheim. Von einer Freundin derselben aus Original-Papieren und andern zuverläßigen Quellen gezogen. Herausgegeben von C. M. Wieland,* 2 vols. (Leipzig: Weidmanns Erben und Reich, 1771). Page references will be to the edition by Barbara Becker-Cantarino (Stuttgart: Reclam, 1983).

2. Two separate English translations appeared in 1776: *The History of Lady Sophia Sternheim,* 2 vols., translated by Joseph Collyer (London: T. Jones); and *Memoirs of Miss Sophy Sternheim,* 2 vols., translated by E[dward] Harwood (London: T. Becket). A new translation by Christa Baguss Britt has recently made the novel available again (*The History of Lady Sophia Sternheim*

[Albany: State University of New York Press, 1991]). For details of the work's publication and reception, see Christine Touaillon, *Der deutsche Frauenroman des 18. Jahrhunderts* (Vienna and Leipzig: Wilhelm Braumüller, 1919) pp. 120–23; and Britt's introduction to her translation, pp. 24–29.

3. See the reactions to the novel collected in the Reclam edition (pp. 363–76). La Roche's female heirs include, to name only a few, Frederike Helene Unger (1751–1813), Elisa von der Recke (1754–1833), Benedikte Naubert (1756–1819), Karoline von Wolzogen (1763–1847), Karoline Wobeser (1769–1807). This women's tradition is the subject of Touaillon's pioneering study, *Der deutsche Frauenroman des 18. Jahrhunderts.* More generally, see the contribution to the recovery of this tradition by Silvia Bovenschen, *Die imaginierte Weiblichkeit* (Frankfurt am Main: Suhrkamp, 1980), esp. pp. 158ff.; and Barbara Becker-Cantarino, *Der lange Weg zur Mündigkeit. Frau und Literatur 1500–1800* (Stuttgart: J. B. Metzler, 1987). Helpful discussions in English may be found in Elke Frederikson, ed., *Women Writers of Germany, Austria, and Switzerland: An Annotated Bio-Bibliographical Guide* (New York: Greenwood Press, 1989), esp. p. xix; and Ward, *Book Production,* pp. 144–45.

4. For an overview of La Roche's life and writings, see the introduction to Britt's translation of *Fräulein von Sternheim* (n. 2 above); Becker-Cantarino, *Der lange Weg zur Mündigkeit,* pp. 278–301; and Jeannine Blackwell, "Sophie von La Roche," in *Dictionary of Literary Biography. German Writers in the Age of Goethe,* edited by James Hardin and Christoph Schweitzer (New York: Bruccoli Clark and Gale, 1991), pp. 154–61.

5. Bergk lists, in this order: Wieland, whom he calls "a true Prometheus among the Germans" (p. 271), Goethe, Thümmel, Müller, Knigge, Musäus, Jean Paul (Richter), Lafontaine, Kotzebue, Spieß, Cramer, Nicolai, Schiller, Fr. Schulz, Langbein, Becker, Sintenis, Hermes, Bouterweck, Starke, Albrecht, Große, Jünger, Jung (Stilling), Klinger, Jacobi, Demme, Huber, Wächter, Wezel, Hippel. (*Die Kunst, Bücher zu lesen,* pp. 270–98). The only woman on the list, [Therese] Huber, Bergk refers to as "he" (p. 295).

6. Bovenschen, *Die imaginierte Weiblichkeit,* p. 197; Becker-Cantarino, "Nachwort," p. 399, and " 'Muse' und 'Kunstrichter,' " p. 582. My discussion of the preface draws heavily on both, and I would not wish this difference in emphasis to obscure that debt.

7. See Lenz's criticism of Wieland's "dumb notes" in the Reclam edition of the novel (p. 372).

8. Becker-Cantarino points out that in their correspondence at the time of the novel's composition Wieland frequently emphasized its utility to women. "Thus is the *Frauenroman* born," she writes. "The work is christened by mentor Wieland and therewith confined to serving the female sex" ("Nachwort," pp. 396–97).

9. Quoted in Sophie von La Roche, *Mein Schreibtisch* (Leipzig: Heinrich Gräff, 1799), pp. 300–2.

10. This occurs later in England. In Clara Reeve's history of the novel, *The Progress of Romance* (1785), women writers still abound, even overshadowing the (now canonical) men. The story of their disappearance—and indeed, of Reeve's—from the history of the novel has yet to be told.

11. Letter to La Roche, April 3, 1805, in *C. M. Wielands Briefe an Sophie von La Roche*, edited by Franz Horn (Berlin: Christiani, 1820), pp. 329–30. Quoted in Becker-Cantarino, " 'Muse' und 'Kunstrichter,' " p. 575.

6. The Uses of Kant in England

1. See chapter 3, p. 60 above.

2. For Bürger's influence on the *Lyrical Ballads*, see Parrish, *The Art of the "Lyrical Ballads"*; Jacobus, *Tradition and Experiment in Wordsworth's "Lyrical Ballads"*; James H. Averill, *Wordsworth and the Poetry of Human Suffering* (Ithaca: Cornell University Press, 1980); John K. Primeau, "The Influence of Gottfried August Bürger on the *Lyrical Ballads* of William Wordsworth: The Supernatural vs. the Natural," *Germanic Review* 58 (1983):89–96; Andrew Nicholson, "*Kubla Khan*: The Influence of Bürger's *Lenore*," *English Studies* 64 (1983):291–95.

3. Wordsworth, *Literary Criticism*, p. 10.

4. Echoes of Taylor's notice may also be heard in Wordsworth's statement in the *Preface* to the second edition of the *Lyrical Ballads* that his object in the volume had been to fit "to metrical arrangement a selection of the real language of men in a state of vivid sensation" (pp. 15–16).

5. Given as the Karl Reinhard edition in 2 vols. (Göttingen, 1796) in *The Letters of William and Dorothy Wordsworth. The Early Years. 1787–1805*, edited by Ernest de Selincourt, revised by Chester L. Shaver (Oxford: Clarendon, 1967), p. 234*n*.

6. Letter to Mrs. Samuel Taylor Coleridge, November 8, 1798 in *Collected Letters of Samuel Taylor Coleridge*, edited by Earl Leslie Griggs (Oxford: Clarendon Press, 1956), I, p. 438. For his (and Wordsworth's) observations on other German writers of the period and on German life and customs in general, see "Satyrane's Letters" in Coleridge's *Biographia Literaria* in *Collected Works of Samuel Taylor Coleridge*, vol. 7, edited by James Engell and W. Jackson Bate (Princeton: Princeton University Press, 1983), pp. 160–206.

7. *The Letters of William and Dorothy Wordsworth: The Early Years*, pp. 233–235.

8. On the "similarity of thought between Schiller and Wordsworth," cf. L. A. Willoughby, "Wordsworth and Germany," *German Studies. Festschrift for H. G. Fiedler* (Oxford: Clarendon, 1938), pp. 443–45. Willoughby's suggestive remarks are not reflected in the scholarship on Wordsworth.

9. "Über Bürgers Gedichte," *Schillers Werke*, 22, p. 257.

10. Cf. Marilyn Butler's interpretation of Wordsworth's project in the *Preface*, in *Romantics, Rebels, and Reactionaries. English Literature and Its Backgound 1760–1830* (New York: Oxford University Press, 1982), pp. 57ff. More consonant with my own reading is Jon P. Klancher's study, *The Making of English Reading Audiences 1790–1832* (Madison: University of Wisconsin Press, 1987), esp. pp. 137–50.

11. Hence the motto Wordsworth placed on the title page of the second edition of the *Lyrical Ballads*: "Quam nihil ad genium, Papiniane, tuum!" which, as "freely" translated by Mary Moorman, asserts: "How absolutely *not*

after your liking, O learned jurist!" (Mary Moorman, *William Wordsworth: A Biography. The Early Years* [Oxford: Clarendon Press, 1957], p. 501).

12. On the conformity of the *Lyrical Ballads* to the "magazine poetry" of the 1790s, see Robert Mayo's pioneering study, "The Contemporaneity of the *Lyrical Ballads*," *Publications of the Modern Language Association* 69 (1954):486–522. Cf. also James H. Averill, *Wordsworth and the Poetry of Human Suffering.*

13. So striking a parallel must raise the question of a direct influence. In his isolation in Goslar in the winter of 1798–99 Wordsworth is not likely to have come across the *Allgemeine Literatur-Zeitung* for 1791 that contained Schiller's review, and the review did not appear in book form until 1802; but Coleridge probably read it (see the echoes of this same passage by Schiller near the beginning of chap. 15 of the *Biographia Literaria;* cf. also Samuel Taylor Coleridge, *The Notebooks,* edited by Kathleen Coburn [London: Routledge and Kegan Paul, 1957], I, entry 787 and *n,* and Appendix A [p. 453]), and Coleridge had a large hand in the conception, if not the composition, of the *Preface.* See his remark to Southey (July 29, 1802) that it "is half a child of my own brain, and arose out of conversations so frequent that, with few exceptions, we could scarcely either of us, perhaps, positively say which first started any particular thought" (Moorman, *William Wordsworth,* I, pp. 492–93).

14. See Wordsworth's account to Coleridge of his conversation with Klopstock during his stay in Hamburg in 1798: "We talked of tragedy. He [Klopstock] seemed to rate highly the power of exciting tears—I said that nothing was more easy than to deluge an audience, that it was done every day by the meanest writers" (Coleridge, "Satyrane's Letters," in *Biographia Literaria,* p. 205). On this impulse in Wordsworth, see also Stallybrass and White, *The Politics and Poetics of Transgression,* pp. 119–24.

15. Stephen Gill believes that Wordsworth may have been forced to draw this distinction so crucial to his poetic by his failure to get his tragedy *The Borderers* staged in 1797 (*William Wordsworth. A Life* [Oxford: Clarendon, 1989], p. 132). He points to Coleridge's letter to Wordsworth in January 1798 about the commercially successful *Castle Spectre* by Monk Lewis: "This Play proves how accurately you [Wordsworth] conjectured concerning *theatric* merit. The merit of the Castle Spectre consists wholly in it's *situations.* These are all borrowed, and all absolutely *pantomimical*; but they are admirably managed for stage effect" (*Collected Letters,* I, p. 379).

16. On Coleridge's construction of the reader, see Robert DeMaria, Jr., "The Ideal Reader: A Critical Fiction," *Publications of the Modern Language Association* 93 (1978):463–74; John R. Nabholtz, "Coleridge and the Reader," *"My Reader My Fellow-Labourer": A Study of English Romantic Prose* (Columbia: University of Missouri Press, 1986), pp. 97–128; Klancher, *The Making of English Reading Audiences,* esp. pp. 150–70; and Deirdre Coleman, *Coleridge and "The Friend" (1809–1810)* (Oxford: Clarendon Press, 1988), pp. 50–62.

17. Page references are to the Shawcross edition included in S. T. Coleridge, *Biographia Literaria,* edited by J. Shawcross (London: Oxford University Press, 1907), II, pp. 219–46, which unfortunately deviates from the text originally published in *Felix Farley's Bristol Journal* not only in matters of punctuation, capitalization, and italicization, but, as John R. Nabholtz has

shown, by misplacing material in the third essay ("The Text of Coleridge's *Essays on the Principles of Genial Criticism,*" *Modern Philology* 85 [1987]: 187–92).

18. For his most substantial thefts, see in addition to the notes in Shaw-cross's edition of the text (n. 17, above), pp. 304–15: René Wellek, *Immanuel Kant in England 1793–1838* (Princeton: Princeton University Press, 1931), pp. 111–14. In his edition Walter Jackson Bate is as circumspect as Coleridge, who, though he mentions other precedents by name in the essays, suppresses *any* mention of Kant (*Criticism: The Major Texts*, enlarged ed. [New York: Harcourt, Brace, Jovanovich, 1970], pp. 364–75). At the opposite end of the spectrum from the anxiety of influence that Bate shares with his hero is the moral outrage that seems to have inspired Norman Fruman's biography, *Coleridge, the Damaged Archangel* (New York: George Braziller, 1971). His stern condemnation is of course no less a product than Bate's adulation of the modern ideology of authorship explored in chapter 2, above. Coleridge's plagiarism merits restudy in this light.

19. Letter to Daniel Stuart, September 12, 1814, in *Collected Letters*, III, p. 534. Founded in 1752, the *Bristol Journal* was one of four weeklies in that city (population 75,000 compared with London's 120,000, according to the 1811 census). See John Evans, *The History of Bristol, Civil and Ecclesiastical; including Biographical Notices of Eminent and Distinguished Natives* (Bristol: W. Sheppard, 1816).

20. Letter to Daniel Stuart, September 12, 1814, in *Collected Letters*, III, p. 535.

21. Nabholtz, "Coleridge's *Essays on the Principles,*" p. 188, n. 1.

22. Letter to Daniel Stuart, September 12, 1814, in *Collected Letters*, III, p. 535. Kant had asserted at the very beginning of the *Critique of Judgment* that as taste is "the faculty of judging of the beautiful," if we wish to understand taste, we must first investigate "what is required in order to call an object beautiful" (p. 37, n. 1).

23. *Principles* thus belongs to the project Coleridge had undertaken so unsuccessfully in his periodical, *The Friend* (1809–10), of "referring Men in all things to PRINCIPLES or fundamental Truths." This had necessitated his placing "all the driest and least attractive Essays" at the beginning, Coleridge rationalizes (in an elaborate "apology" in no. 11 designed to stem the cancellation of subscriptions), just where he ought to have been "se-cur[ing] the confidence of [his] Readers by winning their favour" (*The Friend*, edited by Barbara E. Rooke [Princeton: Princeton University Press, 1969], II, pp. 149–53).

24. E. H. Gombrich, *The Story of Art*, 13th ed. (Oxford: Phaidon Press, 1978), pp. 240–45.

25. For a thorough investigation of Coleridge's "prosaics of deferral," see Jerome Christensen, "The Method of *The Friend,*" in *Coleridge's Blessed Machine of Language* (Ithaca: Cornell University Press, 1981), pp. 186–270.

26. Addison, *The Spectator* (no. 417), vol. 3, p. 562.

27. R. S. Peters and C. A. Mace, "Psychology," *Encyclopedia of Philosophy*, vol. 7 (New York: Macmillan, 1967), pp. 15–16.

28. For an overview of the critical deployment of associationism, see

Martin Kallich, "The Association of Ideas and Critical Theory: Hobbes, Locke, and Addison," *English Literary History* 12 (1945):290–315. Or see his comprehensive treatment, *The Association of Ideas and Critical Theory in Eighteenth-Century England* (The Hague: Mouton, 1970). On Alison, see also his "The Meaning of Archibald Alison's *Essays on Taste*," *Philological Quarterly* 27 (1948):314–24; and Walter John Hipple, Jr., *The Beautiful, the Sublime, and the Picturesque in Eighteenth-Century British Aesthetic Theory* (Carbondale: Southern Illinois University Press, 1957), pp. 158–81.

29. Francis Jeffrey, "*The Excursion, being a portion of the Recluse, a Poem.* By William Wordsworth," *Edinburgh Review* 47 (November 1814):1.

30. Letter to Archibald Alison, July 29, 1808, as quoted by Willi Real, *Untersuchungen zu Archibald Alisons Theorie des Geschmacks* (Frankfurt am Main: Akademische Verlagsgesellschaft, 1973), p. 161.

31. While the first edition of 1790 sold slowly, the second edition of 1811, according to Kallich, was followed up by four more Edinburgh editions, in 1812, 1815, 1817, and 1825, with many cheap reprints being issued in other literary centers in England and America until 1879 ("The Meaning of Archibald Alison's *Essays on Taste*," pp. 314–15).

32. Archibald Alison, *Essays on the Nature and Principles of Taste* (New York: Harper and Bros., 1860), pp. 20–21. Subsequent page references will be given in the text.

33. Francis Jeffrey, "*Essays on the Nature and Principles of Taste.* By Archibald Alison," *Edinburgh Review* 35 (May 1811):10. Subsequent page references will be given in the text.

34. See Stanley Fish's reformulation for our own times of this crucial insight into the nature of interpretation in "Interpreting the Variorum," *Is There a Text in This Class?* (Cambridge, Mass.: Harvard University Press, 1980), pp. 171–73.

35. John Clive, *Scotch Reviewers. The Edinburgh Review 1802–1815* (Cambridge, Mass.: Harvard University Press, 1957).

36. René Wellek, *A History of Modern Criticism 1750–1950,* II (New Haven: Yale University Press, 1955), p. 114.

37. Ideas that exerted as much authority as Alison/Jeffrey's for so long merit more scholarly attention than they have received since the Coleridgean perspective achieved hegemony. For a penetrating assessment of some of the consequences of this partiality, see Norman Fruman's review of the recent Princeton edition by James Engell and W. Jackson Bate of the *Biographia Literaria:* "Review Essay: Aids to Reflection on the New *Biographia,*" *Studies in Romanticism* 24 (1985):141–73. A useful survey of the scholarly "sides" taken in the struggle between Coleridge and Jeffrey may be found in Clive, *Scotch Reviewers,* pp. 151–65. The "facts" of the controversy may be found in David V. Erdman and Paul M. Zall, "Coleridge and Jeffrey in Controversy," *Studies in Romanticism* 14 (1975):75–83.

38. On the earlier opposition of Burke, Usher, and Reid to the associationist model, see Martin Kallich, "The Argument against the Association of Ideas in Eighteenth-Century Aesthetics," *Modern Language Quarterly* 15 (1954):125–36.

39. Jeffrey considers the huge differences in ideals of female beauty an especially strong argument for the associationist model: "Think what different and inconsistent standards would be fixed for [female beauty] in the different regions of the world;—in Africa, in Asia, and in Europe;—in Tartary and in Greece;—in Lapland, Patagonia and Circassia. If there was any thing absolutely or intrinsically beautiful, in any of the forms thus distinguished, it is inconceivable that men should differ so outrageously in their conceptions of it. . . . [I]f it were actually and inseparably attached to certain forms, colours or proportions, it must appear utterly inexplicable that it should be felt and perceived in the most opposite forms and proportions, in objects of the same description. On the other hand, if all beauty consist in reminding us of certain natural sympathies and objects of emotion, with which they have been habitually connected, it is easy to perceive how the most different forms should be felt to be equally beautiful" (p. 18).

40. Coleridge continues in an equally Kantian vein: "The BEAUTIFUL is thus at once distinguished both from the AGREEABLE, which is beneath it, and from the GOOD, which is above it: for both these have an interest necessarily attached to them: both act on the WILL, and excite a desire for the actual existence of the image or idea contemplated: while the sense of beauty rests gratified in the mere contemplation or intuition, regardless whether it be a fictitious Apollo, or a real Antinous" (p. 239).

41. Nabholtz's illuminating observations on *Principles* ("My Reader My Fellow-Labourer," pp. 119–28) are flawed by his assumption that the work's every detail somehow furthers Coleridge's project of teaching readers to read "actively" by continuously erecting nearly insurmountable barriers to their understanding him (by means of the "passive" reading habits they have acquired reading novels, newspapers, and magazines). Such "no-fault" reading of the master afflicts Coleridgeans more than it did Coleridge.

42. *Bristol Gazette*, September 1, 1814. I wish to thank Marie Mulvey Roberts for locating this letter for me.

43. Coleridge's response to his critic "Cosmo," published in the *Bristol Journal* for September 10, 1814, merits quoting in this context because it is so characteristic of his way of dealing with criticism. Rather than adjust his pedagogy, he tends to become defensive and to retaliate either by showering abuse on his critics or by diverting their attention through a humorous display of erudition—or both simultaneously, as here, where he identifies the author of the criticism as probably just an "ambitious Sign-painter," and then unleashes a stream of insult that concludes:

> In short, till this Nauseist of "mere mechanic ingenuity" shall have proved himself capable of writing three periods consecutively without some offence against either Grammar, Logic, History or good Manners; I must content myself by admonishing him, Nil, nisi lignum, oblinire; which may be interpreted, keep to thy own Ladder Friend! (on which Hogarth in his Beer Street has immortalized one of thy Predecessors) and pray Heaven to preserve thee from Envy, Hatred, Uncharitableness and all the vices, that might finally translate thee to a far less honourable one.

(To the Editor of "Felix Farley's Bristol Journal," September 10, 1814, in *Collected Letters,* III, pp. 526–27).

44. Coleridge's translation, as included in the sixth chapter of *Biographia Literaria (Collected Works,* vol. 7, pp. 114–15).

45. See his remark to Humphry Davy: "I do not write in this Work for the *Multitude*; but for those, who by Rank, or Fortune, or official Situation, or Talents and Habits of Reflection, are to *influence* the Multitude." It is noteworthy that when he goes on to characterize his project in *The Friend*—"I write to found true PRINCIPLES, to oppose false PRINCIPLES, in Criticism, Legislation, Philosophy, Morals, and International Law"—it is in opposition to the project he associates with periodicals like Jeffrey's *Edinburgh Review*: "But of English Readers three fourths are led to purchase periodical works in the expectation of gratifying these passions [above all, curiosity]—even periodical works professedly literary—of which the keen Interest excited by the Edingburgh [sic] Review and it's wide circulation, yield a proof as striking, as it is dishonorable to the moral Taste of the present Public. All these Readers *I* give up all claim to" (December 14, 1808, *Collected Letters,* III p. 143).

46. See no. 11 of *The Friend,* edited by Rooke, II, p. 150.

47. See no. 1 of *The Friend,* edited by Rooke, II, p. 5.

48. Letter to Thomas Poole, January 28, 1810, in *Collected Letters,* III, p. 281. Coleridge goes on to promise "preparatory to writing on any chosen Subject [to] consider whether it *can* be treated popularly, and with that lightness & variety of illustration which form the charm of the Spectator." But note his resolve unraveling as he continues:

> If not, next whether yet there may not be furnished by the *results* of such an Essay Thoughts & Truths that may be so treated, & form a second Essay—3rdly. I shall always, *besides* this, have at least one No. in 4, of rational entertainment, such as were Satyrane's Letters: as instructive as I can, but yet making entertainment the chief Object in my own mind—. But lastly, in the Supplement of the Friend I shall endeavor to include whatever of higher & more abstruse meditation may be needed as the foundations of all the Work after it—and the difference between those, who will read & master that Supplement, & those who decline the toil, will be simply this—that what to the former will be *demonstrated Conclusions,* the latter must start from as from *Postulates* and (to all whose minds have not been sophisticated by a Half Philosophy) *Axioms.*

By the end of his promise Coleridge's resolve has succumbed completely to the impulse to pursue metaphysics.

49. See n. 45, above.

50. Letter to Richard Sharp, September 27, 1808, in *The Letters of William and Dorothy Wordsworth. The Middle Years,* p. 242.

51. Ibid., p. 242.

52. See also the sonnets this episode inspired: "A Plea for Authors, May 1838" and "A Poet to His Grandchild. Sequel to 'A Plea for Authors.'" For

the details of Wordsworth's involvement, see the introduction by W. J. B. Owen to Wordsworth's writings on copyright in *The Prose Works of William Wordsworth,* edited by W. J. B. Owen, vol. 3 (Oxford: Clarendon Press, 1974), pp. 303–6. See also Paul M. Zall, "Wordsworth and the Copyright Act of 1842," *Publications of the Modern Language Association* 70 (1955):132–44; Mary Moorman, *William Wordsworth: A Biography. The Later Years* (Oxford: Clarendon Press, 1965), pp. 550–55; and Richard G. Swartz, "Patrimony and the Figuration of Authorship in the Eighteenth-Century Property Debates," *Works and Days* 7(2) (1989):29–54.

53. *The Kendal Mercury,* April 14, 1838. In *The Prose Works of William Wordsworth,* vol. 3, p. 312.

54. *The Prose Works of William Wordsworth,* vol. 3, p. 318.

55. *The Statutes of the United Kingdom of Great Britain and Ireland, 5 & 6 Victoria,* 1842, Cap. 45 (London: Her Majesty's Printers, 1842), pp. 404–5.

WORKS CITED

Abrams, M. H. *The Mirror and the Lamp.* Oxford: Oxford University Press, 1953.
———. *Natural Supernaturalism.* New York: W. W. Norton, 1971.
———. "Kant and the Theology of Art." *Notre Dame English Journal* 13:75–106, 1981.
———. "Art-as-Such: The Sociology of Modern Aesthetics." *Bulletin of the American Academy of Arts and Sciences* 38(6):8–33, 1985.
Addison, Joseph. "The Pleasures of the Imagination." In Joseph Addison and Richard Steele, *The Spectator,* vol. 3. Edited by Donald F. Bond. Oxford: Clarendon Press, 1965.
Adler, Mortimer J. *How to Read a Book.* Rev. ed. New York: Simon and Schuster, 1972.
Alison, Archibald. *Essays on the Nature and Principles of Taste.* New York: Harper and Bros., 1860.
Alsop, Joseph. *The Rare Art Traditions: The History of Art Collecting and Its Linked Phenomena Wherever These Have Appeared.* Princeton: Princeton University Press, 1982.
Altick, Richard D. *The English Common Reader. A Social History of the Mass Reading Public 1800–1900.* Chicago: University of Chicago Press, 1957.
Arac, Jonathan. *Critical Genealogies: Historical Situations for Postmodern Literary Studies.* New York: Columbia University Press, 1987.
Armstrong, Nancy, and Leonard Tennenhouse, eds. *The Ideology of Conduct.* New York: Methuen, 1987.
Assmann, Aleida. "Die Domestikation des Lesens. Drei historische Bei-

spiele." *LiLi. Zeitschrift für Literaturwissenschaft und Linguistik* 57/58:95–110, 1985.

Averill, James, H. *Wordsworth and the Poetry of Human Suffering.* Ithaca: Cornell University Press, 1980.

Barthes, Roland. "The Death of the Author." In *Image-Music-Text.* Edited and translated by Stephen Heath. New York: Hill and Wang, 1977.

Battersby, Christine. *Gender and Genius.* Bloomington: Indiana University Press, 1989.

Batteux, Charles. *Einschränkung der schönen Künste auf einen einzigen Grundsatz.* Translated from the French by Johann Adolf Schlegel. Leipzig: Weidmann, 1751.

———. *Die schönen Künste aus einem Grunde hergeleitet.* Translated from the French by P. E. B[ertram]. Gotha: J. P. Mevius, 1751.

———. *A Course of the Belles Lettres; or, The Principles of Literature.* Translated by John Miller. London: B. Law, 1761.

———. *Les beaux arts réduits à un même principe.* In *Principes de la littérature,* vol. 1. Göttingen and Leyden, 1764.

Baumgarten, Alexander Gottlieb. "Meditationes philosophicae de nonnullis ad poema pertinentibus." Master's Thesis, 1735; reprinted as *Reflections on Poetry.* Translated by Karl Aschenbrenner and William B. Holther. Berkeley: University of California Press, 1954.

———. *Aesthetica.* Frankfurt, 1750; reprinted Hildesheim: G. Olms, 1961.

Beardsley, Monroe. *Aesthetics from Classical Greece to the Present: A Short History.* Birmingham: University of Alabama Press, 1966.

Beaujean, Marion. *Der Trivialroman in der zweiten Hälfte des 18. Jahrhunderts.* Bonn: H. Bouvier, 1969.

Becker, Rudolf Zacharias. *Das Eigenthumsrecht an Geisteswerken, mit einer dreyfachen Beschwerde über das Bischöflich-Augsburgische Vikariat wegen Nachdruck, Verstümmelung und Verfälschung des Noth- und Hülfsbüchleins.* Frankfurt and Leipzig, 1789.

Becker-Cantarino, Barbara. " 'Muse' und 'Kunstrichter': Sophie La Roche und Wieland." *Modern Language Notes* 99:571–88, 1984.

———. *Der lange Weg zur Mündigkeit. Frau und Literatur 1500–1800.* Stuttgart: J. B. Metzler, 1987.

Berghahn, Klaus L. "Volkstümlichkeit ohne Volk?" In Reinhold Grimm and Jost Hermand, eds., *Popularität und Trivialität.* Frankfurt am Main: Athenäum, 1974.

Bergk, Johann Adam. *Die Kunst, Bücher zu lesen. Nebst Bermerkungen über Schriften und Schriftsteller.* Jena: In der Hempelschen Buchhandlung, 1799.

———. "Bewirkt die Aufklärung Revolutionen?" In Zwi Batscha, ed., *Aufklärung und Gedankenfreiheit. Fünfzehn Anregungen, aus der Geschichte zu lernen.* Frankfurt am Main: Suhrkamp, 1977.

Berleant, Arnold. "The Historicity of Aesthetics." *British Journal of Aesthetics* 26:101–11, 195–203, 1986.

Beyer, Johann Rudolph Gottlieb. *Ueber das Bücherlesen, in so fern es zum Luxus unsrer Zeiten gehört.* Erfurt: Sumtibus Georg. Adam. Keyser, 1796.

Blackwell, Jeannine. "Sophie von La Roche." In James Hardin and Christoph

Schweitzer, eds., *Dictionary of Literary Biography. German Writers in the Age of Goethe.* New York: Bruccoli Clark and Gale, 1991.

Borchmeyer, Dieter. *Die Weimarer Klassik.* Königstein/Ts.: Athenäum, 1980.

Borges, Jorge Luis. "The Analytical Knowledge of John Wilkins." In *Other Inquisitions, 1937–1952.* New York: Simon and Schuster, 1964.

Bosse, Heinrich. *Autorschaft ist Werkherrschaft.* Paderborn: Ferdinand Schöningh, 1981.

Boulby, Mark. *Karl Philipp Moritz: At the Fringe of Genius.* Toronto: University of Toronto Press, 1979.

Bourdieu, Pierre. *Distinction: A Social Critique of the Judgement of Taste.* Translated by Richard Nice. Cambridge, Mass.: Harvard University Press, 1984.

Bovenschen, Silvia. *Die imaginierte Weiblichkeit.* Frankfurt am Main: Suhrkamp, 1980.

Brantlinger, Patrick. *Bread and Circuses: Theories of Mass Culture as Social Decay.* Ithaca: Cornell University Press, 1983.

Brauer, Johann Nikolaus Friedrich. *Erläuterungen über den Code Napoléon und die Großherzoglich Badische bürgerliche Gesetzgebung,* vol. 1. Karlsruhe, 1809.

Brooks, Cleanth, and Robert Penn Warren. *Understanding Poetry.* New York: H. Holt, 1938.

———. *Understanding Fiction.* New York: Appleton-Century-Crofts, 1943.

Bruford, W. H. *Germany in the Eighteenth Century: The Social Background of the Literary Revival.* Cambridge: Cambridge University Press, 1935.

Bürger, Christa. *Der Ursprung der bürgerlichen Institution Kunst.* Frankfurt am Main: Suhrkamp, 1977.

Bürger, Christa, Peter Bürger, and Jochen Schulte-Sasse, eds. *Aufklärung und literarische Öffentlichkeit.* Frankfurt am Main: Suhrkamp, 1980.

———, eds. *Zur Dichotomisierung von hoher und niederer Literatur.* Frankfurt am Main: Suhrkamp, 1982.

Bürger, Gottfried August. *Gedichte.* Göttingen: J. C. Dieterich, 1778; 2d ed., 1789.

———. "*Lenora.* A Ballad, from Bürger." Translated by William Taylor. *Monthly Magazine* i: 136–37, March 1796.

———. *Briefe von und an Gottfried August Bürger,* 4 vols. Edited by Adolf Strodtmann. Berlin: Gebrüder Paetel, 1874.

———. "Herzens-Ausguß über Volks-Poesie." Part 2 of "Aus Daniel Wunderlichs Buch." In *Werke in einem Band.* Edited by Lore Kaim and Siegfried Streller. Weimar: Volks-Verlag, 1962.

———."Vorschlag dem Büchernachdrucke zu steuern." In *Sämtliche Werke.* Edited by Günter Häntzschel and Hiltrud Häntzschel. Munich: Carl Hanser, 1987.

Butler, Marilyn. *Romantics, Rebels, and Reactionaries. English Literature and Its Background 1760–1830.* New York: Oxford University Press, 1982.

Campe, Joachim Heinrich. "An Joseph den Einzigen." *Deutsches Museum* (February):101–4, 1784.

———. *Moritz. Ein abgenöthigter trauriger Beitrag zur Erfahrungsseelenkunde.* Braunschweig: Im Verlage der Schulbuchhandlung, 1789.

Cella, Johann Jakob. "Vom Büchernachdruck." In *Freymüthige Aufsätze*, vol. 1. Anspach: B. F. Haueisen, 1784.

Christensen, Jerome. *Coleridge's Blessed Machine of Language*. Ithaca: Cornell University Press, 1981.

Clive, John. *Scotch Reviewers. The Edinburgh Review 1802–1815*. Cambridge, Mass.: Harvard University Press, 1957.

Coleman, Deirdre. *Coleridge and "The Friend" (1809–1810)*. Oxford: Clarendon Press, 1988.

Collins, Jim. *Uncommon Cultures: Popular Culture and Post-Modernism*. New York: Routledge, 1989.

Coleridge, Samuel Taylor. "On the Principles of Genial Criticism Concerning the Fine Arts, More Especially Those of Statuary and Painting, Deduced from the Laws and Impulses Which Guide the True Artist in the Production of His Works." In *Biographia Literaria*, vol. 2. Edited by John Shawcross. Oxford: Oxford University Press, 1907.

———. *Collected Letters of Samuel Taylor Coleridge*. 6 vols. Edited by Earl Leslie Griggs. Oxford: Clarendon Press, 1956–71.

———. *The Notebooks of Samuel Taylor Coleridge*. Edited by Kathleen Coburn. Vol. 1, London: Routledge, 1957; vol. 2, New York: Pantheon, 1961; vol. 3, Princeton: Princeton University Press, 1973.

———. *The Friend*. Edited by Barbara E. Rooke. In *The Collected Works of Samuel Taylor Coleridge*, vol. 4. Princeton: Princeton University Press, 1969.

———. "On the Principles of Genial Criticism Concerning the Fine Arts." In Walter Jackson Bate, ed., *Criticism. The Major Texts*, enlarged ed. New York: Harcourt, Brace, Jovanovich, 1970.

———. *Biographia Literaria*. Edited by James Engell and W. Jackson Bate. In *The Collected Works of Samuel Tayler Coleridge*, vol. 7. Princeton: Princeton University Press, 1983.

Cosmo [pseud.] "To the Editor of the Bristol Gazette." *Bristol Gazette* (September 1, 1814).

Cross, Nigel. *The Common Writer: Life in Nineteenth-Century Grub Street*. Cambridge: Cambridge University Press, 1985.

Danto, Arthur. "The Artworld." *Journal of Philosophy* 61:571–84, 1964.

Darnton, Robert. *The Great Cat Massacre*. New York: Basic Books, 1984.

Dau, Rudolf. "Friedrich Schiller und die Trivialliteratur." *Weimarer Beiträge* 16(9):162–89, 1970.

Dauber, Kenneth. *The Idea of Authorship in America: Democratic Poetics from Franklin to Melville*. Madison: University of Wisconsin Press, 1990.

Davidson, Cathy N. *Revolution and the Word: The Rise of the Novel in America*. New York: Oxford University Press, 1986.

———, ed. *Reading in America*. Baltimore: Johns Hopkins University Press, 1989.

DeMaria, Robert, Jr. "The Ideal Reader: A Critical Fiction." *Publications of the Modern Language Association* 93: 463–74, 1978.

Derrida, Jacques. "Economimesis." *Diacritics* 11:3–25, 1981.

Eagleton, Terry. *The Function of Criticism: From the Spectator to Post-Structuralism*. London: Verso, 1984.

———. *The Ideology of the Aesthetic.* Oxford: Basil Blackwell, 1990.

Ehlers, Martin. *Ueber die Unzulässigkeit des Büchernachdrucks nach dem natürlichen Zwangsrecht.* Dessau and Leipzig, 1784.

Eisenlohr, Ch. F. M. *Das literarisch-artistische Eigentum und Verlagsrecht mit Rücksicht auf die Gesetzgebungen.* Schwerin: F. W. Bärensprung, 1855.

———, ed. *Sammlung der Gesetze und internationalen Verträge zum Schutze des literarisch-artistischen Eigenthums in Deutschland, Frankreich und England.* Heidelberg: Bangel and Schmitt, 1856.

Engelsing, Rolf. "Die Perioden der Lesergeschichte in der Neuzeit." *Archiv für Geschichte des Buchwesens* 10:cols. 945–1002, 1970.

———. *Der Bürger als Leser. Lesergeschichte in Deutschland. 1500–1800.* Stuttgart: J. B. Metzler, 1974.

Erdman, David V., and Paul M. Zall. "Coleridge and Jeffrey in Controversy." *Studies in Romanticism* 14:75–83, 1975.

Evans, John. *The History of Bristol, Civil and Ecclesiastical; including Biographical Notices of Eminent and Distinguished Natives.* 2 vols. Bristol: W. Sheppard, 1816.

Eybisch, Hugo. *Anton Reiser. Untersuchungen zur Lebensgeschichte von K. Ph. Moritz und zur Kritik seiner Autobiographie.* Leipzig: R. Voigtländer, 1909.

Feder, Johann Georg. "Neuer Versuch einer einleuchtenden Darstellung der Gründe für das Eigenthum des Bücherverlags, nach Grundsätzen des natürlichen Rechts und der Staatsklugheit." *Göttingisches Magazin der Wissenschaften und Litteratur* 1(1):1–37; 1(3):220–42; 1(3):459–66, 1780.

Fichte, Johann Gottlieb. "Beweis der Unrechtmässigkeit des Büchernachdrucks. Ein Räsonnement und eine Parabel." In *Sämtliche Werke*, vol. 3, pt. 3. Edited by J. H. Fichte. Leipzig: Mayer and Müller, n.d.

———. *Die Grundzüge des gegenwärtigen Zeitalters.* Edited by Fritz Medicus. Leipzig: Fritz Meiner, 1908.

Fish, Stanley. *Is There a Text in This Class? The Authority of Interpretive Communities.* Cambridge, Mass.: Harvard University Press, 1980.

Fontius, Martin. "Produktivkraftentfaltung und Autonomie der Kunst: Zur Ablösung ständischer Voraussetzungen in der Literaturtheorie." In Günther Klotz, Winfried Schröder, and Peter Weber, eds., *Literatur im Epochenumbruch.* Berlin: Aufbau, 1977.

Foucault, Michel. "What Is an Author?" In Josué V. Harari, ed., *Textual Strategies: Perspectives in Post-Structuralist Criticism.* Ithaca: Cornell University Press, 1979.

Frederikson, Elke, ed. *Women Writers of Germany, Austria, and Switzerland: An Annotated Bio-Bibliographical Guide.* New York: Greenwood Press, 1989.

Fruman, Norman. *Coleridge, the Damaged Archangel.* New York: George Braziller, 1971.

———. "Review Essay: Aids to Reflection on the New *Biographia.*" *Studies in Romanticism* 24:141–73, 1985.

Geyer-Ryan, Helga. *Der andere Roman. Versuch über die verdrängte Ästhetik des Populären.* Wilhelmshaven: Heinrichshofen, 1983.

Gieseke, Ludwig. *Die geschichtliche Entwicklung des deutschen Urheberrechts.* Göttingen: Otto Schwartz, 1957.

Gilbert, Sandra M., and Susan Gubar. *The Madwoman in the Attic.* New Haven: Yale University Press, 1979.

Gill, Stephen. *William Wordsworth. A Life.* Oxford: Clarendon Press, 1989.

Goethe, Johann Wolfgang. "Die schönen Künste in ihrem Ursprung, ihrer wahren Natur und besten Anwendung, betrachtet von J. G. Sulzer." In *Goethes Sämtliche Werke.* Jubiläums-Ausgabe in 40 Bänden, vol. 33. Edited by Eduard von der Hellen. Stuttgart und Berlin: Cotta, n.d.

———. *Dichtung und Wahrheit.* In *Werke.* Hamburger Ausgabe in 14 Bänden, vol. 9. Edited by Erich Trunz. Hamburg: Christian Wegner, 1955.

———. *Goethes Briefe.* Hamburger Ausgabe in 4 Bänden, vol. 1. Edited by Karl Robert Mandelkow. Hamburg: Christian Wegner, 1962.

———. *Faust.* Translated by Walter Arndt and edited by Cyrus Hamlin. New York: W. W. Norton, 1976.

Gombrich, E. H. *The Story of Art,* 13th ed. Oxford: Phaidon Press, 1978.

Gottsched, Johann Christoph. *Versuch einer critischen Dichtkunst,* 4th rev. ed. Leipzig: B. C. Breitkopf, 1751.

Gräff, Ernst Martin. *Versuch einer einleuchtenden Darstellung des Eigenthums und der Eigenthumsrechte des Schriftstellers und Verlegers und ihrer gegenseitigen Rechte und Verbindlichkeiten. . . .* Leipzig: Gebüder Gräff, 1794.

Habermas, Jürgen. *The Structural Transformation of the Public Sphere.* Translated by Thomas Burger. Cambridge, Mass.: MIT Press, 1989.

Haferkorn, Hans Jürgen. "Der freie Schriftsteller." *Archiv für Geschichte des Buchwesens* 5:cols. 523–712, 1964.

Hamburger, Käte. "Nachwort. Schillers ästhetisches Denken." In Friedrich Schiller, *Über die ästhetische Erziehung.* Edited by Käte Hamburger. Stuttgart: Reclam, 1965.

Hauser, Arnold. *The Social History of Art,* vol. 3. New York: Random House, n.d.

Heinzmann, Johann Georg. *Appell an meine Nation über Aufklärung und Aufklärer. . . .* Bern: Auf Kosten des Verfassers, 1795.

Herder, Johann Gottfried. "Auszug aus einem Briefwechsel über Ossian und die Lieder alter Völker." In *Von deutscher Art und Kunst. Einige fliegende Blätter.* Hamburg, 1773.

———. *Vom Erkennen und Empfinden der menschlichen Seele.* In *Herders Sämmtliche Werke,* vol. 8. Edited by Bernhard Suphan. Berlin: Weidmann, 1892.

Hesse, Carla. "Reading Signatures: Female Authorship and Revolutionary Law in France, 1750–1850." *Eighteenth-Century Studies* 22:469–87, 1989.

———. "Enlightenment Epistemology and the Laws of Authorship in Revolutionary France, 1777–1793." *Representations* 30:109–37, 1990.

Hipple, Walter John, Jr. *The Beautiful, the Sublime, and the Picturesque in Eighteenth-Century British Aesthetic Theory.* Carbondale: Southern Illinois University Press, 1957.

Hirsch, E. D. "Two Traditions of Literary Evaluation." In *Literary Theory and Criticism: Festschrift in Honor of René Wellek.* Bern: Peter Lang, 1984.

Hirschman, Albert O. *The Passions and the Interests: Political Arguments for Capitalism before Its Triumph.* Princeton: Princeton University Press, 1977.

Hoche, Johann Gottfried. *Vertraute Briefe über die jetzige abentheuerliche Lesesucht und über den Einfluß derselben auf die Verminderung des häuslichen und öffentlichen Glücks.* Hannover: Chr. Ritscher, 1794.

Hohendahl, Peter Uwe. *The Institution of Criticism.* Ithaca: Cornell University Press, 1982.

Holub, Robert C. "The Rise of Aesthetics in the Eighteenth Century." *Comparative Literature Studies* 15:271–83, 1978.

Horace. "The Art of Poetry." In *Horace for English Readers.* Translated by E. C. Wickham. Oxford: Oxford University Press, 1903.

Hospers, John, and Anita Silvers, eds. "Aesthetics and the Histories of the Arts." *The Monist* 71(2), April 1988.

Huyssen, Andreas. *After the Great Divide: Modernism, Mass Culture, Post-Modernism.* Bloomington: Indiana University Press, 1986.

Jacobus, Mary. *Tradition and Experiment in Wordsworth's "Lyrical Ballads".* Oxford: Clarendon Press, 1976.

Jaszi, Peter. "Toward a Theory of Copyright: The Metamorphoses of 'Authorship.' " *Duke Law Journal* 1991:455–502.

Jeffrey, Francis. *"Essays on The Nature and Principles of Taste.* By Archibald Alison." *Edinburgh Review* 35:1–46, May 1811.

———. *"The Excursion, being a portion of the Recluse, a Poem.* By William Wordsworth." *Edinburgh Review* 47:1–30, November 1814.

Jentzsch, Rudolf. *Der deutsch-lateinische Büchermarkt nach den Leipziger Ostermeß -Katalogen von 1740, 1770 und 1800 in seiner Gliederung und Wandlung.* Leipzig: R. Voigtländer, 1912.

Jolles, Evelyn B. *G. A. Bürger's Ballade "Lenore" in England.* Regensburg: Hans Carl, 1974.

Kallich, Martin. "The Association of Ideas and Critical Theory: Hobbes, Locke, and Addison." *English Literary History* 12:290–315, 1945.

———. "The Meaning of Archibald Alison's *Essays on Taste.*" *Philological Quarterly* 27:314–24, 1948.

———. "The Argument against the Association of Ideas in Eighteenth-Century Aesthetics." *Modern Language Quarterly* 15:125–36, 1954.

———. *The Association of Ideas and Critical Theory in Eighteenth-Century England.* The Hague: Mouton, 1970.

Kant, Immanuel. "Idee zu einer allgemeinen Geschichte in weltbürgerlicher Absicht." *Berlinische Monatsschrift* 4:385–411, November 1784.

———. "Beantwortung der Frage: Was ist Aufklärung?" *Berlinische Monatsschrift* 4:481–49, December 1784.

———. "Über die Vulkane im Monde." *Berlinische Monatsschrift* 5:199–213, March 1785.

———. "Von der Unrechtmäßigkeit des Büchernachdrucks." *Berlinische Monatsschrift* 5:403–17, May 1785.

———. *Kant's Briefwechsel,* vol. 1. Edited by Rudolf Reicke. Berlin and Leipzig: Vereinigung wissenschaftlicher Verleger, 1922.

———. *The Critique of Judgment.* Translated by J. H. Bernard. New York: Macmillan, 1951.

Kaplan, Benjamin. *An Unhurried View of Copyright.* New York: Columbia University Press, 1967.

Kernan, Alvin. *Printing Technology, Letters, and Samuel Johnson.* Princeton: Princeton University Press, 1987.

Ketzer, Hans-Jürgen. " 'Ihr letztes Ziel ist es, daß sie Vergnügen verursachen sollen.' Zu einer ästhetischen Theorie der populären Künste und ihren Anfängen bei Gottfried August Bürger." *Weimarer Beiträge* 33:1145–58, 1987.

Kiesel, Helmuth, and Paul Münch. *Gesellschaft und Literatur im 18. Jahrhundert.* Munich: C. H. Beck, 1977.

Kivy, Peter. "Recent Scholarship and the British Tradition: A Logic of Taste—the First Fifty Years." In George Dickie and R. J. Sclafani, eds., *Aesthetics: A Critical Anthology.* New York: St. Martin's Press, 1977.

Klancher, Jon P. *The Making of English Reading Audiences 1790–1832.* Madison: University of Wisconsin Press, 1987.

Kleist, Heinrich von. *Sämtliche Werke und Briefe,* vol. 2, 2d ed. Edited by Helmut Sembdner. Munich: Carl Hanser, 1961.

Klischnig, Karl Friedrich. *Erinnerungen aus den zehn letzten Lebensjahren meines Freundes Anton Reiser. Als ein Beitrag zur Lebensgeschichte des Herrn Hofrath Moritz. . . .* Berlin, 1794.

Knigge, Adolf Freiherr von. *Über den Büchernachdruck. An den Herrn Johann Gottwerth Müller, Doktor der Weltweisheit in Itzehoe.* Hamburg: Benjamin Gottlob Hoffmann, 1792.

Koller, Benediktus Joseph von. *Entwurf zur Geschichte und Literatur der Aesthetik, von Baumgarten bis auf die neueste Zeit.* Regensburg: In der Montag und Weißischen Buchhandlung, 1799.

König, Dominik von. "Lesesucht und Lesewut." In Herbert G. Göpfert, ed., *Buch und Leser.* Hamburg: Ernst Hauswedell, 1977.

Krause, Christian Sigmund. "Über den Büchernachdruck." *Deutsches Museum* (May):400–30, 1783; (June):487–514, 1783.

Kreuzer, Helmut. "Gefährliche Lesesucht? Bermerkungen zu politischer Lektürekritik im ausgehenden 18. Jahrhundert." In Rainer Gruenter, ed., *Leser und Lesen im 18. Jahrhundert.* Heidelberg: Carl Winter, 1977.

———, ed. *Der Autor. LiLi. Zeitschrift für Literaturwissenschaft und Linguistik* 42, 1981.

Kristeller, Paul Oskar. "The Modern System of the Arts." In Morris Weitz, ed., *Problems in Aesthetics,* 2d ed. New York: Macmillan, 1970.

La Capra, Dominick. *History and Criticism.* Ithaca: Cornell University Press, 1985.

Lanckorónska, Maria, and Arthur Rümann. *Geschichte der deutschen Taschenbücher und Almanache aus der klassisch-romantischen Zeit.* Munich: E. Heimeran, 1954.

La Roche, Sophie von. *Pomona für Teutschlands Töchter.* Speier, 1783–84.

———. *Mein Schreibtisch.* Leipzig: Heinrich Gräff, 1799.

———. *Geschichte des Fräuleins von Sternheim.* Edited by Barbara Becker-Cantarino. Stuttgart: Reclam, 1983.

———. *The History of Lady Sophia Sternheim.* Translated by Christa Barguss Britt. Albany: State University of New York Press, 1991.

Lessing, Gotthold Ephraim. *Laokoon oder über die Grenzen der Malerey und Poesie.* Berlin: Bey Christian Friedrich Voß, 1766.

————. *Hamburgische Dramaturgie*, 2 vols. Hamburg: In der Lessing und Bode unterhaltenen Druckerei, 1769.

————. *Gesammelte Werke*, vol. 9. Edited by Paul Rilla. Berlin: Aufbau, 1968.

————. *Briefwechsel über das Trauerspiel*. Edited by Jochen Schulte-Sasse. Munich: Winkler, 1972.

————. "Leben und leben lassen. Ein Projekt für Schriftsteller und Buchhändler." In *Werke*, vol. 5. Edited by Herbert G. Göpfert. Munich: Carl Hanser, 1973.

Levine, Lawrence W. *Highbrow/Lowbrow: The Emergence of Cultural Hierarchy in America*. Cambridge, Mass.: Harvard University Press, 1988.

Linguet, Simon Nicolas Henri. *Des Herrn Linguets Betrachtungen über die Rechte des Schriftstellers und seines Verlegers*. Translated by Philipp Erasmus Reich. Leipzig, 1778.

Lipking, Lawrence. *The Ordering of the Arts in Eighteenth-Century England*. Princeton: Princeton University Press, 1970.

Little, William. *Gottfried August Bürger*. New York: Twayne, 1974.

Luther, Martin. "Vorrhede und Vermanunge." In *Fastenpostille. Martin Luthers Werke*. Kritische Gesamtausgabe, vol. 17, pt. II. Weimar: Hermann Böhlaus Nachfolger, 1927.

Lutz, Hans. *Schillers Anschauungen von Kultur und Natur*. Berlin: E. Ebering, 1928.

McCarthy, John A. "The Art of Reading and the Goals of the German Enlightenment." *Lessing Yearbook* 16:79–94, 1984.

McFarland, Thomas. *Originality and Imagination*. Baltimore: Johns Hopkins University Press, 1985.

McKendrick, Neil, John Brewer, and J. H. Plumb. *The Birth of a Consumer Society: The Commercialization of Eighteenth-Century England*. Bloomington: Indiana University Press, 1982.

Martens, Wolfgang. *Die Botschaft der Tugend. Die Aufklärung im Spiegel der deutschen moralischen Wochenschriften*. Stuttgart: J. B. Metzler, 1968.

Mason, John E. *Gentlefolk in the Making: Studies in the History of English Courtesy Literature and Related Topics from 1531 to 1774*. Philadelphia: University of Pennsylvania Press, 1935.

Mayo, Robert. "The Contemporaneity of the *Lyrical Ballads*." *Publications of the Modern Language Association* 69:486–522, 1954.

Mendelssohn, Moses. "Betrachtungen über die Quellen und die Verbindungen der schönen Künste und Wissenschaften." In *Gesammelte Schriften*, vol. 1. Edited by F. Bamberger et al., continued by Alexander Altmann. Stuttgart: Fr. Frommann, 1972.

Meusel, Johann Georg. *Das gelehrte Teutschland; oder, Lexikon der jetzt lebenden teutschen Schriftsteller*, 5th ed. Lemgo: Meyerische Buchhandlung, 1796–1834.

Miller, Nancy K. *Subject to Change*. New York: Columbia University Press, 1988.

Minder, Robert. *Glaube, Skepsis und Rationalismus. Dargestellt aufgrund der autobiographischen Schriften von Karl Philipp Moritz*. Frankfurt am Main: Suhrkamp, 1974.

Moorman, Mary. *William Wordsworth: A Biography*, 2 vols. Oxford: Clarendon Press, 1957–65.

Moritz, Karl Philipp, ed. *Magazin zur Erfahrungsseelenkunde. Als ein Lesebuch für Gelehrte und Ungelehrte*, 1783–93.

———. *Reisen eines Deutschen in England im Jahre 1782*. Berlin: Friedrich Maurer, 1783.

———. *Anton Reiser. Ein psychologischer Roman*. Berlin: Friedrich Maurer, 1785–94.

———. *Andreas Hartknopf. Eine Allegorie*. Berlin: Friedrich Unger, 1786.

———. *Über eine Schrift des Herrn Schulrath Campe und über die Rechte des Schriftstellers und Buchhändlers*. Berlin, 1789.

———. *Reisen eines Deutschen in Italien in den Jahren 1786 bis 1788*. Berlin: Friedrich Maurer, 1792–93.

———. *Travels, chiefly on foot, through several parts of England, in 1782. Described in letters to a friend by Charles P. Moritz, a literary gentleman of Berlin, translated by a lady*. London: For G. G. and J. Robinson, 1795.

———. Über die bildende Nachahmung des Schönen." In *Schriften zur Ästhetik und Poetik*. Edited by Hans Joachim Schrimpf. Tübingen: Max Niemeyer, 1962.

———. "Versuch einer Vereinigung aller schönen Künste und Wissenschaften unter dem Begriff des in sich selbst Vollendeten." In *Schriften zur Ästhetik und Poetik*. Edited by Hans Joachim Schrimpf. Tübingen: Max Niemeyer, 1962.

———. *Werke*, vol. 2. Edited by Horst Günther. Frankfurt am Main: Insel, 1981.

Müller, Klaus-Detlef. "Schiller und das Mäzenat. Zu den Entstehungsbedingungen der *Briefe über die ästhetische Erziehung des Menschen*." In Wilfried Barner, Eberhard Lämmert, and Norbert Oellers, eds., *Unser Commercium. Goethes und Schillers Literaturpolitik*. Stuttgart: J. G. Cotta, 1984.

Muller-Seidel, Walter. "Schillers Kontroverse mit Bürger und ihr geschichtlicher Sinn." In *Formenwandel. Festschrift für Paul Böckmann*. Hamburg: Hoffmann und Campe, 1964.

Müller von Itzehoe, Johann Gottwerth. *Siegfried von Lindenberg*, 5th rev. ed. Leipzig: Carl Friedrich Schneider, 1790.

———. *Komische Romane aus den Papieren des braunen Mannes und des Verfassers des Siegfried von Lindenberg*. Göttingen: Johann Christian Dieterich, 1788.

Nabholtz, John R. *"My Reader My Fellow-Labourer": A Study of English Romantic Prose*. Columbia: University of Missouri Press, 1986.

———. "The Text of Coleridge's *Essays on the Principles of Genial Criticism*." *Modern Philology* 85:187–92, 1987.

Nicholson, Andrew. *"Kubla Khan*: The Influence of Bürger's *Lenore*." *English Studies* 64:291–95, 1983.

Nicolai, Friedrich. *Das Leben und die Meinungen des Herrn Magister Sebaldus Nothanker*. Edited by Fritz Brüggemann. Leipzig: Reclam, 1938.

Pape, Helmut. "Klopstocks Autorenhonorare und Selbstverlagsgewinne." *Archiv für Geschichte des Buchwesens* 10: cols. 1–268, 1970.

Parker, Rozsika, and Griselda Pollock. *Old Mistresses. Women, Art and Ideology.* New York: Pantheon, 1981.

Parrish, Stephen Maxfield. *The Art of the "Lyrical Ballads."* Cambridge, Mass.: Harvard University Press, 1973.

Patterson, Lyman Ray. *Copyright in Historical Perspective.* Nashville: Vanderbilt University Press, 1968.

Payne, Harry C. "Elite versus Popular Mentality in the Eighteenth Century." *Studies in Eighteenth-Century Culture* 8:3–32, 1979.

Pears, Iain. *The Discovery of Painting. The Growth of Interest in the Arts in England 1680–1768.* New Haven: Yale University Press, 1988.

Perthes, Clemens Theodor. *Memoirs of Frederick Perthes; or, Literary, religious, and political life in Germany, from 1789–1843. From the German of Clement Theodore Perthes,* 3d ed., 2 vols. London and Edinburgh: T. Constable, 1857.

Peters, R. S., and C. A. Mace. "Psychology." In Paul Edwards, ed., *Encyclopedia of Philosophy,* vol. 7. New York: Macmillan, 1967.

Plant, Marjorie. *The English Book Trade: An Economic History of the Making and Sale of Books.* London: George Allen and Unwin, 1939.

Plumb, J. H. "The Commercialization of Leisure in Eighteenth-Century England." In *The Birth of a Consumer Society.* Bloomington: Indiana University Press, 1982.

Plumpe, Gerhard. "Eigentum—Eigentümlichkeit." *Archiv für Begriffsgeschichte* 23:175–96, 1979.

———. "Der Autor als Rechtssubjekt." In Helmut Brackert and Jörn Stöckrath, eds., *Literaturwissenschaft.* Reinbek bei Hamburg: Rowohlt, 1981.

Pölitz, Karl Heinrich Ludwig. *Die Aesthetik für gebildete Leser.* Leipzig: J. C. Hinrich, 1807.

Pope, Alexander. "Essay on Criticism." In Hazard Adams, ed., *Critical Theory since Plato.* New York: Harcourt, Brace, Jovanovich, 1971.

Primeau, John K. "The Influence of Gottfried August Bürger on the *Lyrical Ballads* of William Wordsworth: The Supernatural vs. the Natural." *Germanic Review* 58:89–96, 1983.

Pütter, Johann Stephan. *Der Büchernachdruck nach ächten Grundsätzen des Rechts geprüft.* Göttingen: Vandenhoeck, 1774.

Real, Willi. *Untersuchungen zu Archibald Alisons Theorie des Geschmacks.* Frankfurt am Main: Akademische Verlagsgesellschaft, 1973.

Reeve, Clara. *The Progress of Romance.* Colchester, 1785; reprinted, New York: Facsimile Text Society, 1930.

Reich, Philipp Erasmus. *Zufällige Gedanken eines Buchhändlers über Herrn Klopstocks Anzeige einer gelehrten Republik.* Leipzig, 1773.

Richardson, Jonathan. *Discourse on the Dignity, Certainty, Pleasure and Advantage of the Science of a Connoisseur.* London, 1719.

Ritter, Joachim. "Genie." In Joachim Ritter, ed., *Historisches Wörterbuch der Philosophie,* vol. 3. Basel: Schwabe, n.d.

Robertson, J. G. *A History of German Literature,* 6th ed. Edited by Dorothy Reich. Elmsford, N. Y.: London House and Maxwell, 1970.

Rorty, Richard, J. B. Schneewind, and Quentin Skinner, eds. *Philosophy in History*. Cambridge: Cambridge University Press, 1984.

Rose, Mark. "The Author as Proprietor: *Donaldson v. Becket* and the Genealogy of Modern Authorship." *Representations* 23:51–85, 1988.

Rosenfeld, Hellmut. "Zur Geschichte von Nachdruck und Plagiat." *Archiv für Geschichte des Buchwesens* 11:cols. 337–72, 1971.

Ross, Marlon B. *The Contours of Masculine Desire*. New York: Oxford University Press, 1989.

Said, Edward W. *The World, the Text, and the Critic*. Cambridge, Mass.: Harvard University Press, 1983.

Saine, Thomas P. *Die ästhetische Theodizee. Karl Philipp Moritz und die Philosophie des 18. Jahrhunderts*. Munich: Fink, 1971.

Sauder, Gerhard. "Ein deutscher Streit 1789. Campes Versuch 'moralischen Totschlags' und Moritz' Verteidigung der Rechte des Schriftstellers." In Albrecht Schöne, ed., *Akten des VII. internationalen Germanisten-Kongresses*. Tübingen: Max Niemeyer, 1986.

Sauerland, Karol. "Goethes, Schillers, Fr. Schlegels und Novalis' Reaktionen auf die neuen politischen, konstitutionellen und sozialphilosophischen Fragen, die die französische Revolution aufwarf." In Norbert Honsza, ed., *Daß eine Nation die ander verstehen möge. Festschrift für Marian Szyrocki*. Amsterdam: Rodopi, 1988.

Saunders, J. W. *The Profession of English Letters*. London: Routledge and Kegan Paul, 1964.

Scheible, Hartmut. *Wahrheit und Subjekt. Ästhetik im bürgerlichen Zeitalter*. Bern: Francke, 1984.

Schenda, Rudolf. *Volk ohne Buch. Studien zur Sozialgeschichte der populären Lesestoffe. 1770–1910*. Frankfurt am Main: Vittorio Klostermann, 1970.

Schenker, Manfred. *Charles Batteux und seine Nachahmungstheorie in Deutschland*. Leipzig: H. Haessel, 1909.

Schiller, Johann Christoph Friedrich. *Schillers Briefe*, 7 vols. Edited by Fritz Jonas. Stuttgart: Deutsche Verlags-Anstalt, 1892–96.

———. "Über Bürgers Gedichte." In *Schillers Werke*. Nationalausgabe, vol. 22. Edited by Herbert Meyer. Weimar: Hermann Böhlaus Nachfolger, 1958.

———. "Merkwürdige Rechtsfälle als ein Beitrag zur Geschichte der Menscheit." In *Sämtliche Werke*, vol. 5. Edited by Gerhard Fricke and Herbert G. Göpfert. Munich: Carl Hanser, 1959.

———. "Was kann eine gute stehende Schaubühne eigentlich wirken?" In *Schillers Werke*, Nationalausgabe, vol. 20, pt. 1. Edited by Benno von Wiese. Weimar: Hermann Böhlaus Nachfolger, 1962.

———. *On the Aesthetic Education of Man in a Series of Letters*. Edited and translated by Elizabeth M. Wilkinson and L. A. Willoughby. Oxford: Clarendon Press, 1967.

Schlegel, August Wilhelm. *Die Kunstlehre*. In *Kritische Schriften und Briefe*, vol. 2. Edited by Edgar Lohner. Stuttgart: W. Kohlhammer, 1963.

Schlegel, Friedrich. "Georg Forster. Fragment einer Charakteristik der deutschen Klassiker." In *Kritische Friedrich-Schlegel-Ausgabe*, vol. 2. Edited by Hans Eichner. Munich: Ferdinand Schöningh, 1967.

Schlingmann, Carsten. *Gellert. Eine literar-historische Revision.* Bad Homburg: Gehlen, 1967.

Schmidt, Jochen. *Die Geschichte des Geniegedankens in der deutschen Literatur, Philosophie und Politik 1750–1945.* 2 vols. Darmstadt: Wissenschaftliche Buchgesellschaft, 1985.

Schnabel, Johann Gottfried. *Die Insel Felsenburg,* 4 vols. Nordhausen, 1731–43.

Schulte-Sasse, Jochen. *Die Kritik an der Trivialliteratur seit der Aufklärung.* Munich: Fink, 1971.

———. "Das Konzept bürgerlich-literarischer Öffentlichkeit und die historischen Gründe seines Zerfalls." In Bürger, Bürger, and Schulte-Sasse, eds., *Aufklärung und literarische Öffentlichkeit.*

Schulz, J. G. F. *Firlifimini.* Edited by Ludwig Geiger. Berlin, 1885.

Segebrecht, Wulf. *Das Gelegenheitsgedicht: Ein Beitrag zur Geschichte und Poetik der deutschen Lyrik.* Stuttgart: J. B. Metzler, 1977.

Shaftesbury, Anthony Ashley Cooper, Earl of. *Characteristics of Men, Manners, Opinions, Times.* Edited by John M. Robertson. Indianapolis: Bobbs-Merrill, 1964.

Shaw, Daniel. "A Kuhnian Metatheory for Aesthetics." *Journal of Aesthetics and Art Criticism* 45:29–39, 1986.

Shusterman, Richard, ed. "Analytic Aesthetics." Special issue, *Journal of Aesthetics and Art Criticism* 46:115–223, 1987.

Siskin, Clifford. *The Historicity of Romantic Discourse.* New York: Oxford University Press, 1988.

Smith, Barbara Herrnstein. *Contingencies of Value.* Cambridge, Mass.: Harvard University Press, 1988.

Snell, Reginald. "Introduction." In Friedrich Schiller, *On the Aesthetic Education of Man in a Series of Letters.* Translated by Reginald Snell. New York: Frederick Ungar, 1965.

Sosnoski, James J. "Literary Study in a Post-Modern Era: Rereading Its History." *Works and Days* 5:7–33, 1987.

Stallybrass, Peter, and Allon White. *The Politics and Poetics of Transgression.* Ithaca: Cornell University Press, 1986.

Statutes of the United Kingdom of Great Britain and Ireland, 5 & 6 Victoria. London: Her Majesty's Printers, 1842.

Stewart, Susan. *Crimes of Writing.* New York: Oxford University Press, 1991.

Stolnitz, Jerome. "On the Significance of Lord Shaftesbury in Modern Aesthetic Theory." *Philosophical Quarterly* 11:97–113, 1961.

———. "On the Origins of 'Aesthetic Disinterestedness.'" *Journal of Aesthetics and Art Criticism* 20:131–43, 1961.

Sulzer, Johann Georg. *Allgemeine Theorie der schönen Künste.* Leipzig: M. G. Weidmanns Erben und Reich, 1771–74; 2d enlarged ed. Leipzig: In der Weidmannschen Buchhandlung, 1792–94.

Swartz, Richard G. "Patrimony and the Figuration of Authorship in the Eighteenth-Century Literary Property Debates." *Works and Days* 7(2):29–54, 1989.

Szondi, Peter. "Antike und Moderne in der Ästhetik der Goethezeit."

In *Poetik und Geschichtsphilosophie*, vol. 1. Frankfurt am Main: Suhrkamp, 1974.

Todorov, Tzvetan. *Theories of the Symbol.* Translated by Catherine Porter. Ithaca: Cornell University Press, 1982.

Tompkins, Jane P. "The Reader in History: The Changing Shape of Literary Response." In Jane P. Tompkins, ed., *Reader-Response Criticism: From Formalism to Post-Structuralism.* Baltimore: Johns Hopkins University Press, 1980.

Touaillon, Christine. *Der deutsche Frauenroman des 18. Jahrhunderts.* Vienna and Leipzig: Wilhelm Braumüller, 1919.

Troller, Alois. "Originalität und Neuheit der Werke der Literatur und Kunst und der Geschmacksmuster." In Fritz Hodeige, ed., *Das Recht am Geistesgut. Studien zum Urheber-, Verlags- und Presserecht.* Freiburg i. B.: Rombach, 1964.

Ungern-Sternberg, Wolfgang von. "Schriftsteller und literarischer Markt." In Rolf Grimminger, ed., *Deutsche Aufklärung bis zur Französischen Revolution, 1680–1789.* Munich: DTV, 1980.

"Ursachen der jetzigen Vielschreiberey in Deutschland." *Journal von und für Deutschland* 6:139–43, 1789; 7:498–502, 1790.

Vogel, Martin. "Der literarische Markt und die Entstehung des Verlags- und Urheberrechts bis zum Jahre 1800." In *Rhetorik, Ästhetik, Ideologie. Aspekte einer kritischen Kulturwissenschaft.* Stuttgart: J. B. Metzler, 1973.

Walzel, Oskar. "Das Prometheussymbol von Shaftesbury zu Goethe." *Neue Jahrbücher für das klassische Altertum* 13:40–71, 133–65, 1910.

Waniek, Erdmann. "Karl Philipp Moritz's Concept of the Whole in His *Versuch einer Vereinigung . . .* (1785)." *Studies in Eighteenth-Century Culture* 12:213–22, 1983.

Ward, Albert. *Book Production, Fiction, and the German Reading Public 1740–1800.* Oxford: Clarendon Press, 1974.

Weber, Peter. "Politik und Poesie. Literarische Öffentlichkeit im Übergang zur Kunstperiode." In Peter Weber et al., *Kunstperiode. Studien zur deutschen Literatur des ausgehenden 18. Jahrhunderts.* Berlin: Akademie, 1982.

Weinsheimer, Joel. "Conjectures on Unoriginal Composition." *The Eighteenth Century: Theory and Interpretation* 22:58–73, 1981.

Weitz, Morris, ed. *Problems in Aesthetics*, 2d ed. New York: Macmillan, 1970.

Wellek, René. *Immanuel Kant in England 1793–1838.* Princeton: Princeton University Press, 1931.

———. *A History of Modern Criticism 1750–1950*, vol. 2. New Haven: Yale University Press, 1955.

Wieland, Christoph Martin. "Review of Bürger's *Gedichte*." *Der teutsche Mercur* 3 (July):92–94, 1778.

———. *C. M. Wielands Briefe an Sophie von La Roche, nebst einem Schreiben von Gellert und Lavater.* Edited by Franz Horn. Berlin: Christiani, 1820.

Willoughby, L. A. "Wordsworth and Germany." *German Studies. Festschrift for H. G. Fiedler.* Oxford: Clarendon Press, 1938.

Wilson, R. Jackson. *Figures of Speech: American Writers and the Literary Marketplace, from Benjamin Franklin to Emily Dickinson.* Baltimore: Johns Hopkins University Press, 1989.

Wittkower, Rudolf. "Genius: Individualism in Art and Artists." In Philip P. Wiener, ed., *Dictionary of the History of Ideas*, vol. 2. New York: Scribner's, 1973.

Wittmann, Reinhard. *Buchmarkt und Lektüre im 18. und 19. Jahrhundert.* Tübingen: Max Niemeyer, 1982.

Woodmansee, Martha. "Deconstructing Deconstruction: Toward a History of Modern Criticism." In Martha Woodmansee and Walter F. W. Lohnes, eds., *Erkennen und Deuten*. Berlin: Erich Schmidt, 1983.

Woodmansee, Martha, and Peter Jaszi, eds. *The Construction of Authorship: Textual Appropriation in Law and Literature*. Durham: Duke University Press, 1993.

Wordsworth, William. "Advertisement to *Lyrical Ballads, with a Few Other Poems* (1798)." In *Literary Criticism of William Wordsworth*. Edited by Paul M. Zall. Lincoln: University of Nebraska Press, 1966.

——. "Essay, Supplementary to the Preface." In *Literary Criticism of William Wordsworth*.

——. "Preface to *Lyrical Ballads, with Other Poems* (1800)." In *Literary Criticism of William Wordsworth*.

——. *The Letters of William and Dorothy Wordsworth*. Edited by Ernest de Selincourt, revised edition by Chester L. Shaver. Oxford: Clarendon Press, 1967.

——. Petition to Parliament (1839). In *The Prose Works of William Wordsworth*, vol. 3. Edited by W. J. B. Owen. Oxford: Clarendon Press, 1974.

——. "To the Editor of the Kendal Mercury." In *The Prose Works of William Wordsworth*, vol. 3.

Wurzbach, Wolfgang von. *Gottfried August Bürger. Sein Leben und seine Werke.* Leipzig: Dieterich, 1900.

Young, Edward. *Conjectures on Original Composition in a Letter to the Author of Sir Charles Grandison*. In Edmund D. Jones, ed., *English Critical Essays. Sixteenth, Seventeenth and Eighteenth Centuries*. London: Oxford University Press, 1975.

——. *Gedanken über die Original-Werke*. Translated by H. E. von Teubern and edited by Gerhard Sauder. Facsimile ed. Heidelberg: Lambert Schneider, 1977.

Zall, Paul M. "Wordsworth and the Copyright Act of 1842." *Publications of the Modern Language Association* 70:132–44, 1955.

Zedler, Johann Heinrich. *Grosses vollständiges Universal-Lexikon aller Wissenschaften und Künste*. Leipzig and Halle: Zedler, 1732–50.

Zilsel, Edgar. *Die Geniereligion. Ein kritischer Versuch über das moderne Persönlichkeitsideal mit einer historischen Begründung*. Vienna and Leipzig: Wilhelm Braumüller, 1918.

——. *Die Entstehung des Geniebegriffs. Ein Beitrag zur Ideengeschichte der Antike und des Frühkapitalismus*. Tübingen: Mohr, 1926.

Zinck, Georg Heinrich. *Allgemeines Oeconomisches Lexicon*, 3d ed. Leipzig: Johann Friedrich Glebitsch, 1753.

INDEX

Originality, 35, 38, 39, 40, 52–54, 117, 145
Ownership, *see* Intellectual property

Patronage, 22–23, 37, 41, 43, 48
Perfection, 16, 18, 19, 20, 22, 32, 152*n*13
Perthes, Friedrich Christoph, 46, 49
Piracy, 45–47, 49, 52, 54, 72, 82, 159*n*19, 160*n*28, 166*n*32
Pleasure, 15, 16, 18–22, 31–32, 55, 88, 95, 98, 101, 116, 121–24, 126, 129, 135, 138–39, 143
Poetry: popularity of, 61–62, 70–71, 73, 78, 79
Pölitz, Karl Heinrich Ludwig, 103, 105, 144
Pope, Alexander, 40, 55, 114; *Essay on Criticism*, 37–38
Privilege, 42, 45–46
Professional writer, 22, 37, 40, 42, 45, 59, 108; *see also* Author; Coleridge, Samuel Taylor; La Roche, Sophie von; Moritz, Karl Philipp; Schiller, Johann Christoph Friedrich
Public, *see* Audience
Publishing, *see* Authorship: and publishing practices
Pütter, Johann Stephan, 47, 160–61*n*31

Rabener, Gottlieb Wilhelm, 43
Readers, *see* Audience
Reading: debate 89–102; purpose of, 29, 89–91, 93–97, 106; rise of, 22, 24, 25, 88, 89, 100, 111, 121, 143, 154*n*25, 155*n*28, 167*n*4; strategies, 5, 93, 97–101, 169*n*22; *see also* Audience: effects of art on; Bergk, Johann Adam
Reeve, Clara, 171*n*10
Reich, Philipp Erasmus, 47, 160–61*n*31
Richardson, Samuel, 17, 104
Richter, Jean Paul, 30, 170*n*5
Robertson, J. G., 63

Romanticism, 63
Rose, Mark, 161*n*31
Rousseau, Jean Jacques, 99, 104, 169*n*27

Schelling, Friedrich Wilhelm Joseph, 30
Schiller, Johann Christoph Friedrich, 5, 8, 27, 29–30, 40, 93, 100, 107, 114, 157*n*47, 164*n*15, 165*n*21, 170*n*5; *Don Carlos*, 80, 83; *Fiesko*, 79–80; *The Ghostseer*, 81–82, 90, 166*n*32; historical writing of, 81–83; *Horen*, 57; *Kabale und Liebe*, 79–80; *Naïve and Sentimental Poetry*, 85; *On the Aesthetic Education of Man in a Series of Letters*, 4, 20, 41, 57–59, 72–73, 75–76, 79, 85, 86; *On Bürger's Poems*, 4, 59, 70, 72–79, 85, 95, 113, 115, 117, 118, 167*n*41, 172*n*13; and patronage, 41, 82–85, 166*n*40; on poetics, 4, 57–58, 71, 72–79, 86, 94, 116, 117, 163*n*2; as professional writer, 40, 41, 79–85; and relation to audience, 41, 79; *Revolt of the Netherlands*, 83; *The Robbers*, 40, 79; *Thalia*, 41, 80–82, 166*n*32; theater of, 72–73, 79–80, 82, 85; *Thirty Years War*, 83; Wallenstein trilogy, 85; "What Can a Good Permanent Theater Actually Accomplish?," 72
Schlegel, August Wilhelm, 30, 151–52*n*12
Schlegel, Friedrich, 30, 87
Schleiermacher, Friedrich Daniel Ernst, 55, 100
Schnabel, Johann Gottfried, 156*n*35
Scholes, Robert, 97
Schulz, J. G. F., 22, 170*n*5
Self-sufficiency, 11, 17–22, 32–33, 117, 138
Shaftesbury, Anthony Ashley Cooper, Earl of, 152*n*14

Shakespeare, William, 101, 114, 137
Steele, Richard, 143
Sterne, Laurence, 99, 104
Stolnitz, Jerome, 5–6
Sublime, 95, 128, 130, 131, 132, 135
Sulzer, Johann Georg, 8, 158n4, 163n54

Taste, *see* Audience: tastes of
Taylor, William, 60, 63, 67, 112, 171n4
Tieck, Ludwig, 30
Todorov, Tzvetan, 152n13
Totality, 11, 17, 32, 33, 94, 97–99, 109
Trattner, Johann Thomas, 160n28
Tromlitz, Friedrich Jacob, 10

Wackenroder, Wilhelm Heinrich, 30
Warren, Robert Penn, 98–99
Weitz, Morris, 2–3, 7, 149n4
Wellek, René, 136
Wendler, Johann, 44
Wieland, Christoph Martin, 5, 27, 40, 71–72, 90, 100, 170n5; *Agathon*, 96, 109; Preface to *Fräulein von Sternheim*, 105–8; and relationship with Sophie von La Roche, 8, 103–6, 170n8
Wilkinson, Elizabeth M., and L. A. Willoughby, 163n2
Women, *see* Gender
Wordsworth, William, 37, 144, 172n14; and Bürger's poetic, 60, 112–18, 172n13; and copyright law, 145–47, 177n52; *Essay, Supplementary to the Preface*, 38–39, 117, 147; *Excursion*, 127; *Lyrical Ballads* (including Preface), 38, 60, 11, 113–14, 117, 118, 120, 171n4, 172n11; *Miscellaneous Poems*, 117; poetics of, 113–18, 120, 171n4, 172n15; and popular literature, 113–16, 146; *Prelude*, 20; and role of reception, 114, 116, 117, 118, 127, 145, 147

Young, Edward: *Conjectures on Original Composition*, 39, 53–54; *see also* Authorship: as organic process

Zedler, Johann Heinrich: *Universal-Lexikon*, 42, 45

Designer:	Teresa Bonner
Text:	Ehrhardt
Compositor:	Maple Vail
Printer:	Maple Vail
Binder:	Maple Vail